Fun and Games

My 40 Years Writing Sports

Dave Perkins

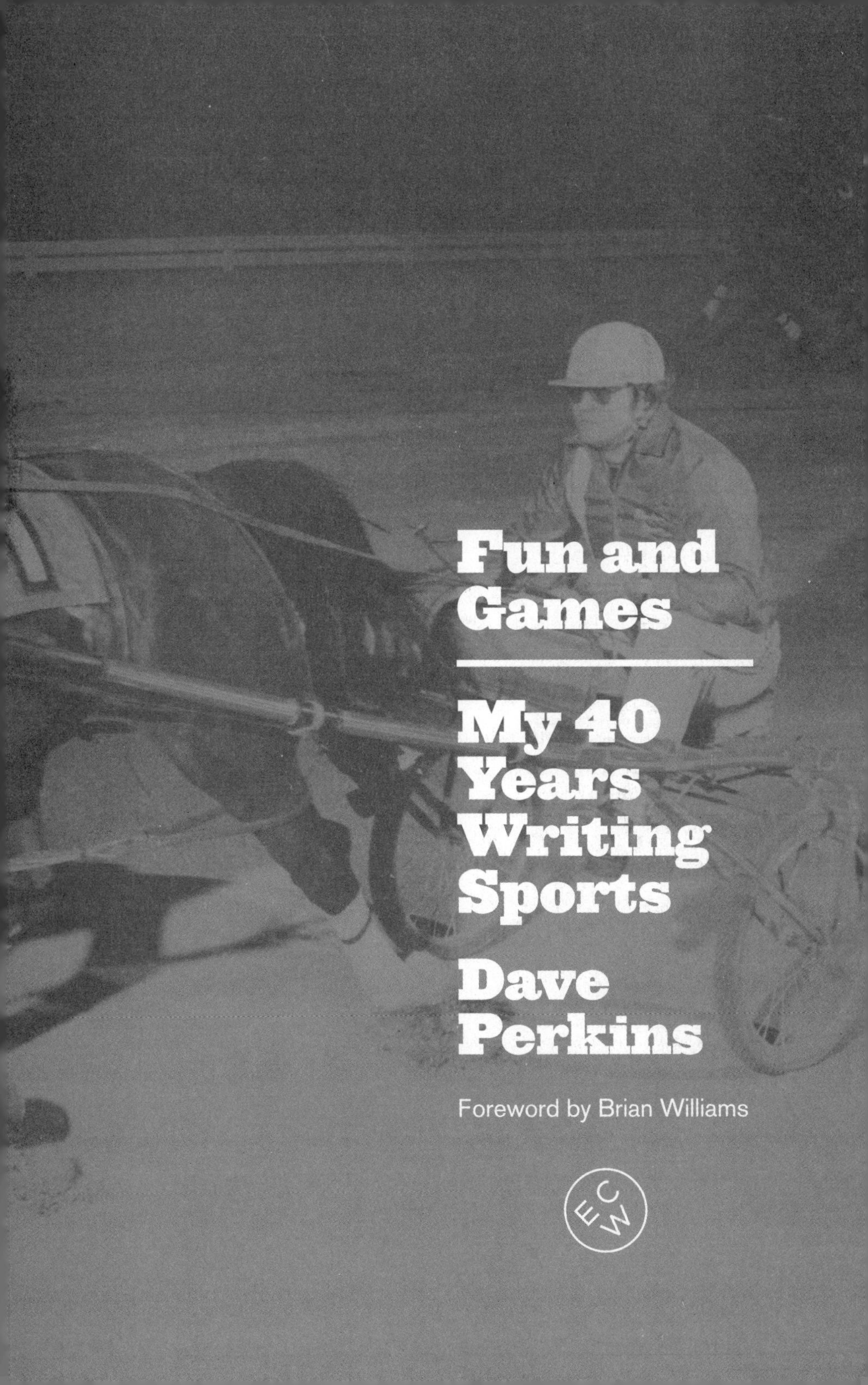

Fun and Games

My 40 Years Writing Sports

Dave Perkins

Foreword by Brian Williams

ECW

Published by ECW Press
665 Gerrard Street East
Toronto, Ontario, Canada, M4M 1Y2
416-694-3348 / info@ecwpress.com

To the best of his abilities, the author has related experiences, places, people, and organizations from his memories of them.

Unless otherwise stated, all photos are from the author's personal collection.

LIBRARY AND ARCHIVES CANADA CATALOGUING IN PUBLICATION

Perkins, Dave, author
Fun and games : my 40 years writing sports / Dave Perkins ; foreword by Brian Williams.

Issued in print and electronic formats.
ISBN 978-1-77041-312-2
also issued as: 978-1-77090-930-4 (PDF); 978-1-77090-929-8 (ePUB)

1. Perkins, Dave. 2. Sportswriters—Canada —Biography. 3. Sports journalism—Canada.

I. Title.

GV742.42.P47A3 2016 070.4'49796092
C2016-902357-5 C2016-902358-3

Cover design: David A. Gee
Cover image: © PeskyMonkey/iStockPhoto
Title page image: Michael Burns

The publication of *Fun and Games* has been generously supported by the Government of Canada through the Canada Book Fund. *Ce livre est financé en partie par le gouvernement du Canada.* We also acknowledge the Ontario Arts Council (OAC), an agency of the Government of Ontario, which last year funded 1,709 individual artists and 1,078 organizations in 204 communities across Ontario, for a total of $52.1 million, and the contribution of the Government of Ontario through the Ontario Book Publishing Tax Credit and the Ontario Media Development Corporation.

Ontario
Ontario Media Development Corporation

ONTARIO ARTS COUNCIL
CONSEIL DES ARTS DE L'ONTARIO
an Ontario government agency
un organisme du gouvernement de l'Ontario

Canada

PRINTED AND BOUND IN CANADA

PRINTING: MARQUIS 5 4 3 2 1

RECYCLED
Paper made from recycled material
FSC
www.fsc.org
FSC® C103567

FOREWORD

By Brian Williams, O.C.

Dave Perkins has the unique ability to write the way he speaks. As a long-time friend and colleague, reading Perkins's outstanding columns those many years in the *Toronto Star* was no different than being in conversation with and listening to Dave over a cup of coffee. Alright, it was actually a beer.

Perkins always observed and reacted to more than the particular story and event he was covering. He was always able to recognize and see the big picture. I witnessed that first-hand at the 2000 Summer Olympics in Sydney, Australia.

Cathy Freeman, Australia's brilliant aboriginal runner, lit the flame in the Opening Ceremony. Later in the Games she competed in the 400-metre event. With the time difference between our two countries, I was not on the air hosting when the women's 400-metre race was run. Dave knew this and suggested we watch the event together. Naturally I assumed we would be seated in the media section at the main Olympic Stadium. However, Perkins with his keen insight saw this as much more than a simple Olympic sprint event. Aboriginal struggles and issues were a part of Australian history, as they have been part of Canadian history. Knowing this, Perkins suggested we watch the event not at the main Olympic Stadium but rather in a downtown restaurant packed with loyal and vocal Australian fans. His reasoning was simple: he wanted to observe both the race and the reaction of the fans. Freeman ran a great race, winning the 400 metres in 49.11 seconds. The restaurant exploded with joy and genuine affection for this remarkable young woman. As the celebration continued, Perkins turned to me and said, "She probably just did more for aboriginal rights in 49 seconds than has been done in decades." You talk about seeing the aforementioned big picture!

I often saved quotes from Dave's columns for use on future occasions. I remember vividly a sentence he wrote that perfectly described the joy and pride I had so often witnessed from Olympic athletes as they entered the main stadium during the Opening Ceremony at both the summer and winter Olympics. He wrote that "Olympic athletes go through life in a convertible with the top down, enjoying the ride." I would use that quote during a future Olympic Opening Ceremony and that one simple sentence was able to not only paint a picture in a column, but allowed viewers to understand what they were seeing.

Whether it is reading about watching the Presidents Cup golf tournament with U.S. President Bill Clinton or attending a Super Bowl, Perkins's ability to paint a picture makes for truly enjoyable reading.

Dave Perkins is not only an excellent writer, he is a highly respected journalist. And believe me there is a world of difference between the two. It is that difference that enables Dave to broaden the picture he paints with his writing and to better be the eyes and ears of the fans.

The stories in this book are told by a master storyteller who creates a window into what often seems like an unreal and dream-filled world.

You will indeed enjoy listening to and having a cup of coffee (or, yes, a beer) with the writer his many friends simply call "Perk."

INTRODUCTION

The gentleman said right up front that he didn't wish me to die, at least not at any time soon. What he hoped for, he said, was that my children got rectal cancer and died, painfully, in front of me. That would serve me right, he was implying, for saying something he did not appreciate about his favourite hockey team.

Well, I thought, *as long as the punishment fits the crime.*

Other emails, always anonymous of course, have more directly wished every possible painful death upon me, or commented freely and usually disparagingly about my appearance, background, family, thought processes, teeth, genitals (a true favourite), hair, hairline, waistline, apparel, choice of friends, immigration status, emigration status and, once, the vehicle I drove. The guy had no idea what I drove, but he just *knew* it was a horseshit car. Occasionally, someone would simply disagree with what I wrote without feeling the need to bear arms. Even more occasionally, they would agree with something I said. My favourite email once told me that while I was right about everything I had written that day, I still was a piece of shit. That kind of suggestion makes a guy feel . . . better?

I think back 30 years, to the time Blue Jays fans were first getting up on their hind legs and making their feelings known en masse to chroniclers. When someone or something in print displeased them, or they merely had what they thought was a better idea, they put thoughts down on paper, addressed and stamped an envelope and went to the post office to mail it. I always figured, since they went to that trouble, that I owed them a read of their thoughts. Hell, sometimes I even agreed with them. The best reader response you can get is the civil one that says, "I believe you're mistaken and here's why . . ." Those often seem to be the ones that feature such antiquities as correct spelling and punctuation, too.

So there you have the opposite ends of one little corner of the newspaper business, a noble but (alas) slowly dying enterprise from which I now am happily retired after 40-plus years of labour. Perhaps people, meaning readers, are dumber and more vicious now than they used to be, or perhaps it's simply the speed and anonymity of the internet that emboldens them to make personal attacks with impunity. I have given up trying to figure it out.

I said I was happily retired and I think I truly am, although every now and then the Blue Jays do something that causes the *Toronto Star* to try to lure me out of my chosen idleness, at least for a day. Plus, I got into the sports-talk radio business as a kind of a poorly paid hobby, doing the minor sidekick act now and then with Bob McCown on his national radio show. I suspect McCown, who is huge within the industry, wanted me around for two reasons: one is that he seems to have fought with every other co-host and parted company with them, as they say at the racetrack; and two, he remembers when he and I played on the same high school football team nearly 50 years ago and, possibly, he suspects I know where some of the bodies are buried.

Nah, not me. I was always better at burying the lead paragraph than bodies.

I began working at the *Globe and Mail* in 1973 while still studying journalism at Ryerson, moved over to the *Toronto Star* in 1977, worked full-time there until 2010, hung around as a freelance weekly sports columnist — the dreaded columnist emeritus, we called them when it was someone else — until 2013 and then went off to do a tiny bit of teaching and have my heart attack. In my time with both papers, I did everything imaginable, starting as agate clerk, copy editor, layout man, slotman, police reporter (very briefly), assistant sports editor, racing handicapper, racing writer, baseball writer, baseball columnist, sports editor and general columnist. That is almost chronologically correct, with my two and a half years as sports editor crammed in between the end of the Blue Jays' first period of glory, in late 1993, to the beginning of, for want of a better description, the Tiger Woods Era in mid-1996. That time as sports editor is better left undiscussed, because neither me nor the job was suited to each other. I used to say I went into the job having zero children and soon had 31 of them. To be fair, you should hear what the staffers say about my time at the tiller.

I would hesitate to call it a highlight of my time as sports columnist at the *Star*, but one moment stands out for mostly ridiculous reasons and centred on Hulk Hogan and professional wrestling. Now, pro wrestling is not a sport, certainly. On the other hand, it is entertainment and it is popular, from time to time, among the masses, although I would guess the mouth-breathing segment of the population would seem to be more keenly appreciative. Regardless, *WrestleMania* was being held at the SkyDome and Hulk Hogan was in town to beat the drums for the show. The sports columnists of Toronto's daily newspapers were invited to some kind of function. Mr. Hogan likewise attended and part of the shtick was that in order to provide gag photographs, he would put headlocks on certain invited guests including the sports columnists, which meant this one. I reluctantly played along, although once in the vise of his arm I was astounded less by Hogan's size than by his miser-

With Hulk Hogan at a WrestleMania *promotion in 1990.*
I can't forget how foul Hogan's breath was that day.

ably foul breath. I have no idea if this was a one-day occurrence or if this was a weapon he used to his advantage in the ring, but Jesus, it was gruesome. I think my eyes were watering.

This was the second instance of contact with pro wrestlers I could have done without. One late night in P.J. Clarke's, the historic watering hole on Manhattan's Third Ave., I was tucking into bacon cheeseburgers with Tom Slater, my *Star* pal and fellow baseball writer. This was the late 1980s; I was still smoking cigarettes and it was still legal to smoke cigarettes in restaurants. (These days, I believe it is a capital offence even to talk about such a thing.) So there we were, at one of the little tables in Clarke's back room and no more than two feet from another tiny table, this one occupied by a very large wrestler named the Million Dollar Man, who was billing and cooing with a very sweet young thing. The wrestler, whose legit name was Ted DiBiase, leaned over and tapped me and asked if he could take one of the cigarettes from my pack, sitting on the table. Help yourself, I told him. He lit up.

Almost immediately, the sweet young thing desired nicotine and Ted again leaned and tapped and asked for a nail. Permission was happily granted. They enjoyed their smokes, they chatted, we chatted and drank and, a while later, came another tap and another request from Ted.

Well, enough was enough, right? Before I thought about the wisdom of my intended response, I had blurted out, "For crissakes, you're the Million Dollar Man. Can't you buy your own goddamn cigarettes?"

This was not entirely clever. With a few possible exceptions, pro wrestlers tend to be steroid-addled monsters of debatable intelligence. And here was I, couple of drinks in me, insulting one of them in front of his girlfriend for about 30 cents' worth of tobacco. Ted's eyes narrowed. He was not pleased. I suspect I realized what I had done, because I laughed nervously and pretended to be joking. If I remember correctly, Slater jumped in and helped defuse the moment by proffering his own pack of smokes. We left shortly afterward.

Other than the state of Hulk Hogan's breath, the only thing I learned from my term as SE is that one word applies to every sports fan who is asked, in surveys and such, what he wants in his sports section. That word is MORE. As in, they want more of what they want and they don't necessarily care what anyone else wants. I kept correspondence for years — until burning it all in a cathartic moment a while back — which made me realize what I was up against when I was fortunate enough to be sports editor of the country's largest newspaper. There were, because I counted and filed them, 131 various written pleas for more coverage. These would come from fans, officials, executives, parents and unidentified strangers, pleading for more information, and not only on the stuff you figured, like hockey, baseball, football, basketball, horse racing etc., which we filled our pages with every day. We called this exercise, "shovelling 10 pounds of shit into a five-pound bag."

I was being urged to devote more space to things like darts, synchronized swimming, Frisbee, martial arts, wrestling (both amateur and professional), skeet shooting, bicycle racing, car racing, motorcycle racing, snowmobile racing, skydiving, orienteering, fishing, hunting and many others. My two favourite letters were from a person outraged because we weren't covering the fireworks events at the Canadian National Exhibition and from someone else, who I always assumed had a straight face when they were adamant that we should have sent a reporter to a chili cook-off. Why should we have covered these two? Because they were "competitions." I was urged to give more space to sports for women, for aboriginals, for amateurs, for the disabled. Many letter writers made compelling arguments. A few made threats. A subdivision of 28 different and separate activities claimed to be "Canada's fastest-growing sport." Which, as most physicists and mathematicians might agree, is a neat trick.

You get the idea. It's why I suggested my time as a sports editor should remain mostly undiscussed, although perhaps I have already failed in that regard.

Anyway, to use one of my favourite words, whatever job I held, I always considered it the best job in town at the moment. I would suggest the quarter century I spent as a sports columnist at a big, rich paper that for the most part spared no expense to do things correctly is undeniably the best job in town, at least for a newspaper stiff. Which is all I ever wanted to be, at least after I got into the business.

I tried to pay attention to the events I covered and while I'm an accomplished talker, I'm a decent listener — and look at the opportunities I had to pay attention. I got close, as the title of this tome suggests, to the greats and the ordinaries of sport over the years while covering (deep breath) 10 Olympics games, 58 golf majors, 10 Ryder and/or Presidents Cups, a dozen Super Bowls, 14 World Series, hundreds of NHL, NBA and MLB postseason games and thousands of regular-season games. Plus thousands of horse races, even a few car races. On the other hand, no tennis, except during one Olympics. Not much curling, either, although I like curling and curlers and wish I'd had more opportunity.

I took pretty good notes and I had a pretty good memory, too, and loved to both hear and tell a good story. There's a little Rolodex somewhere in my head and before age rusts it out, I thought it might be a good idea to put down some of these yarns on paper, or on a screen somewhere or a plastic key or whatever this activity ends up being. I have a little rehearsed patter of favourite stories that I can summon on demand when asked. I have my radio-grade stories and my stories that would get me suspended from the radio. There are inclusions and omissions from both lists.

Caution, to some degree, is not uncommon. Once, speaking to Arnold Palmer after Tiger Woods had hit his fire hydrant and gone through a very public humiliation over his infidelities, I angled toward a question I naïvely thought Palmer might possibly answer. Understand that when it comes to women, the young, dashing Arnold Palmer was positively catnip and, in a theoretical match, he could give Tiger three a side when it comes to female companionship and still beat him like a rented mule.

(An old-time golf pro once told the story that in their very early days as touring professionals, he and Palmer travelled from tournament to tournament, sharing expenses. One night, while splitting a hotel room, the phone rang in the wee hours. The golfer answered it and an angry man at the other end asked if he were Arnold Palmer. Surveying Arnold's empty bed, he assured the man he was not. "I know you're not. That bastard is out right now with my wife. You tell him when he gets back I'm coming down there and I'm going to shoot him." The golfer assured the man he would pass along the message and, before hanging up, added another thought: "Just so you know, I'm in the bed by the window.")

To get back to Arnold this day, I asked him as gently as possible whether he was glad the height of his fame occurred in an era without cell phone cameras and *TMZ* and Instagram sharing your every move with the world, exposing all the 'gotcha' moments. Arnold looked at me, but he didn't want to play. "Not sure what you mean," he said, before eventually adding, "I am sure we all have stories we wouldn't want told unless we were dead — or our wives were."

Some of the subjects of those missing stories are not dead and neither are their wives. So best to let idle lawyers stay idle. There's still plenty to go around. By the way, I'd like to think I'm in the bed by the window.

Dave Perkins

JANUARY 2016

CHAPTER ONE

Midnight Morgue

This felt like an old B movie come to life. It was past midnight, cool and foggy, and where better to look for a missing major leaguer than the city morgue?

There had been no sign of Rick Leach, the AWOL Blue Jay, at any of the downtown Seattle hospitals. Officially, there was zero information; he hadn't been missing long enough to get police excited, although his teammates surely were.

A taxi driver with a sense of adventure had been hired to answer the question: where do you go in this town if you have a little money in your pocket and decide to take a powder?

It was the last week of August, 1987, and the Blue Jays were finishing off a successful West Coast trip in Seattle. It was baseball business as usual as the team assembled in the old Kingdome for game No. 126 of the season.

Leach was a wisecracking utility man, a Rose Bowl quarterback in his college days at the University of Michigan who had switched to baseball and, at this point in his career, was a six-year big-league veteran. A night after counting two hits and two RBIs while enjoying a rare start in right field, his name again was written into the starting lineup by manager Jimy Williams. Only one problem: Leach never showed up at the stadium.

Teammates wondered, increasingly worried. This wasn't like Leach. He was loud, a needler, the kind of guy who kept a team loose, treasured what little playing time he got and always played hard. He also loved to stir the clubhouse pot, and never minded targeting the black players. "Hey, Jesse," he would bellow at Jesse Barfield, the slugging outfielder who led the team (if not the league) in conspicuous consumption. "What are the only French words a black man knows?"

Barfield, warily, would take the bait and say he didn't know, at which point Leach would yell, "Coupe de Ville."

Or else he would turn his attention to Lloyd Moseby, the elegant fashion-plate centre fielder born in the South and brought up in Oakland. "Moseby, I know what you did when you were a kid," Leach would holler, bobbing his head forward and backward as he paraded across the clubhouse. "You were teaching the chickens how to walk."

Leach played it for laughs, always. He delivered his zingers without malice and always tried to make the clubhouse an easier place to inhabit. His teammates generally loved him, one reason so many were so upset when he didn't show.

A new lineup was posted. Reporters, including this one, were shooed upstairs to the press box by the usual pre-game time limits and the Jays officially grew vague about the player's whereabouts. Usually, the Blue Jays weren't like this when they didn't want to talk about something; they would clam up and make themselves scarce, but they wouldn't outright lie to anyone. This time they lied. A travelling PR man, not one of the regulars, said for the record that Leach was back at the hotel curled in a ball, the victim of bad seafood.

This would do as an answer for the early edition stories sent back across the continent to Toronto, but the constant huddling of team officials and lack of specific information had every reporter's radar up. Post-game, a 6-3 Blue Jay win, teammates were upset, with gusts to frantic, about the missing player. Despite a 5-3 trip that kept them in first place in the American League East Division, they packed almost silently for the cross-continent charter flight home and the next day's off-day. Relief pitcher Mark Eichhorn, a friendly and caring Christian, was in tears. "We don't even know he's alive," Ike said, before commencing a prayer.

Wait a second, here: in two hours we go from bad shellfish to a possible toe tag? Really?

My sports editor back at the *Toronto Star*, a wise old newspaper head named Gerry Hall, told me to file whatever story I could assemble, miss the charter flight, hang back in Seattle and search for Leach. Sounds easy, right?

Outside the ballpark, I located a cab driver who wanted to play this particular game and off we went: police stations, hospital emergency rooms, a couple of seedy motels that specialized in short-term stays. Confused night clerks looked at Leach's head shot in the Blue Jays media guide — the only photo I had of the guy — and thought I was putting them on.

After a couple of hours of chasing wild geese like this, I was beginning to lose my enthusiasm. The weather turned cool. The fog settled. It felt like a perfect night for an axe murder. When the cab pulled up in front of an old stone building on a dark street well after midnight, I asked where the hell we were now.

"City morgue," the driver said. "We might as well."

I am certain I did dumber things, or went stranger places, while chasing down stories in four decades of newspaper work. This, happily, turned out to be my one and only morgue visit.

I knocked or rang the night bell and heard footsteps approaching from inside. I thought to myself, if the door creaks open and this sonofabitch is a hunchback, I'm running. He turned out to be an ordinary guy in a lab coat who listened politely to my story and said, yes, we did have a John Doe brought in earlier that evening. Come right in and we'll see if everything fits.

He led me down a corridor and past a door that was marked "Decomposed." I waited while he checked his paperwork, then asked how old my missing right fielder was. "Around 30," I said.

"You're out of luck," he responded, noting that his John Doe was estimated to be in his 40s.

We did not, at that point, share the same definition of the term "out of luck." Happily, I thanked him and scooted back to the cab.

We never did find Leach, of course. He had been in an airport hotel, on some kind of bender, which turned out to be the first we knew of a recreational drug issue for which he later sought treatment. He sheepishly checked in with his wife and the ball club early the next morning. He returned to the Jays, albeit briefly and somewhat subdued. His career was nearly over, but he was far from the craziest guy I ever met in the business. He wasn't even the craziest guy on that ball team.

CHAPTER TWO

At Its Loudest

Often, when people discover how I made my living, they start telling me things about sports they feel I should know. Occasionally, they ask questions. Very occasionally, someone wonders about crowd noise and where and when I heard the most. The answer is easy: No. 1, undeniably, was in Minneapolis at the Metrodome during the 1987 World Series against the St. Louis Cardinals. It was seriously painfully loud. I had a choice seat in the front row of the main press box; I could reach out and slap the heads of the last row of lower-level spectators. Often I needed to fight that very urge. Those people were stupidly loud and the Metrodome roof kept every decibel in.

Right behind that on the tinnitus danger-scale, though, was the early Sunday afternoon in 1998 at Augusta National when Jack Nicklaus was on the prowl. At that stage of his golfing life, at age 58 and with retirement beckoning, Nicklaus was as beloved as ever, but only intermittently magical. Yet for a few holes, as he assembled birdies and his name laddered its way up the leader board, the noise expanded to the point that all around the course, golfers stepped away from their shots, looked toward the man-made thunder and guessed who was making the present very much resemble the past. As I put it in the *Star*:

> *Total strangers in the Nicklaus galleries hugged and high-fived as he stitched together an early quilt of birdies. He said a score of 64 or 65 was needed to get him back to the place he hadn't been in 12 long years, a place most of us (him, too) thought he would never be again.*
>
> *But he almost made an eagle three at the second hole, settling for a three-inch birdie putt. And when he chipped it in for birdie at the next hole, that 64 or 65 didn't seem so far-fetched. And even if it did, who cares? Go Jack!*
>
> *At the par-three sixth hole, playing 200 downhill yards, he knocked a 5-iron to five feet. He was two under par now, looking to go three under, and as he walked to his ball, the scoreboard showed leader Fred Couples had made bogey on the first hole to drop to minus-five.*
>
> *Nicklaus made his fast, edgy little putt to get within two strokes of the top. There is no roof on a golf course, but the roof went off the place anyway.*
>
> *Up he went to the seventh tee, ripping a long, fading drive up the right side of the fairway. Eighty yards to his left, Couples made a birdie at the boomerang second green and Jack was three shots back again. So Nicklaus dropped a wedge 15 feet short of*

> *the cup and rapped home the putt. Two shots back again. Deafness was one glorious possibility.*

Jack's charge petered out when the birdie putts refused to drop, and Mark O'Meara won with a late birdie, but the memory — particularly that noise and particularly at the sixth green after he made that birdie — stays fresh. It was one of what seems like a million Nicklaus moments, because time spent with Jack in the press rooms, where he loved to hold court, was so vivid and educational. Remember, I never saw him win a major (the last one was in 1986 and I didn't begin covering majors for another 10 years), but I heard him queried on them enough times. I recall a questioner casually suggesting that Jack surely couldn't provide specific shot details of a Masters win four decades before, but could he please speak in general about what he could recall. To which Jack replied, "You want club and yardage? For every shot? Because I can give them to you." And no doubt he could.

Some golfers couldn't remember at the end of their round what club they had hit two hours before on a certain hole. Jack not only remembered, but could summon details decades later.

In the 2005 Open Championship at St. Andrews, his final major championship appearances, he went out the only way he could at the Old Course's 18th hole as thousands looked on, many through tears. Part of my description:

> *"I knew that the hole would move wherever I hit it. I always make it on the 18th hole," he said.*
>
> *The hole didn't need to move and Jack didn't always make them, either, even if it seems that way. But he ended with a very proper bang, a 14-footer centre-cut for a birdie at the Old Course that deafened*

the heavens and meant not a thing — he had already missed the cut — but in its own way meant the world to those lucky enough to be there. Nicklaus included.

"I wanted the putt badly," Nicklaus admitted later, but he needn't have bothered stressing that particular point. Anybody who ever watched him, which means pretty much anybody who ever watched televised golf over the past 45 years, knew how much he wanted every one of them.

Pretty much every pro out there, starting with Tiger Woods, who worshipped both the man and his accomplishments, sought an audience with Nicklaus at one time or another, or an invitation to his tournament, or a word on the practice range. Nicklaus loved the role, that of being the paterfamilias of golf, but was always generous with his time. He also was either the teller or the feature of any number of stories.

For instance, in 1972, Lee Trevino, who won a few majors of his own in his day, went head to head with Nicklaus at Muirfield to win an Open Championship by one stroke, but made more money betting on himself at the local legal bookmakers than he earned in purse money. In 2009, Trevino told this story, framing it against that day's tabloids, which had mushroomed some relatively mild comments by Sandy Lyle about Colin Montgomerie into a veritable nuclear attack:

Trevino had travelled from Texas with friends and rented a large house. He threw a victory party that included a visit from the bookmaker, who brought what Trevino called a "suitcase full of cash" to pay everyone off. The house had come complete with a butler named Nicholas. The gentleman's gentleman said he had always wanted a golf lesson and Trevino, before the tournament, had promised he would indeed give him a lesson.

In conversation, a promise to "give Nicholas a lesson" went through the tabloid wringer and came out as a vow to "give Nicklaus a lesson." You can imagine the fun.

I always said I most enjoyed covering golf, of all sports, because there were no night games. It also took me to nice places, just about everyone was civil and the press was usually treated extremely well. As readers possibly know, covering golf tournaments can sometimes be a good game for a lazy man. They bring the leaders into the press room for an interview, then print up the quotes for distribution. The accuracy of the quotes usually is outstanding, although sometimes the sheets are sanitized if something juicy has leaked out. Unless you go out and actually watch golf and seek out individual interviews, you're writing with the pack. Sometimes, there was no way to write anything else, such as the great Carnoustie meltdown by Jean Van de Velde in 1999, the game's greatest, and most entertaining, train wreck. Everyone remembers the gory details, how Van de Velde arrived at the 18th tee of difficult and daunting Carnoustie with a three-stroke lead, then hacked his second shot off a grandstand, into the burn (the tiny walled stream that bisects the course), then the rough and a bunker, making triple bogey and blowing the lead and eventually losing in a playoff to Paul Lawrie. (Lawrie, by the way, had been almost anonymous to *Star* readers through 54 holes; he had been so far back, a record 10 strokes entering the final round, that he hadn't inserted himself into any stories.)

Van de Velde had been both charming and hilarious — certainly not easy in a second language — through three rounds, after which he held a five-shot lead. His Saturday press conference had been legendary:

> *When does Jean Van de Velde back up? When does the world's 152nd-ranked golfer back out of the room waving hello?*
>
> *If anyone thinks it's a joke that a relatively unknown golfer is leading the British Open after three rounds, and leading it by five strokes, no less, well the joke would more or less agree.*
>
> *"I've got the red nose in the bag," he said, an hour after shooting the lights out — make that putting the lights out — against the best field in the world on the toughest course in the world. He sat there cracking jokes and trading one-liners with reporters, yukking it up. In one session, he may have replaced Jesper Parnevik as golf's biggest whoopee cushion.*
>
> *Someone asked him about his sponsorship by the European Disneyland, outside Paris, and he didn't miss a beat: "Well, I test all the rides and then I have to walk around with the characters."*
>
> *What? Him worry?*
>
> *"What kind of pressure can you get in here? It is the biggest tournament ever in the world and I'm in there and I'm a bit ahead of everybody, so what can happen? I can lose it. That's the only thing that can happen."*
>
> *Then he thinks again.*
>
> *"The other is that I can win it."*

> *He probably blows it. He sounds as if he fritters it away.*

He did blow it, of course, although no one could possibly imagine the manner in which he did. The next day's *Star* sounded shocked:

> *Mon dieu. We've found the missing Marx Brother. He plays golf.*
>
> *Jean Van de Velde authorized a French farce of unimaginable proportions by handing away the greatest championship in golf in a brie-brained performance that was comedy turned to tragedy.*

It still might be the most remarkable screw-up I've ever seen — and I watched Kenny Williams run the bases, remember.

Three more things about Van de Velde's meltdown: One, I never heard a louder press-box reaction, before or since. Hundreds of reporters were shrieking in disbelief, most of them Europeans on deadline who had written their stories and sought only final scores before hitting the send button. They certainly didn't have the time to do literary justice to this historical collapse. Plus, now there was a three-man, four-hole playoff that would take another deadline-destroying hour, at least.

Two, my pal Cam Cole, a very good golfer, played the course the next day and went to the spot from which the Frenchman had hit his second shot at 18. (Van de Velde hit a grandstand railing with his second shot and bounced back into long rough, a truly terrible break.) Cam dutifully hit it toward the grandstand. It went in, which meant he could go to the drop zone, from where he pitched and made the bogey that would have won easily for JVV the day before. A month later, Cam caught up to him at the PGA Championship and told him he had, likewise, hit a solid 2-iron that went into the grandstand, instead of bouncing out. "It stayed in?" Van de Velde confirmed. "Lucky bastard!"

The third part is that a man named Chris Smith, a good friend then and now and a former men's captain at Carnoustie who knows every yard of the course, had been marshalling the 18th hole that day. A few weeks later, Van de Velde returned with a film crew to shoot a commercial at the scene of the crime. Smith went out to observe. They began setting up the cameras at the wrong tee box. Smith pointed out the mistake. Van de Velde said they had the correct tee. The two went back and forth and eventually a bottle of Scots whiskey was wagered. Upon checking the video, Smith was, of course, correct. Van de Velde went into town, bought a fine bottle at the local grog shop and returned to the club to share it with members. In the commercial, by the way, he made a double-bogey on the hole using only a putter. Took him five or six tries, but he eventually did it.

CHAPTER THREE

Best and Worst Weeks of the Year

As a kid growing up in the suburbs of Toronto, I liked the Toronto Argonauts. In my high school days, I went to quite a few games and really enjoyed the Canadian Football League. Once I got into, then out of, Ryerson and began a job, I didn't follow the Argonauts too much. This was around the period when the CFL, in a misguided move, blacked out most of its games in the home market. Coupled with a growing interest in wagering on National Football League games, I lost interest almost completely in the CFL. When I started in the sports-writing business, in 1973, the CFL was a good beat. It was No. 2 in Toronto after the Maple Leafs, with horse racing probably No. 3. When the Blue Jays arrived, racing and the CFL suffered. When the NFL got huge, the CFL suffered even more. It became a minor beat, sad to say. I covered relatively few games in my career, but I always enjoyed the CFL, prefer the three-down brand of football as a spectacle and considered it a plum assignment to cover a Grey Cup week. It was traditional and featured great, dedicated fans who were passionate about the game and about being there. They did not resemble the expense-account crowd that clogged Super Bowl venues. Mostly, it was fun and even a non-drinker — rarer to find at a Grey Cup than a bartender known by his last name — knew how to enjoy himself. Or herself, as the case may be.

It also was a time to catch up with press-box friends from across the country and no matter where the game was held, there was a pleasing sameness to it. I did four or five of them, and each time I considered it pound for pound the best week of the year and quintessentially Canadian. Others would suggest the Brier, the national men's curling championship, occupies the same lofty position of respect and inspires rapt enchantment among its chroniclers. I've never set foot in a Brier, but the stories I heard over the years would lead me to support such a premise.

To digress, my only contact with the Brier came via telephone and was a source of great hilarity among several colleagues. I was in Florida covering spring training and had gone to SeaWorld on a day off with my wife and son, who was seven at the time. Now, I am not much for mascots. Hate the damned things. They always seem to seek me out no matter how much I detest them and wish to be left alone by them. It's a long story, but I got into a situation with some kind of fuzzy dolphin that was wandering around SeaWorld, hugging children and such. It wanted to hug me and I kept telling it to piss off. I didn't hit it or anything, but after yet another confrontation I swore at it and called it a bleeping furball and gave it a nudge. It flopped down onto a path and began rolling around and moaning. A security guard came over and started giving me hell for attacking it. This did not exactly calm the situation.

We left SeaWorld not long afterward. Perhaps it was not my finest hour.

The next day, I mentioned the confrontation to some colleagues at spring training, causing great merriment all around. That night, in my motel in Dunedin, the phone rang and it was a gruff voice asking for me. Who the hell was this?

It was another stuffed animal mascot, this one known as the Brier Bear, calling from Nova Scotia or some place. My issues with the SeaWorld mascot had made the rounds and some friends at the Brier enticed the mascot there to call and harass me on behalf of his cousin Fred the Dolphin, or whoever the hell it was. Now I was into it, long distance, with another costumed furball and soon we were insulting each other, somewhat graphically. I am certain alcohol was involved, although not at my end. I could detect howls in the background. Apparently, my friends had me on speakerphone.

To this day I can't see a mascot without heading in the other direction, although the guy who plays the Raptor at Toronto's NBA games, who is really, really good; is a big golf fan and loves to chat. Him I don't mind. Plus he always takes off his dinosaur head when he talks.

The highlight of all my Grey Cups, other than the games themselves, was the legendary 2007 party in Toronto at the home of Argonaut co-owner David Cynamon. It was a toga-themed exercise in fantastic excess, with extraordinary food, drink and sightseeing. It was the first place I ever saw — repeat, saw — thirsty individuals slurp tequila shots off of cheerleaders' bellies. The band Trooper supplied the entertainment. A brief description:

> *Old Caligula himself might have been slightly hung over yesterday, given all the candy dispensed the*

evening before at a remarkable and memorable Grey Cup bash staged at Chez Cynamon. If any of the neighbours were big fans of Trooper, they likely considered "Raise a Little Hell" an appropriate greeting for midnight.

If the Grey Cup is the best week of the year, the Super Bowl, or at least the dozen I covered, represented my least favourite week of the year. It contained the flat-out worst day of my working calendar, namely the so-called Media Day held each Tuesday of SB week. Each team, for one hour in either the morning or afternoon, would make all of its players available in the stadium to the thousands of accredited media. In between the sessions, lunch would be served for several hundred, so these were extensive undertakings.

The press would be penned up outside the stadium, searched by overzealous security and sniffed at by bomb-detecting dogs, until the hour commenced, then released to literally sprint to the various star stations. Only the keeners and rookies ran hard; those of us who had been through it before recognized little of value came out of these gangbangs and didn't bother with the dash to the ringside seats. Star players would have their podiums surrounded. Non-stars would wander around on foot or else sprawl in the stands and draw smaller crowds of notepads and microphones.

This was the best opportunity for crazy people with media credentials — whether they were legit sports reporters or not — to dress up as nuns, the pope, cowboys or *Star Wars* creatures and the like. There were always one or two individuals — sometimes even women — wearing wedding dresses and "proposing" to Tom Brady, or whomever. In short, it was a complete zoo and, occasionally, players would play along with the stupidity. A guy was lucky if he could squeeze in a serious question and obtain a serious answer before someone dressed as a vegetable asked the player to describe his favourite salad, or someone asked a player to engage in a staring contest. Here was one description from 2000, a U.S. election year:

> *When the journalist representing the Cartoon Network asked players which cartoon character they would vote for as president — and they didn't mean Al Gore — you knew it was a case of anything goes. So the crackheads from Empty-V were bouncing around seeking player requests for the next video and the Comedy Channel provocateur was asking players whether you're allowed to make cell phone calls from the huddle and so on.*
>
> *The NFL, which never met a minicam it didn't like, will give a pass to anybody who asks, even to us highly trained professionals, like the guy several years ago who asked Doug Williams how long he had been a black quarterback.*

Media Day also was the day — although not the only day — a few women dressed provocatively to become the centre of attention, because that was their station's style. One veteran was the famous Ines Sainz, the spectacularly cantilevered Mexican sports-TV star who became the media focus (at least) of a couple of Super Bowls.

One year in Miami Beach, the Canadian reporters were assigned to a hotel with the rest of the so-called "international" press. The NFL considered Canadians to be "international" the way some Americans regard a pancake house in the same light. So one day, we were coming out of our hotel and a fire engine–red early 1960s convertible was outside the hotel door. Sitting on top of the back seat were Ines and an equally gorgeous confederate, both wearing little wee bikinis that, added up, would have covered about as much ground as a Kleenex. They were off to one of the team hotels to interview players, or at least those players not put off by such a gruesome sight.

The rest of us laughed and headed off to do our work, which, technically, was not so different from what they were doing. We were all trying to get players to say something interesting or newsworthy. These ladies just looked and dressed differently. So fast-forward to the next morning, on the wrong side of 7 a.m., and I pull into the hotel's breakfast room, seeking coffee and an IV drip. First person I see is Ines wearing sandals that lace up to the thighs, tiny short-shorts and a tight blouse tied at the cleavage in such a way that brought to mind two groundhogs wrestling under a blanket. Needless to say, my eyes were wide open without the aid of coffee.

So what, I thought to myself as I saw Ines head to the buffet, would such a creature allow herself to eat to maintain such a sensational silhouette? Two grapes and a thimble full of weak tea?

Wrong again. She loaded up on bacon and eggs, pancakes, hash browns, fruit, coffee, toast, juice, the whole works. My god, I thought: *she's eating just like a regular guy.*

The look, of course, was her gimmick, her way to stand out in a competitive business that demanded one main return from its on-air personnel: eyeballs and lots of them. In the TV world, how many was far more important than how they were drawn and nothing was off-limits.

One other feature of Super Bowl week was the press availability with the star of the halftime entertainment. They were always big names. One year the feature artist was Shania

Twain, promoting her new album called *Up*. While responding to idiotic prompts from a plant in the crowd about what she intended to sing, she jumped off her chair and pointed skyward and said "Up — where the balls go!" There was a momentary silence in the room at the shameless and ridiculous plug, which I filled by blurting out, "It depends how cold it is." That drew a decent laugh.

Other entertainment pressers in other years, like the Rolling Stones and Paul McCartney, were memorable, but the cream came in 2001 in Tampa — a city whose definition of a swanky restaurant, I wrote, meant any place with non-plastic cutlery. Britney Spears was the headliner, but was a no-show at Wednesday's scheduled press conference. The stage was left to grizzled old rocker Steven Tyler and the freshly scrubbed members of NSYNC, a boy band I had never heard of. The next day's *Star* carried a report that included the following:

> *"They promised us Britney Spears and the little minx didn't show. Gross me out. She stiffed a roomful of reporters old enough to be her, uh, older brothers . . . All we got instead were some harmless children named NSYNC and eventually, after a false start, the lurching entrance of Aerosmith, a pensioner-aged group of rockers. You thought the Raptors look old and slow lately? Man, these guys appeared right out of it.*
>
> *Their duck-lipped leader, Steven Tyler, at least had a few old rock-n-roller-type anarchist lines. Somebody asked one of NSYNC's lads, a curly headed little jasper, something about dating Tyler's daughter — that would be Liv — and Tyler muttered something about putting the family cat in the blender. You had to be there. Even if Britney was not.*

It turned out my "curly headed little jasper" was Justin Timberlake — complete stranger to me at the time of course — and there soon were a ton of angry emails, apparently from teenaged girls and, occasionally, their mothers, calling me vile names and worse.

Timberlake, everyone remembers, got into a jackpot at Super Bowl halftime in 2004 for the famous "wardrobe malfunction." At the end of one song he tore off part of Janet Jackson's dress, exposing a breast, complete with nipple jewellery, for perhaps one second. Naturally, all hell broke loose, although I thought it was a well-designed play and still do. MTV, the music video channel I usually referred to as Empty-V, was promoting the halftime show in opposition to something called the Lingerie Bowl, whose title is self-explanatory. The briefly exposed nipple seemed all too convenient and as outrage mounted over the next 48 hours, I jumped in to prop up the forgotten side:

> *The NFL is in perfect position here: It gets to tut-tut and claim the high moral ground that such a terrible, depraved thing could ever happen on our dime when in reality, the holiness of the $2.5 million commercial spot is not only maintained, it probably is enhanced.*
>
> *You think anyone is ever going to stage a Lingerie Bowl again? You think anyone's going to be stupid enough to take on the greatest god in television, the Super Bowl, with vague promises of pay-per-view titillation? The Super Bowl has already given you the real thing, Bosco. It gave you the Other Jackson. There will be nobody trying to upstage next year's halftime show.*
>
> *It is to laugh, to hear Paul Tagliabue and the blue suits wring their hands about what those ruffians at Empty-V did to our precious halftime. The NFL didn't*

> *know that crotch-grabbing and overt sexuality were the staple of the network's videos? Sure. It's not difficult to believe that no one at the NFL or CBS knew what was coming. It's impossible to believe that.*
>
> *Janet? She had a new record coming out the next day. What could a little extra exposure hurt? Her weepy apologies prolong the matter and don't hurt the cause, either.*

I never changed my mind on that, by the way. I always thought it was a set-up and still do. The words Janet Jackson and Nipplegate set a record for Google searches that stood for several years. Somebody was on the ball.

Generally, the Super Bowls I handled were lousy, one-sided games, with a couple of exceptions. Pittsburgh's late back-and-forth with Arizona in 2009 was a classic, the best I attended. Most memorable might be the 2000 game in Atlanta, in which St. Louis beat Tennessee on a game decided on the final play as a bid for the tying touchdown was tackled a yard short of the goal line. That finish isn't the only reason the game resonates here. One is that Atlanta had a touch of freezing rain a couple of days before the game and the city panicked and hunkered down, shutting schools and cancelling parties and Super Bowl functions and such. On the Saturday afternoon, all stories filed, Stephen Brunt and I sat and had a beer at our hotel bar and watched out the window as cars smashed into each other on Peachtree Street while drivers unsuccessfully tried to deal with unrecognizable (to them) elements. One other is that the Rams were simply so interesting, starting with their quarterback, Kurt Warner, who had been stocking grocery shelves not long before. They also had a strange cat of a defensive end named Kevin Carter, who had delusions about both worshipping and being Superman:

> *The man who fancies himself as Superman, who has a fixation, if not outright obsession, with the comic-book character right down to the point of believing reporters are mild-mannered and referring to his own wife as Lois Lane, used to play as if opposing tackles were coated in kryptonite.*
>
> *You remember kryptonite. Its mysterious power had laid low more superheroes than undercover cops.*
>
> *Carter is 290 pounds of buffed mayhem now, this season's sack leader with 17 and a half — whatever a half-sack is. He believes he is the standard for NFL defensive ends in terms of speed, power, quickness and all those categorical buzzwords. Plus, he thinks he should change clothes in a phone booth.*
>
> *"He's Superman. He will tell you that and if you tell him that he's not, he will chase you and catch you and tell you again that he is," says his friend and fellow Pro Bowler D'Marco Farr, the defensive tackle. "He really believes it."*

Carter wasn't the only source of easy stories that year. Both team owners, namely the Titans' Bud Adams and the Rams' Georgia Frontiere, were borderline nutcases who provided good copy for columnists without even trying hard. Brief references were made to both:

> *The wacko owner, part one: Who could resist the image of Bud Adams brandishing the [AFC title]*

> *trophy and beaming out from underneath a hairpiece that looked as if it were feeding its young yesterday morning? This is the NFL and municipal blackmailers must be rewarded.*
>
> *The wacko owner, part two: Georgia Frontiere inherited the team from her sixth husband, an allegedly Mobbed-up guy whose mysterious death has been worth 20 years of ugly rumours. Then she saw her seventh husband go to jail for tax evasion after he was caught scalping the Rams' Super Bowl tickets years ago. Georgia, also an astrology nut, is convinced she can't lose in Georgia.*

A week's worth of buildups for any one of these overhyped Super Bowl matchups always stretched my creative limits, to be sure. I always itched for the game to arrive, although game days themselves were long and mostly tedious, beginning with bus rides to the stadiums and extensive security checks (particularly after 9/11) before early arrivals. Those early arrivals were always required because we needed to first find our seats in whatever auxiliary press box we had been assigned, and then make sure the telephones we had ordered, and paid a ton of money for, were indeed hooked up and working so we could file our stories. This was a cash cow for the telephone companies, by the way; they used to charge something like $350 to hook up a private line. That would include a fee for the first month of service, even though we needed the damned thing for about six hours. The NFL always looked the other way at this rip-off.

This nonsense changed with the invention of wireless internet service, early in the first decade of this century, although the technology we now take for granted arrived with some serious growing pains. The main press box was always reserved for the competing teams' hometown papers, plus the larger national outlets. Because Toronto had no NFL team, all Canadian writers were always assigned to the auxiliary boxes with the rest of the so-called international press. Fine. In Phoenix in 2008, during the helmet-catch game where the Giants beat the Patriots in a spectacular back-and-forth finale, there were something like 350 reporters in one corner of the upper deck in an auxiliary press box, including me.

Hours before the game, we tested the wireless, for which we were charged a reasonable flat fee. Maybe $50 if I remember correctly. It seemed to work pretty well. And then it went out. It would get back up and running and seem fine. And then it would go out. This continued for a while and approaching kickoff, we were starting to panic because the service was extremely unreliable. Given that no one bothered to order expensive telephone lines any longer, we needed the wireless running smoothly in order to file. We were helpless without it.

The NFL and the local wireless provider assigned their chipheads to sort out the problem and finally it was discovered. The router was in the top row of the section. Sitting in front of it was a German writer, a massive guy from *Der Zeitung* or some such paper. Now take this from someone who is so technologically challenged that he can barely work a zipper, but as I understood it, every time the big German stood up, he did something to the router and it shut down. Something like that.

The solution, once discovered, turned out to be easy. The NFL found the guy another place to sit and kept the space in front of the router empty by putting yellow police tape across the now-empty seats. We all laughed at the absurdity of it, but the wireless worked the rest of the night.

Soon, as technology improved, wireless came to be taken for granted, and it got cheap enough that it was provided free of charge in most places. By the time I came off the road, in 2013, I think the British Open was the last place I went that still charged for wireless access to the internet.

As an aside, when Augusta National first went wireless about 10 years ago, the wireless in the dedicated press building crashed on the first day of the tournament. It couldn't be resurrected and a couple of hundred writers needed to share the few landlines that worked in the building. Well, the Masters communications people were mortified; they imported chipheads — word was a couple of club members dispatched their private jets to pick up more technicians in nearby states — and when we all arrived at work Friday morning, each of the 200 or so press spaces had been hardwired with an Ethernet cable. Plus there was a letter of apology from the golf club, asking forgiveness for Thursday's problem. What a place. There's nowhere like it.

Back to the Super Bowl, which always had one great thing going for it no matter where it was held: the food was always superb. Maybe the boxed lunches provided during the games were standard stuff, but the parties all week for media and sponsors and the like were generously first-rate, including the post-game spread back at the headquarters hotel, to which every media person was invited. Your game credential was always good for admittance and, with the free bar all part of things, it was always a great time. It's the only part of a Super Bowl week I could ever regret missing.

CHAPTER FOUR

Sneaking In to Journalism

Basically, Richard Nixon helped me land my first real newspaper job. To be entirely accurate, it was a combination of Tricky Dick and a bad headline in the *Globe and Mail.*

It was late in the summer of 1973, international intrigue around Watergate was at its peak and my third and final year of my journalism program at Ryerson was commencing. One of our courses was called masthead and involved a few weeks of editing and producing the *Ryersonian*, the daily (Tuesday through Friday) student newspaper. It was a little eight- or, occasionally, 12-page broadsheet that featured student writers, photographers and editors and, now and then, actually could be quite good. I was the editor-in-chief for six weeks and assembled a staff consisting of city, sports, photo and entertainment editors, copy editors, reporters, etc.

On a parallel track, the *Globe and Mail*, in something of a quaint custom, asked Ryerson to send down a six-pack of third-year students for what was lovingly called a two-week "tryout" on the copy desk. There was a certain scouting element to it, of course, but it also was essentially cheap labour for kids anxious to please, even doing some of the grunt jobs a newspaper features.

During my stint as *Ryersonian* editor, my number came up for one of these "tryouts." No worries. I worked on the school paper until it went to bed, usually by about 5:30 p.m., then hustled down to the *Globe* and sat on the copy desk until about 1 a.m. Kids just turned 20 had plenty of energy for such a schedule in those days.

Now, one of my responsibilities as big-chief editor at the *Ryersonian* was to select the topic for, and cause to be written, the lead editorial in the little paper. (We all took this stuff seriously, by the way.) I had decided that Richard Nixon, whose Watergate fingerprints were being revealed line by line pretty much every day, was worthy of a good whack from our earnest little publication. The idea seems ridiculous now, of course, that a mostly flimsy student newspaper in another country could leave any kind of scar, but, again, we took this stuff seriously and we had lived through Vietnam and Kent State and all the other atrocities that reaffirmed, to us anyway, that Richard Nixon was a Bad Man.

In order to pan-fry him properly, though, there was some point of law to be referenced and off I went to the library to pull out books and research it. Something about the executive branch and the judicial branch and the legislative branch and where they all fit on this particular tree. (Nowadays you could do it in 30 seconds on the internet, but in those days it meant time spent thumbing through dusty old books.) I found what I needed, wrote my scathing denouncement of the U.S. president and bolted for the *Globe*. That evening, I had been assigned to the foreign desk, which was literally knee-deep in wire copy about Watergate. The slotman, the maître d' of the copy desk, was having trouble sorting out one or two arcane points and up chirped Perkins, freshly armed with some technical knowledge from his time in the library that very afternoon. Made it sound as if I very casually understood the minutiae about the executive and judicial and so on.

"You know this shit?" the slotman asked. "Then carve this together into something readable."

He threw me a basket of wire copy, which I then proceeded to trim and shape — using scissors and paste, which is how we did it back then — into a useful, coherent story. It ran on the front page and the managing editor, the next day, was complimenting the slotman who, to his endless credit, pointed at little old me and said I was the chief wizard on the topic. For the next two weeks I was, too.

My "tryout" came and went and they kept asking me to come in and work on the foreign desk and sort out the Watergate copy. Five days a week. Between that and editing the *Ryersonian*, I didn't get much sleep, but who cared? The *Globe* began paying me — $21 a day, in cash every Thursday. (I didn't know it then, but this was the way to keep me off the books and out of the union's scope of activity. Later on, I learned about this strategy somewhat painfully.)

The custom at the *Globe* in those days was to handle the early edition of the paper, universally called "the bulldog," by about 7:45 p.m., then break for an hour for dinner. The newsroom pretty much emptied, except for me, who could not afford to eat out. I would sit in the newsroom, reading the freshly printed bulldog, and eat my wrapped-up sandwiches.

One day, a headline in the sports section caught my eye. It said something about the Oakland Athletics closing in on the

East Division pennant. Now, I had always been a huge baseball fan, but it didn't take much of a fan to know this was a dumb mistake, since Oakland wouldn't be in the East Division of anything that didn't start in Japan. I looked around; the newsroom was empty. I didn't even know where the sports department was located, other than a vague sense that it was down yonder hallway. So away I went and not too far away, in a large, messy, glassed-in room with some sporting pictures on the wall, a white-haired man sat, chewing on a cigar, his feet on the desk.

It was a sports editor out of central casting and so was his response when I knocked. The gruff old bastard growled, "Whaddya want, kid?" I gently pointed out the mistake, at which point he jumped to his feet, yelled "Jesus H. Christ!" at me and started bellowing.

I did the only sensible thing. I ran away. Ran back down the hall, back to the foreign desk, got down as low as I could and concentrated on the last of my sandwich, wondering how I had gotten myself into this scrape.

The other troops wandered back from dinner and the rest of the shift began, as usual. New stories replaced old stories and headlines and pictures were changed and newspaper life moved on. At one point, I looked up and there was that old white-haired guy . . . staring at me. He started toward me. I was trapped, felt doomed.

"Are you the kid who showed me that goddamn headline?" he said. I stammered out an apologetic confirmation, at which point he cut me short. "I just came to thank you. You saved our ass. We got it changed before too many papers got out. By the way, who are you?"

He was Jim Vipond, the *Globe*'s long-time and legendary sports editor and, I soon discovered, a fine guy and great boss. When he determined my status as a Ryerson kid on an extended tryout working five nights a week, he asked if I liked, or knew anything about, sports. I croaked out something acceptable and he told me he needed me Saturday night. There was no Sunday paper, but sports needed a junior man to clear the wires, alert editors to breaking news and mark up things like hockey summaries and race results that would be carried over to the Monday paper. (That's one of the things I meant by newspaper grunt work.)

Thus began my salaried foray into big-time sports journalism. The foreign-desk gig dried up, as a new recruit of third-year students showed up to try out. My sports job soon became five and sometimes six nights a week on the sports copy desk. The *Ryersonian* term expired and still I kept showing up at the *Globe* to find my name pencilled in to next week's schedule. I even got a staff mailbox and every Thursday, a chit would arrive in an envelope that would entitle me to go down to the cashier's cage and draw either $105 or $126 in cash, depending whether I had worked five or six days the previous week.

This seemed like all the money in the world to a 20-year-old, who soon spent too much of it on booze on a night off.

Several months into my *Globe* career, I had a free Saturday night and went to the Brunswick House, a venerable tavern that featured cheap beer, loud bands and an interesting client base. I had too many beers and upon leaving, tried to scurry across Bloor Street. A relatively new subway line ran under Bloor, but the old streetcar tracks, while falling into disrepair, had yet to be ripped up. Somehow, I tripped over one track and landed on the other, elbow first. Dislocated it. Friends walked me down to Toronto General and there I spent the night, sobering up and aching. A bandage and sling were added to my wardrobe as I resumed work at the *Globe* and that seemed to be the end of it, until a letter arrived from the hospital a couple of weeks later — along with a bill for something like $700.

I had always been listed on my father's OHIP for previous hospital sojourns for broken wrists and fingers and a messed-up knee as a kid. For this emergency room visit, I had handed in the same card I had used for years. Except my father had died the year before and I hadn't obtained any coverage of my own despite being a "working" man. Shaken, I took the letter and bill into work. I asked advice from a copy editor named Bill Luscombe — a brilliant if pedantic guy with words who taught me more about the English language than anyone this side of Shakespeare. Luscombe, who also happened to be the union's shop steward, said I had been working there long enough to surely be covered by the company hospital plans, etc. He walked me down another hallway to a tiny office. It was the newspaper guild office, where the union head listened politely to my story and then asked two questions: Who the hell are you and HOW LONG have you been working here?

Too late to make a long story short, but this was the union officially discovering me and likewise finding the paper had been hiding me and paying me in cash and denying me benefits and so on, all in strict contravention of the contract. The union went crazy and the upshot turned out to be that given my time already spent in full-time employment, I had therefore officially passed my six-month "trial" period and I was to be considered a full-time employee entitled not only to overtime and benefits but also to back-dated overtime and benefits. And, of course, the paper needed to pay my hospital bill and enroll me in the various benefit plans immediately and so on.

None of this made management too happy, of course. Clark Davey, the managing editor, called me in and yelled at me for being a troublemaker and said I would never amount to anything. He said — actually said to my face — that he considered Ryerson people "too stupid" to ever help him. I asked why, therefore, did the *Globe* always request Ryerson send down waves of third-year students for "tryouts?" His answer was for me to get out of his office.

Welcome to the business.

The *Globe* gig was my first regular job, but was not actually my maiden voyage on a newspaper. Earlier that summer of 1973, I had a decent idea for a freelance piece. I noticed the Yankees brought up a pitcher named Dave Pagan from Nipawin, Saskatchewan. A Canadian pitching with the lordly Yankees! What a story. I called the three Toronto newspapers to pitch the idea. The *Star* said no, we have our own baseball writer who will do it. The *Globe* wasn't interested. At the *Sun*, sports editor George Gross said he would love to have it and that if it was any good and the paper ran it, he would give me $100 for it. I called the Yankees and arranged for a press pass, jumped in my car and headed down. Gas was cheap and by taking the back highways I avoided the tolls of the New York State Thruway. I could make the trip for $100, no problem. I got a cheap motel outside New York and headed to Yankee Stadium.

It couldn't have worked better. A PR man named Marty Appel set me up with a pass and ushered me into the office of manager Ralph Houk. He called me "podner" and asked me if I wanted a drink. Pagan was great to talk to and I filled my notebook. The Yankees were playing the White Sox that weekend and I witnessed a small piece of history; knuckleballer Wilbur Wood started (and lost) both games of a doubleheader for Chicago and that remains the last time the same pitcher started both games of a major league twin bill.

The next day, Appel told me that when the game ended, I was welcome at the press lounge, to have a drink while the traffic cleared. He told me to sit at a table. I obeyed. In trickled various writers and front-office people and ex-players. The table filled up. Whitey Ford sat down beside me. Yogi Berra was over there. People started telling stories. I sat there, slack-jawed and silent, sipping a Coke while they pounded back whiskey and told more stories. How good was this?

At one point, Whitey Ford leaned over and said to me, "Where ya from, kid?" I croaked out "Toronto" and he said, "Hey, you must know my friend Shopsy." He was referring to Sam Shopsowitz, the bon vivant and fixture among the sporting crowd who also owned the city's largest delicatessen.

"No, I don't know him, but I eat his corned beef," I stammered out, which was pretty much the extent of my contribution to the conversation.

The party broke up, the traffic cleared and I began the drive back to Toronto after this unbelievable day. "This business," I thought to myself, "can be fun. This is the work for me."

Back home, I wrote the story, three days later the *Sun* ran it and George Gross called me in to get paid. My foot was in the door — but not for long. The $100 Gross had promised me was forgotten. "I didn't know you were a student," Gross told me. "I can only pay students $25."

Now, this was wrong. I held firm, spoke of the deal we had agreed to. Gross refused to budge and, knowing George as I later did, I suspect he planned to invoice $100, pay me the $25 and put the rest in his pocket. I told him to keep his $25 because he needed it more than me. Our meeting ended not what you would call amicably. Needless to say, that was the last byline I ever had in the *Sun*.

Watergate was in the news, though. And you know where it led me a few weeks later.

CHAPTER FIVE

Those Blue Jays

For a couple of years there, Kelly Gruber was a very good, if brittle, third baseman for the Toronto Blue Jays. Twice an all-star. Good with fans off the field. Did a lot of charity work. One year, he was nominated for the Lou Gehrig Memorial Award, a spirit/character kind of honour. Gruber was clearly touched even to be mentioned for it. Except, like most ball players of his day, he didn't know a thing about Lou Gehrig other than he was some kind of famous player from caveman days.

"Ask Perk," Lloyd Moseby said to Gruber one day in the clubhouse, after Gruber had wondered aloud about the man after whom the award was named. "Perk knows all that history stuff."

Thus began the 39-cent explanation to Gruber and Moseby about the great Yankee first baseman, one that listed his achievements and concluded with a particular favourite stat:

". . . and one year, 1930, Gehrig had 27 homers and 115 RBIs . . . on the road."

Moseby's head snapped up. "What?"

"Yes, he had 27 homers and 115 RBIs strictly in road games that year. Plus, they played only 77 away games back then, when it was a 154-game season. Gehrig had 175 RBIs overall that season. Plus, you know, 49 times Babe Ruth had just unloaded the bases in front of him. Pretty good year, huh?"

Both Moseby and Gruber shook their heads in admiration, at which point Jesse Barfield happened to walk past.

"Jesse, Jesse. Listen to this," Moseby said, after which I told the same story, ending with the same stat.

Barfield considered the information and said, flatly, "That's impossible."

Assured that it was, indeed, correct and that they could go look it up, Barfield then switched the conversation to his favourite area.

"So how much did this guy make?" he wondered.

Told that Gehrig's best salary was $33,000, Barfield chuckled and put it into his own personal focus: "How good could he have been if he didn't make no cake?"

Postscript to this story: Gruber saw a famous old photograph taken of Gehrig in the Tiger Stadium dugout, looking out at the field wearing a somewhat stoic expression the day his consecutive game streak ended in 1939. On the Jays' next trip into Detroit, Gruber arranged for a photographer to pose him in the same pose Gehrig had assumed, at the same place in the same dugout, nearly 50 years earlier. That always impressed me, that he would arrange such a thing on his own.

Those players — Gruber, Barfield, Moseby — and a handful of others formed the nucleus of the first team I covered for any extended period. I switched from the sports desk to covering baseball in 1985, when the Blue Jays were going to the postseason for the first time in their existence and, for the *Star*, it was all hands on deck.

Initially, with a few weeks left in the season, I started covering the American League West, attempting to locate the team that would face the Jays in the AL Championship Series. I travelled to Kansas City late in the season for a showdown series against the Oakland Athletics. The winner would be in the driver's seat for the demi-pennant. I was to stay with the team that won the series, but it wasn't close. The Royals swept Oakland as George Brett put on a slugging clinic. I remained with the Royals the rest of the season while the Blue Jays clinched the East by beating the Yankees. When those two teams met in the ALCS — what we simply used to call the playoffs — I was part of a *Star* team that included 19 reporters and photographers. No kidding. Nineteen people on one assignment. Sports and news reporters, sports and city-side columnists, photographers and even two darkroom guys to process and send photos on the spot.

It cost the paper hundreds of thousands of dollars in expenses, obviously, but back then most papers, and particularly the *Star*, didn't think about cost; they thought about packing their product with a volume of information that would attract readers and plenty of them. They also knew they would get more than enough advertising to cover any extra expenses. Nowadays, they would think only of the costs involved and would never, ever send anywhere near that many staffers to any assignment. Not possible.

Those 1985 Blue Jays, every fan will remember, blew a 3-1 series lead and lost to the Royals and the most compelling reason, at least to me, was Bobby Cox's mismanagement. The Jays had a very good lefthanded hitter named Al Oliver, playing in the final games of his career, who neutralized Royals closer Dan

Quisenberry, tagging him for the game-winning hit in the series' second game. But Cox pinch-hit for Oliver early in the sixth and seventh games with a lefthander on the mound for Kansas City, and Oliver's late-game absences brought Quisenberry back into the picture as the Royals rallied. I remember Oliver, furious at Cox, leaning on the wall outside the Blue Jays clubhouse after the disaster, his career now freshly over. "Over 2,700 hits in the big leagues and he thinks I got none of them against lefthanders?" Oliver said. He was incredulous at the way he had been misused. He wasn't the only one.

Cox left soon after for the Atlanta Braves. Jimy Williams replaced him as manager. The next year I began covering baseball semi-regularly and went to spring training for the first time in 1987. The highlight that spring was a trip to Puerto Rico to play the Pittsburgh Pirates in a two-game series to honour the late Roberto Clemente. The newspaper guys flew on the team charters in those days — each paper billed for a seat at commercial airline rates — and I remember the charter touching down in San Juan in a thick rainstorm late one night. We got off the plane and there was Vera Clemente, the great player's widow, standing in pouring rain greeting everyone exiting the plane and thanking them for coming. This was a particular thrill for me, to meet Mrs. Clemente. Virtually none of the players had any idea who she was, which is not surprising because few of them, apart from the Latins, had any idea who Roberto Clemente was.

For three days that rain never eased up for longer than a brief period. The teams got out to Hiram Bithorn Stadium briefly, but the field was not playable. Before the teams gave up and flew back to Florida, most of our time was spent at the oceanfront hotel and in the hotel's casino, where one night I went on the hottest-shooting run of my life at the craps table. Jimy Williams stood at the other end of the table while I made several points and threw all the numbers, several of them the hard way. I made about $3,700 — this after starting with $5 line bets — and Williams made more than that. A couple of players were in on the action, too, and as the roll went on all around the table, red $5 chips gradually were replaced by the black $100 items and sometimes by the stack. All except for Dave Stieb, who stood there risking no more than $5 and dragging that every time I made a point. Stieb at the time was the most highly paid player on the team, making nearly $1.1 million. This time, he was excited to make about $60. I was overjoyed by my windfall. Williams was, too. I don't know how much Jimy made in those days, but I know he had a little business on the side back home in Dunedin, Florida, making lamps out of broken baseball bats and selling them in a local hobby shop for $20 or so.

Williams was packed with baseball knowledge. He could explain any element of the game, the proper way to play and where the mistakes, even subtle ones, were made. Like most managers, he hated to review the mistakes portion of it, at least in public. He protected his players, even the ones he couldn't stand, and refused to criticize them. He bristled, at least, at what he considered a contentious question. Once, in Kansas City, he ordered George Brett walked intentionally in the bottom of the ninth, even though Brett represented the potential winning run. An error and a base hit later, or some such combination, and the Royals had rallied to win with Brett, naturally, scoring the winning run. Having witnessed, close-up, Brett's unconscious run late in the 1985 season, I knew it was not a wrong move to walk him. I'd have walked him 100 times out of 100 with the game on the line. It didn't work out this time, but it wasn't wrong.

As reporters assembled, somewhat delicately after such a painful defeat, the question was put (by me) about walking Brett. Before I could finish it Williams was screaming at me, calling me a "second-guessing cocksucker" and to get out of his office and so on. I tried to say I understood his reasons and agreed with them, but he was yelling and in no mood to listen. As I made the clubhouse rounds of players to ask questions, one of them asked what had set the manager off. "I asked him about walking Brett," I answered, to which he responded, "You're not the only one wondering about that."

Williams and I hashed it out the next day and I explained that even if we understood his reasons for doing something, we still needed to ask just so we could hear his explanation. After that incident, Williams and I never had any serious issues. I never thought he much liked me, but he tolerated me and that's all I could ask. I also always thought he altered his personality when he got the job as manager from his more outgoing and happy demeanor as a coach. Some days when he was manager you couldn't pull a pin out of his ass with a tractor, but he surely knew the game. He had a sense of humour that needed more exposure than it received. For instance, in 1987 he got his own Topps baseball card, his first since his 1966 rookie card from his (brief) major league playing days.

"I was on a rookie card with two other guys," Williams told us. "Joel Horner and George Kornreich. Joel Horner had a pretty good career. Kornreich is a peanut farmer now, so I guess two of us did pretty good, cause being a peanut farmer's not too bad."

When those 1987 Blue Jays collapsed in record-setting fashion, blowing the three and a half game lead with seven games to play, including getting swept by Detroit in the final three-game series in Tiger Stadium to miss postseason play entirely (this was before the wild card was introduced), I felt worse for Williams than for anyone else on the team. Because I knew he would take it harder.

There's one particularly vivid memory about that final-week collapse. The rot had set in several days earlier, when shortstop Tony Fernandez had gotten hurt again and then catcher Ernie Whitt broke a rib. Milwaukee, always tough on the Jays, swept them. But, looking back, I now figure the real harbinger of doom arrived on the Thursday, when the team's flight to Detroit took off from Toronto.

A goose was sucked into the engine on takeoff and problems were apparent. There was a foul smell and a bit of smoke in the cabin, flames were spewing out of the engine and the plane was shuddering. The plane got out over Lake Ontario and began dumping fuel. The pilot told us we were going back for a landing in Toronto. The stewardesses went into their blank-faced efficiency mode. David Wells was sitting in the exit row in front of me. The flight attendant calmly explained his duties regarding opening the emergency door and asked him if he understood. Wells's response was simple: "Holy shit!"

There was some handshaking and good-luck wishes, although no panic whatsoever, and the plane came in to land with emergency vehicles clustered near the runway, lights flashing, just in case. The plane got down safely, to a few cheers of relief from some passengers, and we spent a long time waiting for a new plane in a lounge at the airport. There was some heavy drinking going on, and not only among the press. The next flight, three hours later, wasn't exactly relaxing and it was a very tired, very quiet ball team that checked in to its hotel late that night. I remember sidling up to Jimy Williams outside the elevator and murmuring that he had more than a few players who seemed to be looking for mama. Williams just nodded. Whether this had anything to do with getting swept by the Tigers we can never know. But it surely couldn't have helped.

It isn't possible to discuss those late-'80s Blue Jays without swinging the conversation around to George Bell sooner or later. Bell was the commanding presence on those teams, the loud, funny — both intentionally and not — slugger who dominated every room he entered. He would spar with coaches, players, writers, fans and it wasn't long, in any conversation, before he threatened to "keel" you. Being threatened with assassination was a daily occurrence for most writers; it was as necessary, after a while, as morning coffee. Bell also was the opposite of most players in one regard: the more he did in a game, the less he would talk about it. Some players, you couldn't find them after the game unless they had three hits or drove in big runs. These same phonies, if they'd taken a collar or made a critical mistake, hid from or snarled at any reporter who dared to approach them afterward.

Not Bell. The bigger the hit, the less he would talk about it. He also had more big hits than anyone and after watching the Blue Jays closely for nearly 40 years, I would suggest if I were down one run with the tying run at second base in the bottom of the ninth, it is George, by a nose over Paul Molitor and Jose Bautista, among all Blue Jays, whom I would want at the plate. He didn't always shear off a base hit somewhere to tie the game — no one does — but he did it often enough that he'd be my first choice to get the next opportunity.

Bell had a personal whipping boy in coach John McLaren, a good guy whom he would abuse, and loudly, at every opportunity. McLaren would throw a session of batting practice and Bell would yell at him, mixing in colourful curse words in both English and Spanish. "My kid could throw better than that" would be the nicest thing he ever said to Johnny Mac.

In the clubhouse, Bell would detect McLaren's voice and scream, "No coaches talking when players are talking."

McLaren eventually began handing it right back to Bell at every opportunity. This, naturally, delighted Bell, who never passed a chance to escalate any silly situation. McLaren didn't feel that way in the beginning, though.

"Last year I didn't," McLaren once told me. "It made me feel bad and I talked to him about it. He said, 'Oh, McLaren. I like you. You okay.' I knew he meant it. Now I kind of like his

With Mickey Mantle in 1976. We were all hairier in those days, including Paul Beeston (over Mantle's shoulder in the loud check.)

comments. He's so funny. I never know what he's going to say next. And he keeps the guys loose."

It wasn't only players and coaches he would stick the needle in.

Toronto businessman Michael Firestone was a great friend of team president Paul Beeston and a guy I once called the team's unofficial hood ornament (a description he liked). He also was a friend of Bell's and one winter, he managed to get Bell on skis on a beginner's hill near Toronto. This was after Bell had won the American League MVP in 1987 and had contract negotiations on his horizon.

The next day, Bell called Beeston to say he was trying out for the Dominican ski team and added, "Everything's fine, Paul. I just thought I should talk to you before I go under the anesthetic."

Firestone had a picture taken and sent to Beeston. It was signed by Bell: "Skiing's been berry, berry good to me. Who needs baseball?"

Once, in Yankee Stadium where the customers can be brutal to visiting players, Bell absorbed his usual fan serenades, the ones that urged him to perform a rare biological feat. Chasing a double down the line into the left field corner, Bell had a full cup of beer emptied on him by one thoughtful fan.

The printable parts of Bell's postgame rant concerned unmentionable fans doing unmentionable things and ended with his disgusted declaration that "this place is a zoo."

Then he summoned back the writers to whom he had just granted an audience to amend his last statement.

"No, it's not a zoo," he reconsidered. "At the zoo the animals run away when you look at them."

Baseball humour, while usually never approaching the level of, say, the Algonquin Round Table, tends to be sharp and crude and miles from politically correct. A man who makes a clanking but harmless error might, the next day, arrive at his locker to find a frying pan sitting there affixed with a sign that says something clever like, "Your new glove."

Occasionally the barbs centre on ethnicity and race. Once, Ernie Whitt was pointing out the club's makeup and said, knowing Bell was listening, "We seem to have a lot of cans in this clubhouse." When someone asked him what he meant by "cans," Whitt began listing: "Domini-cans. Puerto Ri-cans. Mexi-cans," with the emphasis on the last syllable.

To which Bell loudly retorted, "How about Ameri-cans?" It broke up the house.

The heartbreak of 1987, when the Blue Jays blew a three and a half game lead with seven to play, including that last-weekend sweep in Detroit, included Bell going 2 for 27 in the collapse, yet still winning the MVP for his 47 home runs and 134 RBIs. But that finish was the preamble to the disaster of 1988, which began in spring training when Bell refused his shift from left field to designated hitter and lay down on the grass near the bullpen rather than accept the DH role when it was his turn to bat in an exhibition game.

All hell broke loose, naturally. Bell's pride was hurt and, from his perspective, he asked everyone to name another MVP in history who arrived at spring training the following season to find he had lost his job. Manager Jimy Williams went nearly berserk; he threatened Bell with a 30-day suspension and $2,000 fine if he did not accept the new role. Bell, who avoided the dugout and lay on the grass outside the left field foul line between at-bats, clearly hated the assignment and took it out on Williams, issuing his famous challenge: "We'll see who's here longer, me or him."

Bell did not know at the time that he had already won. Upper management, which had made the initial decision to get Bell out of the outfield in favour of untried rookie Sil Campusano, didn't back the manager. A quarter century later, Beeston still acknowledged it was the worst mistake he and general manager Pat Gillick ever made.

Williams was adamant that Bell was told, in a mid-winter meeting, he would be the primary DH with perhaps 15 games in left field. Bell insisted he heard it the other way around, that he would be primary left fielder, with 15 games as DH. Gillick was adamant about which way it was presented: "There was no misunderstanding. George may have been asleep, but there was no misunderstanding. There were seven or eight of us in the room, including two of his agents. Everyone knew."

Bell, as usual, had a colourful take on things: "I'm too young to be a DH. I'm only 28. They say it will make my career longer, but 10 years of DH, I'd weigh 250 pounds from eating all those sunflower seeds sitting on the bench."

When Bell hit three home runs on opening day in Kansas City, he was the king again and Williams, whether he knew it or not — and I always suspected he knew full well — was already partly out the door, although it didn't close officially for another 14 months.

There was a particularly ugly incident in Minnesota, when Bell screwed up another play in the outfield and loafed after his mistake. Williams went wild on him in the dugout and yanked him from the game, then benched him for two more. Bell sulked and cursed anyone who came close to him; several other players on the team confided to reporters that both men were out of control. Dugout confrontations soon escalated among other players and Williams lost his grip on things.

That 1988 season turned out horribly for the Jays, who never contended despite drawing close late in the season. Along the way, journeyman Juan Beníquez, whom one club official referred to as "the grandfather of Latin discontent," was released. Beníquez went out with guns blazing.

"This team started to fall apart in spring training with all the changes," he said, referring first and foremost to Bell as DH. "When you've got a team with talent like this, you've got to let the players play.

"The players here are not responsible. The people off the field are . . . someone's not doing his job right here, but it's not the players."

The next year, for whatever reasons, Bell was all sweetness and light in spring training, outwardly friendly with Williams and anxious to please his employers. As I wrote after his first day in camp, *If Beaver Cleaver turned into an axe murderer, the character transformation would compare.*

Fans know the history here. After a 12–24 start, Cito Gaston replaced Jimy Williams as manager, the Jays roared to life and won the demi-pennant, then got humiliated by Rickey Henderson and the Oakland A's in the playoffs. Shortly thereafter, following the 1990 season, Bell departed as a free agent to the Chicago Cubs. He got his money, but he was clearly on the down side of his career. The day he left, I was sad to see him go.

> *He was trying to make friends with a new set of microphones and I overheard him telling one, "Hey, I got a great personality."*
>
> *Yikes. George thinks he's on a blind date.*
>
> *In September, the rest of us thought he was only blind.*
>
> *He had on a Cubs cap and that . . . didn't look any more ridiculous than, say, Tom Henke wearing a dress.*
>
> *Now, I know the Blue Jays have a chance to be a far better team . . . and I know he didn't fit any more and he had to go. I also know we won't have George to kick around any more and already I miss him, because he kicked back. He was fun. He was exasperating, rude, egotistical, profane. Very profane. George uses cuss words like a doughnut shop uses coffee.*

You know George Carlin's seven words you can't say on television? If they took those seven words out of the English language, George Bell is Marcel Marceau — if Marceau could take two and hit to right.

In addition to the great 1987 collapse, the other hugely memorable divisional race for the Jays during my time around them likewise ended in defeat, in 1990, but supplied moments of unforgettable drama.

Down the stretch, for a key game against the Boston Red Sox in Fenway Park, there was question whether Roger Clemens would be activated from the disabled list to pitch against the Jays. He hadn't pitched in 25 days and an hour before the game, Cito Gaston posted two lineup cards — one to face Clemens and one for somebody else. Clemens headed for the bullpen to see if he could go. So, too, did the press, to witness the test run:

At 2:55 p.m., he took a baseball, dug a hole on the mound, sighted bullpen catcher John Marzano and, with thousands of bleacher creatures braying, threw his first pitch 10 feet in the air, over the screen into the Toronto bullpen. Nerves, plain and simple.

He threw a few pitches, stopped, stretched, threw a few more. He began to throw hard. The fans — I have never seen this before — ordered quiet within their ranks. They wanted to hear the ball pop the catcher's mitt. It did. They screamed. Then they shut up and listened again.

Clemens began firing hard, harder. Each loud splat brought a louder response.

"I left a lot of good fastballs in the bullpen," he said

> *later. "The fans' reactions fired me up. I was ready 10 minutes too early. I had to stop, take a breather."*

He threw six shutout innings, left with a 6-0 lead and the Jays' loss dropped them two games behind with four to play. They won the next day and opened a series in Baltimore, one game back, but lost to drop to dormie — two games back with two to play.

In old Memorial Stadium, Fred McGriff bombed a solo homer with two out and two strikes in the ninth inning for a 2-1 win. The Jays descended into the boxy old clubhouse to watch the Red Sox play the White Sox. A Boston win and the Jays' season was over. A Chicago win would delay the decision to game 162.

> *The team, half in uniform and half in towels, congregated in front of the TV. There were those who could watch and those who couldn't bear to. Half the team left early, which makes you wonder.*
>
> *"My job is done. There is nothing I can do about the game. Why should I watch the TV?" Tony Fernandez wondered, although there are thousands of us who could tell him why.*
>
> *Life or death from 500 miles away. No one could remember seeing anything like it. The '67 Red Sox won the pennant by hearing the Tigers lose. They listened over a telephone and radio hookup that time. It's better to see it than hear it, though. You see it, you believe it.*
>
> *Those who stayed agonized as the game stretched to the 11th inning, with George Bell the lead cheerleader. Bud Black, who had pitched eight innings for*

the Jays, left to shower in the 10th but dashed out, head full of lather, when he heard a roar. It was Ellis Burks flying out to end the inning with the bases loaded.

The White Sox ultimately won it 3–2 in 11, sending the Jays soaring. The next evening, the Orioles got them. In the ninth inning, the game tied 2–2, the stadium scoreboard video cut to Fenway Park in the ninth, where the White Sox, down a run, had two on and two out. Ozzie Guillen hit a line drive to right that looked like two runs and the ball game. It was the ball game, all right. Tom Brunansky dove and made a sliding catch to end the game and the Jays' season. Moments later Mickey Tettleton creamed a Tom Henke fastball and the Orioles won 3–2.

There was one absurd moment to the drama in 1990, provided by Junior Félix, a physically talented but mostly miserable player who was less than popular with his teammates and manager(s), for certain. (Years later, after Félix had bounced around, the Marlins released him and the Jays, needing an outfielder at the time, were asked if he was on their radar. Cito Gaston, still managing, was succinct: "Let me just say if he's here, I hope I'm not.") Anyway, in mid-September that year, with the Jays still mathematically alive, Félix went from cubicle to cubicle before the game, handing out envelopes. Someone opened it and handed it to me with the words, "You've got to be kidding me." It was an invitation to Junior's wedding, set for a few weeks hence — the same night set aside for the fourth game of the World Series. A player on a contender would need to be pretty much brain dead to do that, so no surprise it was on Junior's résumé.

Touring the SkyDome in 1988, before finishing touches were applied, with Star *baseball writers Allan Ryan and Neil MacCarl.*

Several other players from that Blue Jays era stood out, for various reasons, but three in particular were a big part of covering that team. First was Lloyd Moseby, a terrific individual with a sense of flair and fashion. He was a street-tough Oakland kid, perceptive and smart. Got all the jokes and delivered more than a few of his own. When his time with the Jays was up, shortly before they moved out of terrible, old windswept Exhibition Stadium and adopted an entirely new look in the SkyDome, Moseby was philosophical.

"Nine years I played in pajamas in the world's worst ballpark. Now we're getting real uniforms and a real stadium and I'm not going to get a chance to be part of it," he said.

As a Blue Jays beat writer, we used to do off-season visits for long feature stories. One year, I went to Texas to visit with Cliff Johnson, for instance. Ended up helping him unload hay from his barn while he told me to watch out for rattlesnakes. Thanks very much. One other year I went to visit Moseby at his home outside Sacramento. It was a great visit. We played golf and took in a Kings game — he was the first absolute NBA basketball nut I ever met — and he talked openly about the way he had fallen out of favour with the Jays. I was sorry to see him go when he departed.

Next on this list was Tom Henke, who was as close to just-plain-folks as any big-leaguer I ever dealt with. He was a simple guy, honest and straightforward, who happened to throw a baseball pretty well. Never high-hatted anyone. I don't know if John Wayne was his role model, but he had that same direct, uncluttered approach to life. Once, U.S. President George Bush — Bush the elder, if you're scoring at home — was due to tour the clubhouse in Texas, where his son, the future president, was a co-owner. Now Henke was a true-blue American, the kind of guy who supported the troops before it was fashionable to slap on that bumper sticker. Someone asked Henke what he would say to Bush, and he was prepared:

> *"I'll say, 'Mr. President, it takes a big dog to make 100 pounds.'"*
>
> *Uh, Tom, 100 pounds of what?*
>
> *"Of dog," he answered. Anyone who didn't know better would think Henke was lefthanded.*

Henke arrived in 1985 to solidify the bullpen; he was always a fan favourite, but was deemed expendable after Duane Ward arrived and demonstrated closer's ability. For a couple of years, they were an impregnable one-two punch, although eventually they didn't get along. Each was clearly envious of the other's save chances and thought he should have been getting the close-out opportunities. Henke, in particular, had endured a couple of very public salary disputes with the Jays and seldom felt appreciated in his later years with the team. One night in Texas, Henke got so carried away that he threw his glove in anger when a Jays teammate hit a home run in the top of the ninth inning and turned a three-run lead into a four-run lead, thereby eliminating the save opportunity for which he had been warming up.

Despite this kind of occasional petulance, Henke never seemed to lose favour with the fans, although when he was rinsed by the team, in the afterglow of the first World Series win, there was precious little outcry from the customers. He was a very good relief pitcher on good teams, though, and like Ward, when he blew a save opportunity he would stand at his locker and answer all the questions. From what I can remember, neither one ever ran and hid, something you can't say for too many others in that clubhouse.

The other guy who stood out, in thought and deed, if less

in word, was Dave Stieb, who still gets this vote as the greatest Blue Jay of them all. Although Stieb was not the best player — that would be Robbie Alomar, who was there for only five years — he, in this estimation, had the greatest Blue Jays career, in a photo finish with Roy Halladay and Carlos Delgado. Granted, Jose Bautista might end up passing them all one day, and so might Josh Donaldson in the distant future, but not yet.

Stieb, though, was a handful to deal with. He didn't like to talk to the press and always considered himself hard done by. He thought he was the unluckiest guy in the world, always talking about bloopers and bleeders as the hits that beat him. In his own mind, he never gave up a line drive and never had much defence played behind him. Once, after a fingernail job in 1987, a 4-3 win pulled out by a bloop single in the bottom of the ninth inning, Stieb broke new ground. Almost.

"They hit some balls hard, but right at people," Stieb said. Then he smiled wide. "With that kind of luck over the next four or five years, I think it will even out."

Stieb's glares at erring infielders were legendary and seldom appreciated. There were times in spring training when he would be on the golf course with clubhouse guys or, worse, writers, because he didn't have games with teammates. I used to think, well, you reap what you sow. Steve Milton of the *Hamilton Spectator* was tight with Stieb and he once boiled it all down succinctly after Stieb, one of the first to get a monster contract, built a beautiful custom home on the shores of Lake Tahoe. "He probably has the only $3 million house in the world without a guest room," Milton suggested.

In retrospect, I think Stieb was simply shy. He had a difficult childhood, didn't trust many people and wasn't always at ease in an interview. What a pitcher, though. He should have won at least two, possibly even three, Cy Young Memorial Awards.

It also was to my endless regret that after seeing Stieb throw a few one-hitters, including those memorable back-to-back near no-hitters broken up with two out in the ninth inning, I wasn't on the trip to Cleveland when he finally threw his coveted (and insanely well deserved) no-hitter.

The first heartbreak, the one in Cleveland in September 1988, was painful to behold:

> *Stieb came within one strike of pitching the first no-hitter in Blue Jays history last night, but a shocking bad-hop single by Julio Franco ruined it with two out and two strikes in the ninth inning.*
>
> *Stieb now knows . . . exactly what it takes for a no-hitter: "A lot of luck," he said afterward.*
>
> *He didn't get it. Jays were bolting out of their dugout and Stieb turned and watched with fist clenched as Franco's grounder, as routine as they come when it left the bat, took one, two hops to Manny Lee at second base. Lee was in his crouch, waiting to pick it cleanly.*
>
> *Suddenly, Lee was leaping. The ball hit an invisible roadblock and bounded high, perhaps two feet over Lee's glove and into short right field. Ernie Whitt collapsed to his knees and punched the ground. Stieb spun on his heel — and laughed.*
>
> *"The ball looked like it hit where a nose guard fell," Jimy Williams said, alluding to the Browns game played in the stadium a few days before.*

In his next start, virtually the same thing happened. Stieb had two out in the ninth against Baltimore, another no-hitter on the boil, when Jim Traber lofted a little broken-bat pop down the first base line that fell just fair and just beyond the reach of first baseman Fred McGriff. It was staggeringly cruel punishment for a pitcher who certainly didn't deserve it and I couldn't think of a single question to ask when that one was over. A couple of years later, he went one better with a perfect game against the Yankees and two out in the ninth inning, before Roberto Kelly hooked a slider to left for a double. By that time, it was ridiculous. I was never a staunch fan of Stieb the individual and we had some great shouting matches over the years based on what I wrote about his performances and deportment — reports whose tone he seldom agreed with. But I had tremendous respect for his pitching.

Years later, when Stieb was attempting a comeback and the Jays had given him a small opportunity, he was sitting in the bullpen at the SkyDome, the season almost played out and his career all but over, when the very young Roy Halladay took a no-hitter into the ninth inning. With two out, Halladay yielded a home run to Bobby Higginson of the Detroit Tigers, a no-doubt rocket to left that shocked the roaring SkyDome crowd into silence. The home-run ball sailed directly to the Jays bullpen where, in the ultimate irony, Stieb reached up and caught it. You couldn't make that one up.

CHAPTER SIX

Finally, Right Side Up

I always got a kick out of the beginning of a set-up column for the 1993 World Series, a screed that has long-since disappeared down the fish-wrapping tubes of history, but one that always struck me as being almost spooky in its prescience. Not that anyone cared at the moment, of course.

After years of painful disappointments, the Blue Jays had won the World Series in 1992 and, despite changing some 40 percent of the team, they were right back in it the next season. One of the team's new faces, and a relatively minor contributor over 110 at-bats, given that he had suffered a broken arm early in the season, was a shortstop named Dick Schofield or, more precisely, Dick Schofield Junior. His father, with the glorious nickname Ducky, had been a similarly minor contributor (102 at-bats) as a utility infielder with the 1960 Pittsburgh Pirates, the team that appeared woefully outgunned by the mighty Yankees, yet somehow defeated them in seven games despite being outscored 55-27. It was knowledge and appreciation of those 1960 Pirates, by the way — a sense of what was improbable yet possible on a ball field — that I often cited as being critically lacking in many Blue Jay players. Those talented Blue Jays teams from the years 1985 through 1991 had been unable to get over the final competitive hurdles, those seasons always ending with dismaying thoughts of various-sized jackpots that had been left on the table.

Here's how part of that piece read, and remember when it was written we didn't know what we know now about the way the Series ended, with Joe Carter's ever-replayed walk-off home run:

> *... Probably the single most recallable moment in World Series history, at least since television began casting its eye over every pitch of every game, was Bill Mazeroski's monumental home run in the bottom of the ninth inning of the seventh game in 1960. It beat the Yankees.*
>
> *Lives there a North American who has not seen — and several times — the footage of Maz's off-balance, one-armed, dazed meander through the fans to a knot of human happiness at home plate?*
>
> *"I don't know how many times I have seen that tape. I expect I'll see it again this weekend," says Dick Schofield, the Blue Jays very occasional shortstop. "But if you look closely, down in the corner, one of the guys waiting at home plate for Mazeroski is my dad. He's No. 11.*
>
> *"If you didn't know he was No. 11 you wouldn't know anything about him even being there, but I see him every time I see that tape."*

> *Because the first Dick Schofield was a part of Bill Mazeroski's home run, then that moment lives on here, in the 1993 World Series, through his son, the second Dick Schofield.*
>
> *"Maybe," says Dick II, "someone will hit a home run in the ninth inning and I'll be out there and in the picture."*

Nine days later, this is exactly what happened. Carter hit his three-run homer off Mitch Williams, the Blue Jays had won their second consecutive World Series, Tom Cheek produced his landmark call — "Touch 'em all, Joe. You'll never hit a bigger one in your life!" — and there, in the joyful mob at home plate, was Dick Schofield Jr., just the way he had figured it and I had written it.

When the dust settled, I remember pulling out still photos of the welcoming committees at home plate, receiving both Mazeroski and Carter, and both Schofields, father and son, are clearly visible. It might not be *Twilight Zone* stuff, but it's close.

Speaking of *Twilight Zone*, the fourth game of that Series, the 15-14 win by the Blue Jays over the mostly bearded and scraggly haired Phillies, certainly would need to be considered the most bizarre World Series game in history. Part of that reason was a strange and occasionally twisted Toronto pitcher named Todd Stottlemyre who, almost literally, started the craziness.

Now, Stott was a pretty good pitcher and later in life became a legendary stock picker and made bushels of money as a financial consultant and such. But as a player, he was a tightly wrapped guy and occasionally a wild man. He was one of the Blue Jays we used to say was even-money to end up in a tower with a high-powered rifle. (We were sort of kidding.) Once, in an ordinary game story, I tossed off a reference to him as Norman Bates

Stottlemyre and no one even blinked or said a word. He laughed. Nowadays, you make some kind of reference like that and the Twitter world would explode — even though very few Twitter types would have any idea who Norman Bates is. Another time, Stottlemyre was suspended or on the disabled list or something and for reasons that escape me now he spent a game in the press box fetching coffee for the writers and becoming genuinely interested in how we did our jobs. He insisted on wearing a fedora and having an unlit cigarette dangle from his lip. One other time, on the disabled list, he was almost literally going crazy and said, for the record, "Why not change the name of the thing from disabled list to insane list? Being on it drives you [bleeping] insane." For Stott, that was more of a putt than a drive.

American League pitchers, almost to a man, always fantasized about themselves batting and running the bases, as National League pitchers did. Stottlemyre ordered custom-made bats and always wore turf shoes when he wasn't pitching, in case he was called on to pinch run. (Cito Gaston, constantly reminded by the pitcher of his availability, just smiled.) In Game 4 of the 1993 World Series, Stottlemyre started, but he couldn't find the strike zone, despite being gifted with a 3-0 lead in the top of the first inning. He promptly walked four men. Before he was yanked in the second inning, he got a chance to run the bases and somehow landed face-first in a slide that took out a chunk of his chin. As it was reported the next day:

> *. . . First, you need to know that Stott is not necessarily with us at all times. This is a guy, understand, who goes fishing and ends up putting a fishhook through a finger trying to get it out of a mistakenly hooked alligator's back. He's a good guy and has a sense of humour — one that will come in awfully handy*

whenever last night is mentioned — but his elevator does not necessarily go all the way to his penthouse out on the mound. Or, apparently, on the base paths. Still, Stottlemyre is the star so far of the 1993 World series. That's in a twisted, Fellini-movie kind of way.

He couldn't pitch worth two hoots — who could? — but he made up for that by knocking himself cold running the bases. Stott scraped a patch of skin off his chin that might have been bigger than [umpire] Charlie Williams's strike zone, then he bled all over the mound.

. . . You know being on base in the World Series would be too much of a stage for Stott to be remotely close to sensible, so when [Phillies pitcher Tommy] Greene walked him — professional courtesy, it was suggested — you know Stott's biological clock was ticking. With two out, Robbie Alomar punched a single to centre and for some unfathomable reason, Stott tried to go to third. He was out, and out easily, despite a belly-flopping headfirst "slide" into the mud. After Stottlemyre had raised himself to one elbow from his bloody puddle, trainer Tommy Craig checked on his facilities. When the trainer held up fingers and asked how many, Stott replied, "Three and oh."

(It's a moment on the podium of the Blue Jays' goofiest base-running moments in history, right up there with two journeys destined to live forever in YouTube history: Lloyd Moseby's incredible back-and-forth dash around the bases and Kenny Williams's fantastic knockout of third-base coach John McLaren after Kenny got confused on the base paths. That was something that happened regularly, by the way.)

One other element from that 1993 championship was the

early August addition of Hall of Famer Rickey Henderson, although he was rather inconsistent during his time in Toronto and part of that was due to his refusal to steal bases unless and until he had been given his favourite number, 24, which belonged to reserve outfielder Turner Ward. Henderson arrived when the Jays were in Yankee Stadium and his arrival was impressive, to say the least.

> *A long white stretch limo pulled up at Yankee Stadium and something suggested this probably was not Darnell Coles or Turner Ward arriving for work.*
>
> *Right, it was Rickey showing up like that. How else could he? Rickey does not take the subway. Rickey, if he chooses, buys the subway. But he does not ride it.*
>
> *Within minutes of his official presentation to a heavily panting press, it became readily apparent that the Blue Jays have never had one like him before.*
>
> *They have had great players and they have had characters. They have had style-masters and they have had centre-ring performers. They have had arrogant jerks and they have had fun-loving clowns. But they never had them all at once in the same package. Not until now.*
>
> *He talks fast. He talks the way a kid showing off on the piano plays "Chopsticks." Rickey is a hot tub full of words; you just pick a topic and lower yourself in gently. But Rickey is not to be quoted so much as be experienced.*

But part of the experience was this: he really did want that 24 and did not steal a base his first week in Toronto. I called him out after he finally stole one:

For a while there, while Rickey and Ed Sprague were tied in career stolen bases as a Blue Jay — each with zero — it appeared the Blue Jays had hired Michelangelo to paint their garage instead of, uh, a masterpiece.

Eventually, it became a story that he wanted his 24 and Rickey willingly fed that particular beast, suggesting Ward had

With the great baseball announcer Ernie Harwell, shortly before the 1992 World Series began. PHOTO COURTESY OF KEN FAUGHT.

been offered up to $35,000 to swap laundry. In reality, when teammates had begged Ward to just give him the damned number so he could get back to playing his game, Ward caved in and traded it for a pair of custom cowboy boots and a dozen new Henderson-style bats that Ward fancied. Henderson eventually became a productive part of the offence, although it was clear that he had the talent to simply pick his spots.

The 1993 World Series victory was an entirely expected event and not only because Toronto had a stacked team with the highest payroll in baseball. It was a team of all-stars, calmly and efficiently managed by Cito Gaston, with enough turnover from the '92 champions that there were plenty of hungry hearts on the team, including Paul Molitor and Dave Stewart, to name two of the higher-profile additions.

The 1992 collection had been different, a team that was very good early, but began struggling, especially its pitching staff, in the second half of the season. That skid eventually ended with the arrival of David Cone, who was outstanding down the stretch, eating innings and allowing the pitching staff to regain its equilibrium.

The ALCS turned, as every fan remembers, on Robbie Alomar's dramatic home run in Oakland off Dennis Eckersley. What I most remember about that game is the majority of the Toronto press being assigned to the auxiliary press box in the upper deck in Oakland on a bright sunny day. It was impossible to see our computer screens, much less make out what we were trying to write. We were begging for cardboard boxes from the concession stands, in order to rig up shields to place over the screens. Anything to help. Most of the writers gave up and retreated to the press workroom under the stands, thus witnessing Alomar's historic home run — still the biggest in franchise history, in this view — on television along with the rest of the world.

That 1992 World Series was always recalled not only for Otis Nixon's final-out bunt in the 11th inning of Game 6, which pitcher Mike Timlin had been warned about by Gaston in a pre-batter visit, but also because some dumb kid in the U.S. military had flown a Canadian flag upside down in the pre-game ceremonies. It was a mistake that very few people noticed at the time, but Canadians back home went nuts when television replayed the slight.

This was in the days before the internet was everywhere. There was no social media to instantly grasp public moods. What there was in those days was people phoning newspapers to complain. The *Star* switchboard was stuffed with outraged callers. I checked in with the sports desk in the first inning on another matter and was told that the phones were ringing non-stop with angry complaints, with no let-up in sight. I looked around and saw Howie Starkman, the Jays' long-time standout public relations man, and Rich Levin, who worked in the baseball commissioner's office. I told them what I had heard from back home, that people were going wild about the flag flap. Levin was astounded. He scurried away. Two innings later, when the magnitude of the problem had been widely ascertained, the commissioner's office issued a statement and an apology. So did some local politician. But it couldn't be contained and bloomed into an international incident, one that ended up with the White House issuing regrets.

The mistake was widely viewed, by many Canadians, as part of a great anti-Canadian plot, one that had begun years ago by umpires and league officials to deny a Canadian team a championship and yada yada. People who bought into this particular conspiracy could not be persuaded to accept any other reality. At times, it seemed, every single ball and strike call was accused of being a manipulated result. There was a revisitation of this paranoid phenomenon when the Blue Jays finally made the playoffs again, in 2015. No doubt it will happen again in the future if and when they reach the postseason again.

I remember a former ump and terrific guy named Marty Springstead, who at one point in the early 1990s was the supervisor of American League umpires. In New York, I usually drank at P.J. Clarke's, and one night I was in there with Marty and we were having a cup of tea and shooting the breeze about baseball and other things. At one point, Marty stunned me by saying, "You know something? I'm secretly rooting for the Blue Jays. I hope they win the World Series. I am so damned sick of hearing how the umpires are working against the Canadian team. I'm tired of it. It makes my life difficult. At least if they win I'll never have to hear it again." He stressed that this was off the record and it has always been — until now. I did see Marty at Toronto's World Series party, after the locale had shifted north, and reminded him of our cocktail conversation. He just laughed and held up two crossed fingers.

There's one other moment from that 1992 World Series, which fans probably don't know. It concerned the ninth inning of the sixth game, when the Jays were leading 2-1 and three outs from winning the whole thing. Against Tom Henke, the Braves got two on and two out. Otis Nixon lined a single to left field and Candy Maldonado charged the ball and threw home. Except Maldonado's throw was wild and high. Jeff Blauser scored the tying run as the ball hit high off the screen behind home plate. The ball was still in play, though, and the Jays quickly recovered it and Lonnie Smith retreated to third base. He expired there as Ron Gant flied out for the third out. Two innings later, Dave Winfield's two-run double drove in the winner for the Jays.

What no one knew was that before the World Series, Major League Baseball had ordered some minor changes to the Atlanta ballpark. One problem was that the screen behind home plate wasn't high enough; workmen extended it upward by three feet. It was in this extra three feet that Maldonado's throw hit — and stayed in play. Without the extension, the throw would have sailed up the netting and out of play, the Braves' runners would have been awarded one extra base and we would have had ourselves a seventh game.

It's not quite the same as wondering what would have happened if Lee Harvey Oswald couldn't get the window opened, but who knows how it all would have turned out?

CHAPTER SEVEN

Are You Nuts?

After four decades of writing about sports and travelling to some of its memorable events, a common question arrives, usually with an answer supplied.

Someone will inevitably ask, "What's the best thing you ever covered?" before immediately supplying his or her own answer. "I'll bet it was Mike Weir's Masters win." Or "I'll bet it was Joe Carter's home run to win the World Series." Or "I'll bet it was the Jays' first World Series." Or something about Usain Bolt, etc.

My own answer always seems to disappoint someone, but it is this: by an eyelash over several outstanding events, it is the 2003 Presidents Cup played over the Fancourt course in George, South Africa.

It's kind of a personal thing and probably involves several factors. One is the considerable distance travelled to a beautiful and exotic (at least to me) part of the world. Two would be the quality of competition; this was a fantastically competitive event decided by a back-and-forth meeting on the 18th green, with those few of us in the press who had made the long journey standing nearby on the green collar and listening to every word. (Captains Gary Player and Jack Nicklaus eventually hammered out a draw and joint possession of the trophy as an acceptable result, with the International team clamouring to play the next morning to break the tie and the U.S. side, or most of it, itching to get on the plane and get home.) Three would be the presence of Nelson Mandela. It really was magical to see him in person and feel the reverence for him. Four was the wonderful vacation I stitched on to both ends of the event and five would be a stupid gaffe I made that ended with Tiger Woods looking at me as if I had six heads and asking me the simple question, "Are you nuts?"

There was very little press coverage from North America, but the Toronto papers in 2003 were crazy for Mike Weir, certainly. He had won the Masters and two other PGA Tour events and was rated No. 4 in the world. He also had been a mainstay on previous Presidents Cup teams and loved the event, so it was easy to justify the expense involved. (Of course, this was back in the day when papers were not scared to spend money.) The *Star* sent me, the *Sun* sent Ken Fidlin and the *National Post* sent Cam Cole. We were friends and had shared numerous houses around the world already, at the Masters, U.S. Open and Open Championships. We met up in South Africa, me after spending a couple of days in Cape Town, a knockout city, and enjoyed every minute of the experience, covering a great event and getting in some golf ourselves at one of the resort's other courses.

As is the custom with Ryder and Presidents Cup, the golfers' wives and girlfriends are invited and are part of the show. And here's where I got in trouble. Several of the U.S. wives, including Tiger's (at the time) girlfriend Elin Nordegren, were photographed together watching golf. The photo, which I never saw until much, much later but went out on the wires that moment, was framed in such a way that in front of Elin, a very large engagement ring decorated a hand that appeared to be hers, but (I later discovered to my horror) actually belonged to someone to one side of her who had otherwise been cropped out of the picture.

Normally, I do not notice such things. However, back at One Yonge Street, one of the smart young ladies employed by the paper did glance at the photo and assumed that Tiger had popped the question and dropped the ring on his GF. She sent me an email wondering why this had not been made into more of a story, given that Woods was, you know, probably the most visible athlete in the world at the time.

Damn right, I said to myself. I cleverly avoided bringing up the subject at his official press conference — why share the scoop with the rest of the world, eh? — and hustled out beside him after it was over. Now, I wouldn't say in those days that there was any kind of connection with Tiger Woods. He distrusted the press and kept up a wall, spoke in stock phrases and seldom, if ever, gave anyone anything worth using. He vaguely knew where I was from because back in the day he had attended (and once won) the Canadian Open, and at other places I was always asking him Canadian-themed questions. Plus he did some corporate events in Toronto and liked a certain cigar store I was familiar with in town. A couple of years before, in Buenos Aires for a World Golf Challenge event, he had looked at me in the press room, thousands of miles from home, and asked why the hell I had come so far for this thing.

Anyway, that day in George I sidled up to him and said

something conspiratorial like, "Looks like congratulations are in order."

He looked at me blankly. "What? Why?"

"The ring," I said. "You gave it to Elin, right?"

Now he stared again and shook his head. "Are you nuts?"

It was obvious from his reaction that I was. I mumbled apologies and said something about bad information and wandered away.

The irony of it turned out to be that Woods did indeed have a ring ready to go and was taking Elin away on safari or to a game ranch or something the week after the Cup to pop the question. Doubtless, my out-of-left-field question had got him thinking there had been a leak, or something.

Naturally, when all got sorted out, my original informant was mortified and I was slapping myself for pursuing a line of inquiry I had not checked out. It could have been worse; I could have gone public with it.

The competition itself at that Presidents Cup was spectacular. There was a match between Kenny Perry and Nick Price that might have been the best match nobody ever heard of. Three times Perry went 3-up and three times Price battled back, including winning holes outright at 15, 16 and 17. When Price missed a five-foot putt on 18, allowing Perry to beat him 1-up, Price, as nice a gentleman as ever swung a golf club, snapped his putter in frustration and genuinely agonized. That competition ended memorably, after three holes of a playoff, with Woods facing local hero Ernie Els and with daylight fast receding and reporters kneeling on the edge of the green. Woods rolled in a bendy 15-footer, forcing Els to halve from about half that distance. In near darkness, Els made what he called the biggest putt of his life. Nicklaus, admitting he could no longer see the hole, and Gary Player hashed out the unprecedented result — usually a tie results in the previous winner retaining the Cup, rather than sharing it — with input from their teams, gathered on separate sides of the green. Never anything quite like it.

Two postscripts from that Presidents Cup. One is that I stayed another 10 days in South Africa, toured Soweto, spent three glorious days at a game resort called Sabi Sabi, saw all kinds of animals, including a pack of lions mere yards away, had a semi-scary encounter with a deadly black mamba, and dropped off a bag full of medical supplies at a Canadian-funded school out in a rural area. I had become interested in a project, run by a woman in Vancouver, that built schools and dug wells and so on in isolated parts of Africa and arranged to participate. Basic medical supplies, such as bandages and insect repellants and cotton swabs and the like, were cheap but necessary. Visiting that small school room, which proudly waved a Canadian flag, and meeting the kids and teachers was a great way to spend a day.

I also played some golf at a course called White River, where the water hazards contained crocodiles and the bush was not to be entered under any circumstances. This kind of warning, I discovered, is the best way to keep shots straight. I also attempted to get on a course called Leopard Creek, but they were not impressed enough by my plea to allow me to play.

Fast-forward about four months, to next March and I'm on the practice range at Bay Hill, talking to someone, and Ernie Els walks over. Ernie, a friendly guy, knew I was one of the very few reporters who had made the trek to Fancourt. He asked, "So what did you think of my country?"

I told him what a wonderful time I had enjoyed, and gave him the 39-cent recap of my trip, including Cape Town, Soweto, Sabi Sabi and so on. Ernie was especially impressed by a stay at Sabi Sabi. He asked if I played golf. I told him White River and he asked if I had been able to play Leopard Creek, which was his course.

"No," I told him. "I tried and told them why I was there, but they wouldn't let me on."

"Why didn't you phone me?" Els responded. "I'd have got you on."

This made me burst out laughing. As if I would have Ernie Els's phone number at my fingertips. I told him next time I would love to call him. Uh, what number would that be?

Another moment endures from a Presidents Cup. This one concerns a sour-dispositioned golfer named Woody Austin, who was part of the U.S. Team at the Presidents Cup at Royal Montreal in 2007.

I had first been exposed to Austin's misery a few weeks earlier at a PGA Championship at Southern Hills in Tulsa. He was another JAG — golf shorthand for Just Another Guy — who had gotten hot for a while and made some money and got briefly into the sport's stratosphere. Tiger Woods was in front at Southern Hills, but Austin, a former bartender and bank teller with a history of injuries and poor eyesight, was making him work for it. Austin was the story everybody in the press room wanted to write, certainly before Sunday. Nobody wants to write the same story — in this case Woods — four days in a row and when Austin came into the press room for his post-match interview, the place was jammed. Here, instead of Woods and his boring, next-to-useless quotes, was somebody we could work with.

Except that Austin didn't want to play. He kept saying no one cared about him and how we all only cared about Woods and wanted to write about only Woods and so on. It was totally backward to reality, but that was his view and he stuck to it. Kept complaining about the amount of coverage Woods received and how the rest of them were second-class citizens. None of this makes for interesting reading in the next day's paper, by the way.

So on to Royal Montreal and Austin still had it stuck in his craw that everybody was against him. On one hole, he needed to play a shot from the edge of a lake. I was across the lake watching and couldn't believe it when he took an off-balance swing and lurched backward — right into the lake. Almost totally submerged, he popped up, drenched, while the crowd roared and other players covered their faces lest they be photographed laughing. I began beetling around the lake to get a closer view, went around a stand of trees that had a blocked view of the incident and came upon another game at a tee box going the opposite direction. Two caddies I recognized saw me coming and asked, "What the hell just happened over there?" I told them about Austin getting dunked and the crowd going crazy. Both caddies broke into wide grins and one said, "That looks good on him." Which told me Austin wasn't exactly the most popular guy in the team room, either.

Too bad, too, because Austin, who handled the gaffe with aplomb and even donned a snorkel the next day, was a kind of everyman who did well to get on the PGA Tour, won a few tournaments and some money and could have been an inspiring guy. What's that old line? Sometimes you need to go along to get along.

There was another Presidents Cup story left over from a previous event, held in 2000 at the Robert Trent Jones Club in Northern Virginia, not far from Washington, D.C. (The PC began in 1994 on even-numbered years, but when 9/11 pushed the 2001 Ryder Cup back to 2002, the PC switched to the odd-numbered years commencing in 2003.)

Bill Clinton still was U.S. president in 2000 and being a golf fan, he had some presence at the event. He had his own little tent complex isolated on a hill, overlooking the 16th green. He could sit out and watch golf, perhaps 100 feet away, although he was seldom there.

On the second day of competition, I went out to the 16th green to watch the matches come through. That hole was a pivotal par-five with lots of birdies available. I sat down all alone in a little roped-off area reserved for press and fired up a nice cigar. It happened to be a Cuban traveller I had brought with me. As if anyone would know.

A few minutes later, with the first group of golfers heading for the 16th tee, a man with a wire in his ear came over and flashed a credential and examined my golf credential. He said my name and affiliation into this shoulder radio and politely told me I had two choices: leave now or sit here for at least 90 minutes, under the watchful gaze of him and his colleagues, until all the matches had come through. I wasn't worried. This clearly was the Secret Service and by now they knew how much I had left on my mortgage. They knew I was just a dumb sportswriter and no threat to anyone. I stayed.

A while later, Clinton arrived at his little tent, which was about 100 feet away and up the hill from me. He waved to a few cheering spectators and sat on his little deck; nobody between me and him. He fired up a cigar. He looked around. He saw me, with my own cigar. He waved his cigar and gave me a thumbs-up. I waved my cigar. I, stupidly, shouted up to him, "I bet yours isn't Cuban."

Clinton laughed and looked only mildly confused. Two guys

with wires in their ears glared at me. I guess I was admitting to displaying contraband while plunked down close to a sitting president. Not the smartest move, eh? I turned around and watched golf. Bill didn't stay long and the boys left me alone.

Still, that wasn't the closest I ever got to a world leader unless you count lunch with Paul Godfrey and who would? The next summer, I was in Moscow watching the International Olympic Committee award the 2008 Summer Games to Beijing, with Toronto as the (thank God) runner-up. I had been strongly opposed to a Toronto Olympic bid, but that's not part of it. *Star* colleague Jim Byers and I made the trip and it was fascinating; Moscow is a fully cultured city. The subway stations are like art galleries. We inhaled all the culture we could, which included scoring a couple of tickets for an IOC function to be held at the Bolshoi Theatre. I am no ballet guy, but I always subscribed to the idea that if you are watching the best in the world at what they do, whatever it is they do, you'll probably enjoy it and at least learn something. So we knotted up the neckties and went to the Bolshoi.

We had decent seats in the orchestra, four and three seats in from the main aisle, which was on our right. At post time, with the orchestra tuning up, suddenly the house lights went out, the congregation rose, the conductor raised his baton, poised to start conducting, and a spotlight turned on. Pretty much on me, as a matter of fact. I looked to my right and there were two empty chairs and beside them, in the middle of the corridor, stood Vladimir Putin. Good old Rootin' Tootin' Putin, as I had called him in the *Star* the day before.

He had two security goons a step behind him, both of them looking around intently, including looking at me with *don't move* written all over their faces. Putin stared straight ahead, his eyes narrowed. He looked like a guy who would kill someone with

Leaning on the batting cage in Moscow, of all places, in 2001.
There was a semi-pro baseball league operating there in those days.

his bare hands just for sport. The orchestra began playing the Russian national anthem, which is a stirring piece of music at all times, and here, part of a packed house at the Bolshoi, with Rootin' Tootin' six feet from me, it sent big chills up my sturdy bits and made me want to march to Leningrad. I will admit that Putin, possibly, does not recall standing so close to me.

CHAPTER EIGHT

They Call Me Woody

The 2003 Masters is best remembered by practically every Canadian as the year Mike Weir beat Len Mattiace in a playoff to record the first major championship by any Canadian male. Having been there and walked many of those 73 holes with Weir and his entourage, it's remembered that way here, too. But it also brings to mind a tale about a woman named Martha Burk and a nut named Woody.

Martha Burk, you might remember, was a high-ranking member of the National Organization for Women and from time to time would wave a familiar banner about complete lack of women members at Augusta National Golf Club, a failing (if that's what it was) not rectified for another decade. This particular field had been well plowed in previous years, but with little result. Every year, one or two reporters would bring it up at the club chairman's press conference, held each

Wednesday of Masters week. Through clenched teeth, the chairman would reaffirm the club's position that membership matters are private and we do not comment on them and so on. With that past stonewalling in mind, this year Burk was planning a large protest outside the grounds of Augusta National for the Saturday morning of Masters week. So I trooped out to a parking lot on Washington Road (a lot owned by Augusta National, by the way) with my pal Cam Cole of the *National Post*, plus a load of other reporters, to see if any news happened.

The short answer was not much, at least from Martha. She gave the same sensible but old speech and drew a predictably approving response from a small posse of supporters. What was out of the ordinary, though, was a young man, probably late 20s, camped down in front of the speaker's podium, goofing on Martha and carrying a sign. One side said, "Make My Dinner." The other said, "Iron My Shirts."

Martha tried dismissing the clown, but he would heckle a little and wave his sign and the TV cameras, lacking any other action, gave him plenty of airtime. After Martha finished her piece and departed, reporters closed in on the sign-waver. It went this way when asked to identify himself and I kid you not.

"Well, my name is Heywood, but my friends call me Woody," he said, earnestly enough.

"Well, Woody, what's your last name and where are you from?"

"My last name's Yablomb and I'm from Atlanta," he said, stressing the "ya" and the "blomb."

Cam and I looked at each other. Yablomb? What kind of name was this? Someone asked him to spell it.

"J-A-B-L-O-M-E," he said, again earnestly, at which point Cam and I closed our notebooks and wandered away, shaking our heads.

The guy's name was Heywood Jablome? (Say it slowly: hey would you blow me.)

We chuckled at the time we had just wasted, went back to watch Mike Weir and thought nothing of it again. Nothing, that is, until the next day and the day after that, when first the Atlanta paper and then *USA Today* identified the dope and quoted him BY NAME.

This, of course, was one of the oldest tricks in the book, to give out a phony name and see if anyone was dumb enough to bite. (Not long afterward, the *Toronto Star* had a naïve kid on the news side who quoted someone named "Hugh Jazz" about some matter of civic importance.) Doubtless it still happens, but when Woody pulled it off with a couple of big-time newspapers, I feared for the future of journalism.

Speaking of Cam Cole, I spent a lot of miles and a lot of time and played a lot of golf and drank a lot of beers with Cam, who writes sports as well as anyone in this country and probably most other countries, if you care to compare. We shared a lot of houses and cooked a lot of meals together at dozens of golf tournaments around the world, although I did most of the cooking because I was always finished first. I never had anything but admiration for Cam's finished product, but he was a bleeder over the keyboard. I whizzed through my work, wrote quickly and filed quickly and that always used to drive him nuts. Then again, he usually had much more space to fill and was more of a craftsman.

Cole, though, provided one memorable newspaper moment certainly through no fault of his own, but one that still gets writers in some press boxes, when the intersection of two timelines gets terribly tangled, to mumble about the Cam Cole Timing Award.

Most people, if they thought about it, know that today's newspaper was written last night, at the latest. Monday's news appears in Tuesday's paper and by the time the Tuesday paper arrives, if there's a mistake or something's outdated, it's too late to do anything about it. The deadline was many hours ago and the papers have all been printed.

So, one day in October 1999, Cole had stitched together a notes column. Those are the columns you write when you don't really have an entire column, so you assemble a little of this and a little of that, lead with your best note and turn your attention to tomorrow's effort. A PGA Tour golf tournament had been held a week or two previously in Vancouver and Payne Stewart, the two-time U.S. Open champion, had competed. But Stewart had behaved badly toward a volunteer; something about the wrong can of soda pop being delivered at a press conference or something. There had been a bit of a scene and Cam wrote a mildly inflammatory notebook item on it, a gentle nudge about golf pros behaving badly.

No big deal, except as the day advanced back east, it turned out there was a terrible air tragedy unfolding. A private jet was flying by itself out of Florida, on automatic pilot with all passengers and crew apparently unconscious after a cabin air-system malfunction. Aboard the jet was Payne Stewart. The world was tuned in to the impending disaster, but nobody could do anything. Eventually the plane ran out of fuel and crashed. All lives were lost, including Stewart's, a terrible tragedy, to be sure. Meanwhile, out on the streets that very day was Cole's paper with a mild rip on Stewart about a can of pop.

The outraged and how-dare-you phone calls started. No one understood, or cared to understand, that this had been written and filed about 18 hours previously and that it was all a terrible coincidence and that such a minor matter would never be written in place of a proper obituary. Cam was pilloried and no amount of explanation could ease reader scorn.

Like all reader shitstorms, it blew over eventually, because people can easily find something else to get themselves worked up about. His colleagues treaded lightly before bringing up the subject. For a few days at least.

The reality is, it could have happened to any of us and some variation probably has landed on most of us in the business. And imagine if it happened today, in the age of instant worldwide social media, where everybody can know everything instantly and a certain element of society, searching far and wide for gotcha moments, takes great pleasure in being offended by things that don't concern them. Cam would've received death threats from the tinfoil-hat crowd, for sure.

Occasionally, an embarrassing error that was entirely understandable, given the disjointed cultures, would emerge from the press room. At Hoylake in 2006, Tiger Woods had been in the press room talking about a certain iron shot that he had mis-hit that came out fluttering and diving. He described it as being "like a Niekro knuckler." That kind of baseball reference, to Phil Niekro and his trick pitch, certainly registered with all the North American reporters. Later, a couple of uncomprehending British friends asked if we could explain, which we did. But somebody forgot to tell the young lady, a local, who recorded every press conference and transcribed the tape. An hour later, when the transcriptions came out, there was Woods being quoted about "Negro knuckles."

A while back, Lee Trevino referenced the legal betting shops in Britain, which I always loved, being a betting man of some practice. Once, wandering down the street in Lytham the night before a British Open began, I saw Mark Calcavecchia, terrific golfer and very good guy, head into a bet shop. I followed him. There he was at the window, pounding away.

Calc was a past champion at the Open. I wasn't too sure of his recent form, but he was something like 100 to 1 to win the tournament. But many other wagers were available, including betting on which player in each three-man group would have the lowest score. Calc's three-ball game the next day didn't seem entirely daunting. I loaded up. He went out and shot 74, or something equally disappointing. I tore up my tickets and wondered how much he had lost.

Not long after, at the Canadian Open, I ran into Calc exiting the locker room. Off the record, I had to ask. I told him the story about Lytham and wondered what he had based his optimism on.

"Oh, hell, I wasn't betting on myself," he said. "I couldn't beat anybody, the way I was playing. But there were a couple of other three-ball games I liked and I thought I'd take a shot."

Let that be a lesson to myself, I figured. You don't know what you don't know. I also rationalized the loss — and what gambler doesn't? — by remembering that a year or two before, I had been in the press room late on a Wednesday when Tom Lehman, the defending champion, mentioned that he had hurt his back or neck or something and didn't expect much; he would hit the first tee shot almost ceremonially as defending champion, but he might not make it all the way around.

On the way home, the bet shop was still open. There was Lehman, the news not yet out, as heavy favourite in his three-ball game. One of his opponents (if I remember right) was an amateur, so I loaded up on the third guy and laughed all the way to the bet shop the next day after cashing in substantially. A true gambler would shrug and say it all evens out in the end.

Still with golf, a friend named Ted Maude always told a good and harmless story and it deserves repeating. Ted was a former golf professional who got into course management and course financing later in life, but as a younger man he played on various tours before landing a dream job — club pro at the Ocean Course in the Bahamas. Part of the deal was use of a home that bordered the first fairway. As Ted tells the story, the new pro was meeting some of the members and one of them, it turned out, was actor Sean Connery, then at the height of his fame as James Bond. They got talking and Connery, who was serious about golf, said he had a swing issue. Maude guided him to the range and they set about combatting whatever flaw it was. Afterward, they were going to have a drink, but Connery was besieged by autograph hunters and well-wishers and such and lamented that he couldn't get much time out of the spotlight. Maude pointed to his nearby back yard and said they could have a drink there and no one would bother them. Soon they were sitting out having a pleasant cocktail, Connery talking golf and Ted trying to talk movies, when they heard a vehicle pulling into the driveway. It's my wife, home with the groceries, Ted said. Connery jumped up and strode around the corner of the house. Ted's wife, who knew nothing of anyone, much less a movie star, in her yard, heard only a familiar voice that said in its familiar dense Scots burr, "Could I help you with the groceries, Mrs. Maude?" She was even more startled to look up and find James Bond himself grabbing a couple of bags and heading for the kitchen. Not the kind of thing that happened every day. Too bad she didn't have her cell phone camera with her.

There's one more yarn involving the actor, this one told by Nick Price at an Open Championship. Price was at Royal Birkdale talking with Lorne Rubenstein, the erudite and accomplished Canadian golf journalist with whom he was quite friendly. A couple of other Canadians joined the chat circle and Price mentioned that he had recently enjoyed a delightful visit to Canada with his wife, spending a few days in one of the luxurious cabins at Redtail, a private club in southwestern Ontario with a very nice links-style golf course and terrific amenities, including residences that had already played host to the Queen on one of her Canadian visits. There were only a handful of club members, mostly rich and famous, and access to the course and facilities was strictly by member invitation.

Price and his wife thoroughly enjoyed their few days and the morning they were due to leave their cabin, she asked if it were possible to stay an extra day. Price said he would go see and headed down to the clubhouse to ask. There, a young woman perused the bookings list and said, "Apologies, Mr. Price, but that cabin has been booked for tonight by Mr. Sean Connery." As Price told us with a laugh, the message was clear: you may have won two British Opens, but James Bond is coming. Please get out.

CHAPTER NINE

The Terminator as Editor

I covered enough big fights that circumstances tend to blur, but I do remember when we were in the Mandalay Bay in Las Vegas to cover Lennox Lewis fighting Hasim Rahman for the heavyweight championship in November 2001. I was in a great seat, last row of the ringside press section. Right behind me were some celebrities and it turns out we — meaning both A-listers and the forlorn press types — all needed to enter and exit through the same restricted access point. I had set up my computer during the preliminaries and wandered out the closest exit to a celebrity-clogged passageway that led to the men's room. Rounded a corner and bumped right into — Meg Ryan.

Now, Meg was famously easy on the eyes, at least on the big screen. This time, she looked a little, shall we say, wasted. She was travelling with Tracey Ullman and Carrie Fisher and they surely appeared to have been partying (and good for them;

that's their business). "Excuse me. Hope you're all right," I said, or some such nonsense, after our minor collision. She mumbled something I couldn't understand. I said, "Well, okay. And by the way, you never call any more and you never write." Then I headed off to the men's room, chuckling at my own audacity and leaving behind one confused trio.

Back at my seat before the big fight, Meg and the girls were down the row. I waved. Meg looked away. Over my right shoulder were Arnold Schwarzenegger and his wife, Maria. Over my left shoulder was my favourite actor since I was a little kid, Sidney Poitier. I leaned back and had a nice chat with Sidney and at one point I said to him, "I'se gwine build you a shappel." This, of course, was his famous line from *Lilies of the Field*, for which he won the Oscar decades before. To his credit, he just laughed at this damned fool with a press pass; he clearly had been dealing with idiot fans for a long time and knew how to handle them.

The fight went. One thing about fights in Las Vegas. They tended to take place on Saturday nights, beginning shortly after 11 p.m. in the eastern time zone. My deadline, at the time, was about 11:35. So it was necessary to watch the rounds and write like mad in the one-minute break between rounds, a kind of play-by-play we call running copy. When the fight ended, there usually was no more than a couple of minutes to put a quick top on it, then send it in. An hour later, there was time to assemble a better, rewritten story with quotes and such for the later editions of the paper.

Sitting on my right was Jim Morris, who worked for the Canadian Press, the national wire service. Now, wire-service reporters were always quick writers, used to hashing together strings of facts and getting them on to the wire in a heartbeat. Morris was there because Lewis, while fighting under a British flag, was loosely considered Canadian since he grew up in Ontario, where his mother still lived. There was a lot of interest in his fights, especially after he won the heavyweight championship of the world, although he had lost the belt to Rahman in a stunning upset in April that year, and this night in Vegas was the rematch.

So the fight ended. (Lewis clobbered Rahman to regain his title.) It was a couple of minutes to deadline. Morris was pounding away. I was pounding away. Suddenly an enormous head appeared right between ours, and a voice, sounding exactly like the Terminator, said to Morris, "You've got a typographical error, hah hah hah."

Jesus, it was Arnold Schwarzenegger and he was reading our screens.

Morris, a veteran pro, to his credit never turned his head and simply said, "Hey, Arnold. We're on deadline. Fuck off."

The gigantic head laughed and disappeared.

A few seconds later, we hit the "send" keys almost simultaneously and then paused for breath, hoping we had dispatched some kind of lucid report. Arnold and Maria had gone. Sidney had gone. The party girls had gone. Morris and I looked at each other and sighed, our blood pressures starting to drop after an intense couple of minutes.

"Did I just really tell Arnold Schwarzenegger to fuck off?" Morris asked.

"Yes," I answered. "I think you just became a legend."

Fights in Las Vegas were almost always very cool events to cover. There is nothing in sports, or at least nothing in the sports I covered, as electric as the moments before a big fight in Vegas, when they turn off the house lights and there's suddenly no one in the ring except the two fighters under spotlight. There's a palpable tingle in the air, on the skin. The only event that comes close is that dead-silent moment when the starter is poised to fire his pistol over eight crouched runners before the 100-metre dash at an Olympics or world track and field championship. And that moment only comes close to a big fight.

For all of my Vegas fights, I was lucky enough to travel and work with Stephen Brunt, one of the very best and most knowledgeable boxing writers, who was always generous about sharing information. We had some good times there setting up fights although, again, the deadlines were always a grind.

Brunt and I were in the house the night in 1997 when Mike Tyson bit off part of Evander Holyfield's ear and imagine that development occurring only a few minutes before deadline. Here's how it came out in the *Star*, written on the fly:

> *Mike Tyson is boxing's man of letters. The two he once knew best were K and O. Now they are D and Q.*
>
> *In one of the more bizarre moments in boxing history, Tyson last night was disqualified for twice biting Evander Holyfield's ears, tearing off a chunk of one of them and spitting it out in a bloodthirsty moment the sport may never live down.*
>
> *Clearly out of control, Tyson responded to a second-round head butt — one ruled accidental but clearly not thought so by Tyson — that opened a cut over his right eye with a huge chomp from a clinch midway in the third round. Holyfield literally jumped around the ring in pain.*
>
> *After a delay and a second Tyson penalty point — he had lost one earlier for a push — the fight was resumed. However, in the first clinch, as the third round was ending, Tyson, who came out for the round without his mouthpiece, sank his teeth in again and referee Mills Lane halted matters.*

Naturally, the way the fight ended set off a ruckus. Handlers from both camps brawled in the ring and fans got involved. Several extracurricular participants were led away in handcuffs. The temperature stayed on simmer and the ugliness culminated two hours later, with rival gangs trading gunfire just outside the casino. Brunt and I were just leaving a wide hallway heading into the back of the casino when we heard a soft pop-pop-pop and, moments later, saw an enormous stampede of people fleeing the front of the casino. We saw craps and blackjack tables overturned, customers ducking behind them for cover and the braver (or stupider) ones scooping up armloads of chips — although the regular surveillance cameras were on and the casinos eventually tracked down every single thief who thought he could fill his pockets with impunity.

Tyson eventually was suspended for inciting the mayhem with his bite, Nevada finally having had its fill of his behaviour and banning him for at least a year. Still, as I wrote after the official hearing, what did they expect? Mike had been out of control for a while now:

> *It's not like he bit the Queen, or Ken Dryden, or someone really important. He and Evander Holyfield were engaged to beat the whiz out of each other, for the great enjoyment of the masses, and [Tyson] went a little nutso at the prospect of certain defeat. Yes, that is terrible, etc. But it seems to fall into the area of a race-car driver going too fast.*

I always suspected his true penalty from Nevada was for messing with the "drop," the term casinos use for the amount of money they would win from gamblers before and after the big fight that drew the high rollers to town.

Now fast forward a couple of years. Tyson was pretty much out of the picture and Lennox Lewis had apparently beaten Holyfield in New York to win the heavyweight championship, except that fight was scored as a draw. Many observers detected the fine hand of Don King, the all-seeing promoter, arranging such a convenient outcome. As I wrote before the rematch in Vegas:

> *One story floating here . . . concerns the Holyfield-Lewis draw, the one that smells like old salmon.*
>
> *When Tyson bit off Holyfield's ear in June of 1997, there was vast and serious mayhem afterward. There was gunfire and casinos were abandoned and a lot of big houses didn't enjoy near the "drop" they were supposed to.*
>
> *With the casinos so upset (the story goes) they needed a make-good. And because fans love to bet on fights here, and because a draw is a bettable option that hardly anyone ever plays, the draw was the gift. Everyone who bet on either Holyfield or Lewis lost their money. The casinos won big.*
>
> *A fairy tale? Far-fetched? Sure. The casinos wouldn't screw around on something they knew had been tampered with. A quarterback catches a cold and they take a game off the board here.*

The majority of fights I covered were in Las Vegas, although I followed Lewis around a little and saw him hammer Michael Grant in Madison Square Garden, which was a cool assignment. My father had been a great boxing fan and in the late 1950s and early 1960s, he would drive to New York to see fights at the old Madison Square Garden on Eighth Avenue. He wasn't a big fan of the heavyweights; his favourites were a couple of great middleweights, Emile Griffith and Dick Tiger. Now and then, he would take me along with him on his New York journeys. Kids weren't allowed into the fights, but he would take me to Yankee Stadium or, in 1962 when the Mets were born, to the Polo Grounds, where the terrible expansion team played its first two seasons. (It's because of these trips I saw Roger Maris hit four home runs in a doubleheader in 1961, the year he broke Babe Ruth's record with 61 homers, then the next summer saw Willie Mays, returning with the San Francisco Giants to play centrefield in the Polo Grounds, where his legend had begun. Great memories to have.) Once, my father took me into Jack Dempsey's Restaurant on Broadway, where Dempsey used to sit just inside the front door, greeting tourists and signing autographs and such. I shook hands with the Manassa Mauler himself. I was eight or nine years old at the time. Then, 40 years later, I was covering a fight in the Garden. I always thought my old man, who died when I was 19, would have liked that.

One other memorable fight I covered was held in Memphis, of all places, Lewis against Mike Tyson in the summer of 2002. It was a weird place to have a fight, but this was during Tyson's suspension in Nevada, and Memphis, driven by a hick of a mayor who wanted his burg to go big time, put up $12 million to hold the fight there. There had been a wild press-conference brawl five months previously, when the fight was announced in New York, during which Tyson actually bit a chunk out of Lewis's leg and screamed obscenities at reporters. Despite this, and possibly because of insanely priced tickets in a far-from-rich city, the arena was one-third empty, even though the mayor was carrying on, interrupting press conferences and trying to fan civic pride in order to sell tickets to cover the municipal guarantees. The fight was nothing but a curiosity; Tyson's best fist fighting days were long over, dulled by his prison stint and his in-ring meltdowns. His uncontrollable personality was subdued by fight week. (I always suspected he was heavily medicated by this point.) Further to the general malaise of the fight, Lewis carried the wrong — i.e. non-American — passport and simply wasn't a very compelling champion. It was a tough fight to sell. As I wrote going in:

> *Tyson, history has demonstrated, usually can play whatever role will play well at any moment — whether the raging bad dream, the pensive and well-read student of the game, the happy guy who sings to children, or a racially motivated powder keg. Whatever the situation dictates, he provides. This week, he needs to be the guy to talk about because Lewis tends to be duller than* The English Patient.

Lewis dominated and scored an eighth-round knockout, but it was winding down for him, too. Within two years, he retired. With him went my career as a boxing writer. And Meg Ryan never did phone.

CHAPTER TEN

It Wasn't Always Sports

Occasionally, writing sports led to writing something else entirely. Or at least experiencing something miles out of the ordinary. The biggest worldwide story I ever got involved in, I suspect, was followed by an even bigger worldwide story that I was at least witness to, although not working at. They happened three weeks apart, believe it or not, and I have yet to discover anyone else who was on hand for both events.

The first was the World Series earthquake, which struck moments before the third game of the 1989 baseball championship. I was in Candlestick Park in San Francisco, wobbling around on a cane with my right leg in a brace, having tripped and torn knee cartilage at some point during the first round of the baseball playoffs, as the Blue Jays were eliminated by Oakland. When the earthquake hit, I was on a corridor just outside one of the upper-deck auxiliary press rooms. I gave a lurch and immediately thought my cane had snapped, but it hadn't. Then I surveyed the nearby parking lot and the ground seemed to be rolling. Uh-oh. I looked up and the top few rows of Candlestick Park, hanging out over the concourse where I was, were gently rippling, the concrete flaking off in tiny pieces, almost as a fine dust. I got into a doorway and thought to myself: So this is what an earthquake is like. Now I know.

I got a quick phone call out to my wife Debra, saying not to worry, and another to the office telling them I would get back to them when I had something to dictate, then gathered up my computer bag and headed down a flight of steps. I got into a VIP parking lot, which contained a few players still in uniform and their families, and quickly hooked a ride with a local TV crew that was chucking its equipment into its vehicle and preparing to head for the Bay Bridge. The two TV guys, whose names I never learned, took pity on this hobbling guy, his leg straight and wrapped up, and let me ride in the back of their vehicle. Initial information was that the bridge had collapsed, although it turned out to be only one section that was down. I got plenty of information from their radio and they let me out on the edge of downtown, while they headed out onto the bridge as far as they could get. I wandered the streets at my reduced speed, taking notes and interviewing confused citizens, cops, storekeepers out on the sidewalk waiting for the aftershocks to roll through. At every pay phone that was still working — no cell phones in those days — I called the office and dictated fresh observations. I was one of those old-time newspaper guys who never went out on assignment without a roll of quarters; you never knew when you would need to feed the pay phones. The quarters came in handy that night for the couple of hours I was able to work, before eastern deadlines shut down the paper for the night.

I was staying at the Berkeley Marina Marriott, on the east side of San Francisco Bay, and with the Bay Bridge closed, the only way to get there in my rental car, which I had parked downtown, was the long way: through San Francisco to the Golden Gate Bridge, north past Sausalito toward San Rafael, then the 580 highway across the top of the bay, past San Quentin prison, through Richmond and south to Berkeley. That took a couple of hours on packed roads. In San Fran, I had run into a baseball buddy, Yankee writer Tom Pedulla, who likewise was staying in Berkeley and didn't have a car and was wondering how to get home. So at least I had company on the journey. When we got near Berkeley, we were pretty much out of adrenaline, but were hungry and thirsty. We found a Thai restaurant without power, the owner doing his best to cook and serve as much food as he could before it spoiled. We had a terrific meal, washed down with slightly warm beer, in the middle of the night. It was one of those meals that tasted far better than it should have.

The next day, we scouted the damage on the Oakland side, including the collapsed highway 880, still holding several crushed cars with bodies inside. This sight felt close to home; I had driven that highway several times in the past few days down and back to the Oakland-Alameda County Coliseum for the Series' first two games. The cops regarded a World Series credential as a legitimate press pass and let us inside the taped-off boundaries, up close to the mayhem and destruction. We spent the day filing plenty of stories back to the office. I was proud of one in particular. There was a woman sobbing in front of a small hotel in downtown Oakland, a building whose entire brick face had been shorn off and was lying in the street. It looked like a dollhouse; the pictures were still on the walls of the rooms, but the entire front wall of each room was gone. The woman was so upset because she was a hooker and this was her john

At the Berlin Wall the day after it came down in 1989.
Found a Toronto Blue Jays sticker among the artwork.

hotel. She was lamenting, with its loss, that she would have to go back to working in cars. In terms of human cost associated with the earthquake, this was as telling as any I ran across. The *Star* decided not to run the story; said it wasn't in good taste.

With the World Series postponed indefinitely, I spent three days there, still filing stories on the aftermath of the shake, before being able to get a flight out. I had to come home because the next week, my wife and I were going on vacation. We had booked a self-driving visit to Germany, heading down the Rhine into Switzerland and Austria, and we weren't about to cancel that so I could go back and cover a couple of baseball games in two weeks.

So away we went and had a great vacation, seeing the sights and enjoying ourselves. One night we were drinking beer in a historic Munich brauhaus when we detected a breakout excitement level among the citizens. What was up? Turns out they were going to open the Berlin Wall tomorrow. The East Germans were giving up. The citizenry was ecstatic because Germany apparently was about to be reunited.

This, obviously, was historic. After sobering up, we got in our car and took full advantage of the autobahn's lack of speed limits, zipping the hundreds of miles to Berlin in a matter of hours. We drove through East Germany, under the providence of one of those time-stamped cards they used to give out at the border. (Take too much time and you are arrested for being a spy. Take too little time and you are arrested for speeding.) We fit into our allowable window, apparently, or perhaps this day they simply did not care. When we got to Berlin, the scene was one of joyful mayhem. The wall had been open a few hours and we got to the newly created hole, waving and cheering as the stinky little one-stroke cars put-putted through. Needless to say, there had never been anything quite like this. For the next couple of days we loved every minute of it, loved watching the East

Germans, their eyes wide in astonishment, shopping in West Berlin and exclaiming about things we would never think twice about, such as oranges or those little individual packs of Kleenex. Colour television sets in shop windows drew enormous crowds. Children gobbled chocolate bars, the treats suddenly available in quantities the kids had previously seen only in their dreams.

Our second day there we walked again along the wall and up near Checkpoint Charlie we came across the magnificent cello maestro Mstislav Rostropovich, who was in the late stages of giving an improv concert. I still get chills thinking about the moment. Later on, further down the wall the other way, a young woman with a violin case cleared out a small space and sat on a folding chair. A few more musicians arrived and set up around her. It turned out they were members of the Berlin Philharmonic, and they broke into some Beethoven for the appreciative masses. This was simple, spontaneous joy.

I kept telling myself that three weeks ago I had been limping around a baseball stadium when the ground shook violently. Now here I was, almost halfway across the world, witnessing the almost instant reunification of a country. I wasn't writing anything for the *Star* at that point, which added to the enjoyment and made it a vacation to remember forever.

Probably nothing in my career, or life for that matter, compares to the excitement of those three weeks, from San Francisco to Berlin and back. But there were several magical moments, days that came close to sharing the same kind of place in the memory banks. One happened in Orlando, when all I wanted to do was play golf on my day off.

For a few years, I covered Arnold Palmer's Bay Hill Invitational, an excellent tournament in the middle of the PGA Tour's

Florida swing, that always drew a great field, mostly out of respect for Arnold. The following week, the golfers would head a couple of hours up to Ponte Vedra Beach for the Players Championship, one of the biggies. I very much liked the Bay Hill Club and wanted to play there, so one year I booked a game for myself for the Monday after the Players. I would drive back from Ponte Vedra Beach on the Sunday evening and play Monday afternoon.

That was the plan and it worked nicely. I covered the Players, wrote and filed Sunday evening and drove back to Orlando. Monday about 11:30 a.m., I went out to Bay Hill for a 1:30 p.m. tee time. I went to the range to hit some balls. There was a tiny snack bar there, with a couple of tables. I went over to get a hot dog and who was sitting there, by himself, but Arnold Palmer. Arnold played a little money game with some long-time members every afternoon and was having lunch while waiting to go out.

"What are you doing here?" he asked me, recognizing me as one of the press guys who always attended his tournament. I told him I'd always wanted to play his course and such and was killing time until my tee-off. He said to sit down, kill the time together and tell him what was happening in Toronto. I got something to eat and we sat there for 20 very enjoyable minutes, just chatting. No interviews, no notes, just two golfers (sort of) chewing the fat. Finally Arnold said, "Well, maybe we should hit some balls." Naturally, I froze in fright. He stepped up to his spot, while I moved several spots down the line, having no desire to station my awkward little crank at the ball anywhere near this legend.

That was a pretty cool moment, and here's another from a golf course and involves two of the greatest women in Canadian sport history, plus the country's very best broadcaster.

Canada has one member inducted into the World Golf

Hall of Fame in St. Augustine, Florida. It's the tremendous amateur champion Marlene Stewart Streit, who won international championships from the 1950s, when she was a kid, to the first years of this century, when she was most decidedly not a kid, but still was a fiery competitor used to taking down opponents twice her size and, often, half her age. She also was a good friend, mostly from time spent together with our mutual

Canada's greatest golfer, Marlene Stewart Streit, graciously gave me the ball with which she won the 2003 U.S. Senior Amateur.

friend Glenn Goodwin, the class act who ran the *Toronto Star* Amateur tournament and was always working hard to bring together golf and kids who might not have had a lot of exposure to the game. Marlene and I played the occasional round together and she was always dynamite company.

Another great lady I had run into a million times was Marnie McBean, the most decorated Canadian Olympian of them all when she was a rower, and now a motivational speaker and mentor to Olympic athletes. Marnie also was a beginning golfer and, being a great athlete, she could hit a ball solidly and was quickly picking up the finer points of the game.

Brian Williams, who also knew both ladies, was a regular golf companion for me, and one day I put the four of us together at Angus Glen, which was my club at the time. Marnie and Marlene had never met. The match was men versus women, and let us say we mere men did not embarrass ourselves against a World Golf Hall of Famer and one of Canada's greatest Olympians. Marlene, her eyes narrowed after one of us made a clutch putt late in the day to draw within one hole, knocked in a 30-footer at the 17th hole to close us out, 2 and 1. Brian and I watched helplessly from the edge of the green as she circled the putt, read it stone-faced, and then stroked it dead centre to clinch the match — as if there had been any doubt whatsoever that the ball was going in the hole. We understood what all those opponents of Marlene's must have felt like for all those years. They didn't call her Little Ben — as in Hogan — when she was a kid for no good reason.

As great as the match was, what was truly remarkable that day was watching Marnie and Marlene quiz each other about their sports, about their preparations, about the mental challenges each faced and overcame. How did they handle pressure? How did they know when they were ready to perform their best?

At one point, Brian and I said if we were smart we'd have set up a tape recorder, caught it all for the record and played it back to every young Canadian athlete out there. It would have been the best lesson in how to become a champion that any of them could ever receive. Along the way, too, Marnie was showing Marlene some of her exercise tips and Marlene was helping Marnie with her short game. Fantastic stuff.

Later on, both ladies would be regular attendees and powerful supporters when the Canadian Sports Hall of Fame, which had been rescued from an ignoble end by the tireless work of Sheryn Posen, would stage fundraising dinners and golf tournaments as it came back to vibrancy. That was entirely a credit to Sheryn, by the way. She worked for years to coerce sponsors, politicians, athletes and a few media types to get behind the project. It took years and, because Toronto dropped the ball badly, required a locale change to Calgary for the Hall to finally land in a fine new building that can properly honour and display this country's sporting giants and their artifacts. None of it would have been possible without Posen, who remains a trusted friend and still organizes first-rate events when the urge strikes her.

There's one other day that strikes me as ultra special, and not only because I spent it with my closest friend Dan Loiselle, the long-time track announcer at Woodbine, Toronto's world-class thoroughbred and standardbred racetrack. I was on a hockey trip to Los Angeles, the Maple Leafs playing the Ducks one night and the Kings two nights later. On the intervening day, Santa Anita was racing. Dan, on his off-season at that point, came out to take in the games and set us up for a day at Santa Anita. We had a fine trackside table and it was one of those days I couldn't do anything wrong, picking five winners out of six races and making a bundle. It was such a good day, we drove straight to a golf shop where I had been eyeing a new set of clubs the day before and I bought them.

At Santa Anita, we met all kinds of trainers and prominent owners Dan knew from their trips to Woodbine. One of them was Mickey Rooney, whom he knew from Rooney's many visits to Woodbine over the years. So there we were talking to Mickey Rooney and, to be truthful, Mickey didn't look or smell too good. He was in dirty clothes, he looked a mess, seemed to be about one tick this side of homeless. I'm a huge old-movie guy who can tell you a lot about the old stars and their pictures, and I was kind of shocked: I mean, here was one of Ava Gardner's ex-husbands and he looked like an unmade bed. The offence was compounded, too, when a friend, not much cleaner, rushed up to Rooney, thrust a half-eaten sandwich into his hands and said, "Mick, Mick. I can't finish this. Eat it for me." Whereupon Rooney took a large bite out of someone else's lunch and two enormous globs of mayonnaise leapt out of the sandwich. One stretched down his shirt front and the other lodged itself on the three days' growth of stubble on Mickey's chin. And sat there. He had no idea.

Mickey stood there talking to us, asking Dan how things were going in Toronto and so on, and all I wanted to do was reach out and wipe the mayonnaise off this Hollywood legend's face. Good lord, what an introduction. For years afterward, I couldn't watch Mickey Rooney in a picture, even when he was a fresh-faced teenager hoofing around with Judy Garland 60 years before, without thinking of that mayonnaise.

This was our day to run into Hollywood legends, by the way. That night, staying out in Santa Monica, we walked down to the Santa Monica Pier for a couple of late beers. This was the place where Forrest Gump had finished his run across America in that dumb movie. We came out of the bar to walk back to the hotel, jabbering away, and some guy with a wire in his ear came rushing over to shush us. There was a movie filming a scene right under the pier and we were too loud. We stepped to the railing and looked over, and there was Paul Newman doing something or other. No sign of mayonnaise anywhere, at least.

CHAPTER ELEVEN

Small Potatoes

Four decades worth of newspapering in a big-league town leaves behind a wealth of memories not only of big stories covered around the world, but of wonderful one-off days and of good times with friends, some of them now sadly absent. There are yarns worth saving and repeating in every category and might as well start with the one that was as nutty as any and commenced, of all places, on a Toronto cricket pitch in 1997.

Total disclosure here: I am a closet cricket fan. I possibly could tell you the difference between a googly and deep square leg. I will hunt the sky for the channel that brings me the Indian Premier League, being a big fan of the Mumbai Indians, even though they do not use Chief Wahoo as a logo and more's the pity there, eh? Granted it was a slow day, but I once wrote an entire column on the wonders of Indian cricket pondering if, among other things, cricket bats ever broke (they do) and whether they had announcers who screamed out, à la Phil Rizzuto and Harry Caray, "Holy Cow!" at moments most dramatic. If they did, there would at least be a good reason. (Believe it or not, this line was not entirely fondly received.)

One of the Mumbai Indians' big sluggers was the Master Blaster himself, Sachin Tendulkar. He was India's team captain at the time and was there during the infamous PotatoGate.

At an event called the Sahara Cup in Toronto, India and Pakistan were playing a "friendly" match, which, considering the rampant animosity between the two countries, might have been something of a longshot to start with. The Pakistanis weren't doing well this day and one struggling batsman in particular, named Inzamam-ul-Haq, was being serenaded, in shall we say an ironic sense, by two fans with an electronic loud hailer. What they were saying I had no idea, but suddenly ul-Haq was up in the stands, seeking out his verbal assailants. Next thing you knew, a bat had appeared, source unknown, and he was menacing the customers and swinging away. Cops quickly got into it and given the way India and Pakistan felt about each other, this was a mini-riot potentially escalating toward a worldwide front-page story. I was treating it with all the seriousness it deserved. For a while.

The *Star* had a senior editor there, as a fan, who spoke the language. He was a pretty reliable guy and after the initial hostilities had ceased, he got hold of me and told me what the fans had been saying: they were calling ul-Haq, kind of a roundish fellow, a potato. Really? The guy is willing to start an international incident because someone called him a potato?

Soon, the insult was confirmed from other sources. Earlier in the day, clever fans had taunted Mohammad Azharuddin, India's former team captain, for leaving his wife for a movie starlet, the kind of invasion of personal space that would set off many athletes, yet he managed to stay on the pitch. But potato got the mayhem going.

It simmered for a couple of days. Everybody made with the tuber jokes, about how nobody really got mashed and so on. Tendulkar mostly played the no-comment card, although I caught him giggling and rolling his eyes a couple of times. Ul-Haq was handed a two-game suspension for "bringing the game into disrepute" and a brief but official investigation could not determine how the bat had appeared in the middle of the melee. No one was hurt badly and the police did not lay any charges as diplomats got involved, trying to keep the lid on things.

Tournament organizers tried to pretend that nothing untoward had happened. They announced only that "hooters" — their word for battery-operated megaphones — would no longer be allowed into the stands. This prompted me, in a follow-up column, to write, "What? Hooters have been banned? Wait just a damned minute here, buddy . . . What's that you say? A hooter is a loud hailer? Never mind."

Good times, and mostly because what could have been ugly turned out to be mostly absurd.

The next story is more pathetic than funny, and it led to a man losing his job, although deservedly so in this opinion.

It was the Tim Johnson debacle, which commenced in 1998, when he took over as Blue Jays manager. A former Blue Jays player from the bad old days, Johnson was a guy about whom not a lot was known, other than the fact he was an unspectacular journeyman ball player, the kind who often turn into managers.

It turns out he was a monumental liar, making up tales about his background and about serving in Vietnam (which he did not) and being forced to kill women and children (which he surely did not). The more we looked into Tim Johnson, the more fantastic all the background stories were.

The issue mushroomed from a harmless enough beginning when *Star* baseball writer Jim Byers, a native Californian, ran into Johnson's mother at a function somewhere. Johnson had been telling stories of his childhood, about growing up in a poor and tough section of Los Angeles and fighting his way out. That kind of thing.

Byers mentioned something to Johnson's mother about how proud she must be about the way her son turned out, considering his early environment, and she kind of laughed and said something like, "Oh, is Tim telling those stories again?"

This got some ears up around the *Star*. Byers, myself and baseball writer Geoff Baker began looking into Johnson's claims and found stuff in official biographies that simply wasn't true: for instance, that he was offered a basketball scholarship to UCLA and was a star high school basketball player coveted by several universities after an all-state career. (In reality, he did not play basketball in high school.) Then came the other stuff, about his Vietnam days and even more incredibly, a suggestion that he was dating, and bedding, country singing star Reba McEntire. (His military involvement showed he was a member of the U.S. Marines reserves, but never set foot outside the U.S.) It took a while and plenty of interviews with former coaches and teammates to pin it all down. Along the way, he got into a public dispute with pitching coach Mel Queen, who took offence to, among other things, what he knew were Johnson's repeated bullshit references to Vietnam.

Finally, when we had all the facts we could ascertain, I confronted Johnson with the discrepancies. He admitted there was much incorrect information out there, in official biographies and such, and had never bothered to correct any of it because no one had asked him about it. But he was adamant that he had never made reference to killing Vietnamese women and children in conversation with his ball team. I wrote a front-page column, with Baker handling the news piece, on the gaps between fact and fiction. General manager Gord Ash, who scoffed at our findings when approached for comment before publication, said he did not care about any of it and would pay no attention.

The morning the story appeared, I went down to the SkyDome. Two coaches came over and thanked me for writing what I had written. Those two coaches and one player also said there was only one error: that Johnson had, indeed, talked about killing civilians in speeches to the team. I confronted Johnson again and he got a little grin and said, well, it said right there on the front page that I didn't do it, so I must not have. After that, I never trusted another thing he said and suggested the Jays' next hire be a polygraph expert. The next spring training, after a winter of criticism, including some broadsides from veterans' groups, the story was resurrected by a couple of former Blue Jays players and refused to go away. The Jays, who ignored the reality for months, finally fired Johnson, who left blaming — you guessed it — not himself for all his lying, but the *Toronto Star* and a couple of writers for exposing him.

Still with guys who talked themselves into trouble, we have the ridiculous mayor of Toronto, Mel Lastman. (Lastman left office seven years before Rob Ford, another farcical mayor of Toronto who talked himself into trouble, was elected. We tended to do questionable things in this town at election time. Perhaps still do.)

Now, Lastman was a civic cheerleader who never let the facts get in the way of a rah-rah moment, such as suggesting the

Olympics were guaranteed to be a municipal money-maker and such. He was in the mayor's chair as Toronto sought the 2008 Summer Olympics, a Games earmarked and pretty much guaranteed for Beijing unless, somehow, the Chinese screwed things up. Which was a possibility, given China's despicable human rights record, so Toronto kept the engines running on its bid.

Lastman, of course, got into jackpots on other matters. For instance, he was accused of fathering two children during a 14-year affair with a former employee at his Bad Boy appliance chain. She sued him, claiming he had stiffed her on child support, among other things.

While all this was floating around, and as the International Olympic Committee's site determination vote was approaching, Lastman was quoted as saying he had no urge to visit Africa because not only was he scared of snakes, he was worried he might end up in a pot of boiling water.

Trite and juvenile, yes. Straight out of the 1950s in terms of sophistication. But naturally, the African members of the IOC, plus a few others openly in Beijing's pocket, went nutty. It was a columnist's dream:

> *And you thought Mel Lastman was only scared of child support payments. Now it's snakes, too. And the other kind of hot water.*
>
> *Oooops, the Love Bug mayor has done it again and now the hand-wringers think it might hurt this city's chances to land the 2008 Olympic Games. (But) a few stupid remarks from the mayor of a bid city will be dealt with in the usual fashion. A little gravy in the pocketbook and the pain will be lessened, if not tolerated. The outrage will be mostly over here, with people who don't vote.*

> *[Bid chief] John Bitove being over in Africa laying out the usual forms of bribery — the "aid" to impoverished sporting nations, etc. — is how to win votes and influence people. We need to turn on that great big sporting tap and then keep the juice flowing. If we do that, Lastman becomes exactly what all IOC delegates have had to deal with: A stupid, meddling politician who needs to be worked around. And a few more dollars can always work around most problems.*

By the time the IOC meetings opened in Moscow that summer, Lastman had apologized a hundred times. Yes, his silly attempt at a joke still drew more examination than Beijing's human rights record, which tells you which way the wind was intended to blow. I arrived in Moscow thinking there was at least a chance for Toronto despite him, albeit not much of one:

> *As always, the Games are China's to lose — and lose them it still could. It would be an upset, but look at it this way: If Kim Basinger can win an Oscar for acting, anything is possible. Even Toronto winning an Olympics.*

It turns out Kim did, but Toronto didn't — and surely won't in my lifetime, no matter how long I get to go.

The other grand moment from that journey to Moscow was a live TV interview with Brian Williams, as we awaited the official vote tally, where I answered Brian's question about the impending result by suggesting we couldn't really be sure "because we're dealing with a bunch of crooks here." I later discovered this to be a wildly popular response, although perhaps not with the public broadcaster, which paid the IOC all kinds of money for the right to televise Olympic Games. When Brian was done with me and the vote was announced, he then brought on our pal Paul Henderson, at the time the head of the International Sailing Federation and an IOC member. Henderson, who is forever mixed up with the hockey player who scored The Goal in 1972, was explaining the inner workings of the vote process when a jubilant Chinese backer banged into him, on camera, as he talked. Paulie The Plumber, as Henderson likes to call himself, kept talking as he delivered a sharp elbow to the man's ribs and sent him flying. Gordie Howe couldn't have done it better and Henderson still gets asked about it.

CHAPTER TWELVE

The Brass

It was always the position here that when it comes to sports franchises, the most important player on any team is the owner. Everything flows from the head down and if the owner, whether an individual, a corporation or — perish the thought — a group of well-meaning but often fatheaded individuals who operate through a board of directors, does not set a winning tone, it's not going to happen on the field or rink or court or whatever. One tick below the owner is the team president or general manager, those responsible for the makeup of the roster.

In that regard, let us therefore begin with the most successful ownership/front office combination, the Toronto Blue Jays in those halcyon days when Pat Gillick was the general manager and Paul Beeston was the team president and a very visual representative of the mostly silent owners, who were R. Howard Webster, the Canadian Imperial Bank of Commerce and Labatt, the brewing giant based in London, Ontario. Webster you never saw or heard. The CIBC showed up only after the team got good, boasting in commercials that it was "the bank of the Blue Jays." The brewery was more front and centre; it was always Labatt that delivered cases of Blue and 50 Ale to reporters' hotel rooms during spring training and made no bones about the fact that it considered the baseball team part of its beer marketing strategy.

What these owners were smart enough to do in the team's early days, though, was let Beeston call the fiscal shots and Gillick build the roster within the financial limits given to him.

Gillick, to start with him, was a master surveyor and appraiser of baseball talent. He was a very smart guy with a photographic memory. Fans know all this, of course. They got short with him when he failed to improve some rosters at trade deadlines, once the team became competitive, and he earned the nickname Stand Pat, which he seriously hated. Now, for reasons we could only guess at, Gillick didn't much like the *Toronto Star*. I suspect it was because of the paper's left-leaning bias and occasional outbreaks of clear-cut anti-Americanism. (Hell, many of us who worked there often felt something similar.)

In the middle of the 1993 baseball season, the *Star* had a 34-day strike that included all of us in editorial, and it got to be ugly at times. I walked a picket line around the *Star* building, at the foot of Yonge Street in downtown Toronto. Allan Ryan and Tom Slater, two fellow baseball writers, happened to be on the same picket shift and one day Gillick, a passenger in a car I suspected was driven by Beeston (although he strongly denies being the wheelman), drove around the block with Gillick heckling us through an open window. He was calling us commies and yelling for us to get back to work and so on. He seemed to be having a good time needling us.

Yet Gillick had a tremendously soft side. He would shed tears at even mildly emotional moments. Any kind of award or ceremony at which someone was honoured would cause him to puddle up. When he was being honoured — named to the Canadian Sports Hall of Fame, for instance — he could barely choke out an acceptance speech. He would fly for hours in the off-season to tell a fringe player he was being released or demoted, rather than do it over the phone. That's the kind of guy he was.

He was good about phoning me back when I needed to speak to him, but he seldom gave me anything, although we did get into a decent dispute once. I called him on some matter and he rambled on somewhat about other things. Mentioned a couple of players by name in less-than-glowing terms, something he never did for the record. I briefly suspected he had been drinking, although he was never much of a drinker. He certainly didn't sound drunk; exasperated with certain players was more like it.

I wrote a story, quoting him liberally, and the next day, Gillick was on the radio denying he'd ever said any such thing. Well, that simply wasn't true. I didn't use a tape recorder in those days — few reporters did — but I double-checked my notes and was certain he had been quoted 100 percent accurately. I phoned him to ask him what the hell he was doing denying a conversation reported accurately. He said he didn't say such things to me. I said he not only said what I reported, he also said such-and-such about so-and-so, which hadn't made it into print.

He sounded stunned and asked me: Did you really call me yesterday?

I told him of course I had and gave him the time and once again began quoting his own thoughts to him.

"That was you?" he asked, incredulously.

He began mumbling and stammering. He clearly had mixed me up with a fellow general manager, or a scout, or someone, and hadn't realized he had been talking to a reporter. It was the only time he ever made any such mistake, at least with me. It blew over quickly, as these things do. What the hell. Stuff happens. He was an excellent GM and built playoff teams in Seattle, Baltimore and Philadelphia after his Toronto days, so in a profession that isn't exactly scientific, he ended up with a tremendous record and deserved every kudo he received, including his plaque in baseball's Hall of Fame.

Gillick's finest moments, obviously, came from presiding over the consecutive World Series champions in 1992 and 1993, the former something of a mild upset and the latter widely expected. In the second inning of the fourth game of that '93 set, with the score 6-4 and the game already looking preposterous, Gillick turned to Michael Firestone and Beeston, among other witnesses, and said, "We win this 15-14."

Three hours later, after the score had reached that exact point, the Jays threatened to add another with a leadoff double in the ninth inning. Gillick waved it away.

"We don't need the run. We've already got the final score."

Beeston, the other half of what was often called the dynamic duo, was a tried-and-true Canadian. He got along with Gillick and they worked well together, but I would not say they were great friends. They tolerated each other very well, obviously, and respected each other. It was ownership and Beeston, more than Gillick, who got impatient with the disastrous disappointments of 1985, 1987 and 1989, when the team was good enough to go deeper than it did and exited painfully. It was Beeston who saw 50,000 fans a night jamming into the brand new (as of 1989) SkyDome and insisted the Jays venture into the free-agent waters to add the finishing touches. Gillick wanted to draft and develop and swipe players from other organizations in lopsided trades. He hadn't had much luck with free agents in his limited dealings — try Bill Caudill and Ken Dayley, to name a couple of expensive bullpen flops in the 1980s. After the terrible collapse in the 1991 playoffs, when Tom Candiotti, Gillick's prized late-season acquisition, started in Game 1 and panicked, refusing to throw his knuckleball and getting hammered trying to beat the Twins with curveballs, upper management's patience had run out.

The Jays went loudly into the free-agent market, but Gillick seemed to be kicking and screaming during the journey. When they signed Jack Morris and Dave Winfield in 1991, two cornerstones of the 1992 World Series champion, Gillick and his wife, Doris, were on a beach in the Virgin Islands. It was Beeston prying the rubber band off the bankroll, dickering with the agents and landing the big fish. (A year later it was Paul Molitor and Dave Stewart plucked out of the expensive FA pool and, once again, Beeston was the point man in negotiations.) Gillick was the architect of the roster, certainly, and made the trades that secured critical pieces, but it was Beeston putting on the icing, if you will, with those free agents. It was obvious, even at the time, as a 1991 column on the two huge signings suggested:

> *But what about Gillick, the man who devoted a lot of long, hard years to rooting out prospects in other organizations, drafting and signing the tough signs and building the organization that way?*
>
> *Gillick's on vacation in the Virgin Islands when Morris arrives to chat about, and eventually sign, a $15 million package? Sure, they have phones in the V.I. and Gillick, for certain, would never be far*

> *from one. He'd be a unanimous selection to the Bell Telephone Hall of Fame if there was one.*
>
> *But this is a guy who'd fly to California to tell a back-up catcher how they plan to use him. Beeston, not Gillick, does most of the big-money negotiating, but Pat doesn't want to be there when the biggest signing in club history goes down? Does that figure?*

The only semi-public disagreement between Beeston and Gillick concerned Cito Gaston, whom Gillick kept insisting was "not a candidate" to replace Jimy Williams as manager in May 1989, even when Gaston held the interim tag. Beeston detected early that the players not only loved Gaston, which was nice but not crucially important, but that they played hard for him, which clearly was. Gillick wanted Lou Piniella, to the point that he was willing to negotiate with George Steinbrenner, who demanded that the Jays give up a player or players to the Yankees for the right to hire away Piniella. He was under contract in New York as a "consultant," the job to which George often assigned his fired managers.

Beeston overruled Gillick on Piniella, they named Gaston manager permanently and it worked out rather well. Though not popular with fans until the sensible ones looked back and realized what the team had accomplished under him — and what it did not accomplish both before and after his time at the helm — Gaston had a huge fan in Beeston, to say nothing of the vast majority of players who laboured under him, and he does to this day.

The night the Jays beat Baltimore to win the American League East Division title in 1989, in the boozy aftermath of a well-soaked clubhouse, Gillick and Beeston leaned on each other and told a story. They said they had called Steinbrenner a day or two before and offered him a list of Blue Jay players and told him to pick out four. Steinbrenner asked what they wanted in return.

"Nothing," Gillick said they told him. "That's for not making Piniella available."

Steinbrenner's response was simple: "Fuck you guys."

Beeston, of course, left the Jays to become the president of Major League Baseball, commuting between Toronto and New York. He spent a couple of years there, but didn't see eye to eye with commissioner Bud Selig — I'm being polite here — on things like labour matters. Beeston had a good relationship with Don Fehr, who ran the players' union, and Selig, like all owners, kept wanting to teach those players a lesson with lockouts and hard lines on strikes and such. One of the reasons Beeston was bought out of his contract with MLB and sent home is that he and Fehr could have worked out an agreement to avoid the kind of labour strife that pockmarked baseball for years — and never did one thing to slow down the growth of salaries, which kept pace with the enormous growth of revenues throughout the first decade and a half of the 21st century.

Beeston eventually returned to run the Blue Jays again, long after Ted Rogers, the media giant, had bought the team from Belgian brewer Interbrew S.A. and (Rogers claimed) continued to lose vast amounts of money with Paul Godfrey, an enthusiastic sports fan and former Metro chairman, in charge as president.

There seemed to be promise when Ted took over in September 2000. I welcomed him as follows:

> *Ted Rogers is a bold, aggressive businessman, obviously. I know this every month when I look at my cable bill.*
>
> *If Rogers can work out an agreement . . . and gain*

control of the Blue Jays, he will need to be bold and aggressive.

In this case the old stuff about the devil you know and the devil you don't know can be waived. The sad truth is, under Interbrew S.A. this franchise has nose-dived. A local man with deep pockets is needed to save it from beating the Montreal Expos to Virginia, or wherever it is these teams could end up.

Rogers seldom made himself available to the press. He never returned a phone call and one of the very few times I saw him came two nights into the 2000 season, when he stumbled into the press box, slurring his words and holding a glass of wine. He announced himself thusly: "Hello, I'm the village idiot" and went on a diatribe about the weak (at the time) Canadian dollar. "Don't you remember what happened to Rome and Greece? This country won't even be here in 15 years unless we do something. We have a hell of a currency issue here." Those were his exact words.

His handlers bundled him out of the place and we all looked at each other stunned. What the hell just happened?

He clearly was drunk and rambling, although the *Star* panicked when I wrote that he was drinking, and the managing editor phoned me at home well after midnight to beg me not to write that he was drinking and slurring his words. (This was one more instance, with more later than before, that the *Star* was far more terrified of rich people than it should have been.) I refused to voluntarily change my copy, but they took it out anyway. A little of what remained:

All of Godfrey's good intentions, and those of his new general manager, J.P. Ricciardi, won't do much good if the new owner gets away from his handlers long enough to begin spouting bizarre history lessons to baseball writers. Sometimes billionaire owners behaving (shall we say) strangely can help a ball team. Ted Turner proved that in Atlanta, although he had to bring aboard Jane Fonda to keep the interest level high.

Godfrey hired J.P. Ricciardi as general manager and while Ricciardi had new ideas, he couldn't build a playoff team and drafted poorly, with gusts to terribly. Nor did Rogers (Ted or his company, take your pick) have any idea how to market its own team. In the spring of 2006, with the Leafs and Raptors, as usual, nowhere in contention in the spring, the Jays continued to botch their chance to be relevant.

For a team owned by a media giant, it was clueless in spring training. Couldn't get any games on TV and only a couple on radio — and Rogers owns both stations. The day the Blue Jays played Team Canada, before the World Baseball Classic, Rogers' own sports channel showed the Dodgers and Braves. With the Leafs in the tank by the middle of February (and) the Raptors heading for the first tee after tonight, Rogers missed a big boat this year.

The biggest boat Rogers and his moneyed friends ever missed, though, was the NFL boat.

Talk of an NFL team in Toronto was up and running, however slowly, when I broke into the business in 1973. It surely ebbed and flowed over the years, but it has never gone away and remains a topic of discussion more than four decades later. It really ramped up when Rogers and his neighbour and fellow billionaire, Larry Tanenbaum, got together and tried to get serious. Along with Phil Lind, Rogers' right-hand man and a huge NFL fan, they jetted around North America in Larry's private plane to see games and shake hands and make their intentions known. Then, in 2008, Rogers paid an astronomical $78 million for the right to play host to eight Buffalo Bills games, five of them regular season, to be played over five years in the SkyDome, which Ted had renamed the Rogers Centre soon after buying it for $25 million — something like $585 million less than what it cost to build, most of that taxpayer dollars.

The plan to bring the NFL to Toronto was introduced at a legendarily embarrassing press conference — easily one of the strangest I ever attended — at which Rogers and Bills owner Ralph Wilson, then in his 90s, were openly and gleefully disdainful of the ticket-buying suckers they thought they were going to fleece. Tanenbaum, presumably horrified, sat there stone-faced as Rogers and Wilson rambled on and made jokes about the lack of affordable seats. Turns out that series organizers were charging such ridiculous prices for tickets that they refused to even advertise costs. They wanted fans to sign up for waiting lists to buy tickets, after which a sales representative would call and discuss prices, which started in the hundreds of dollars. Despite announcing "sellouts," the series turned into a huge flop and several thousand seats were given away. It was one of the low moments of sports ownership, even for Toronto, and the series eventually was abandoned early.

It didn't seem possible anyone could lose money on the NFL, but the Rogers/Tanenbaum empire did. That the first game, before a well-padded house, was excruciatingly boring didn't help matters. My post-game column began:

There you have it: The greatest regular-season game in NFL history. At least until they play the second one, which surely can't be as lacking in entertainment value as this field-goal fest.

The Miami Dolphins beat the Buffalo Bills 16-3 before 52,134 witnessing one of those magnificent kneel-down finishes at the Rogers Centre. The good news is that not all of the customers paid the $575 top price for this dog. Plenty of people didn't pay anything, although let's not rush into calling them the lucky ones. Sometimes you get what you pay for.

The Bills . . . once again were so woeful on offence that people named William should sue.

Rogers died not long after that comedy act with Ralph Wilson and in his obituary, I suggested:

It's kind of a shame for Rogers that his final public appearance, if you will, was that ill-advised press conference. He didn't make many friends that day. Similarly, as much as baseball fans should appreciate the fact that he stepped up and bankrolled the Jays in Toronto when nobody else seemed to want to operate the team, he left money on the table there. For a gigantic media mogul, the Jays under Rogers made terrible mistakes: Poor announcers for too long who alienated customers; almost zero spring training coverage; game feeds picked up from other teams. There were times no one would believe this club was owned by a communications giant.

Still, he paid the bills — paid those other Bills, too — and baseball got healthy in Toronto again under

> *his command, however distant he was as an owner. Things are better now than when he first bought the club. He built an empire, or at least caused it to be built. Now we will see how much of it endures.*
>
> *Keeping the empire going turned out to be Beeston's job. After honing his golf game slightly, sitting on various boards of directors around town, and raising the profile significantly as significant driving force behind the Centre for Addiction and Mental Health, Beeston replaced Godfrey as president. He insisted, both publicly and privately, that he had no long-term designs on the job and was in it only temporarily:*
>
> *Beeston, who is 63 — born exactly the same day as that other Canadian icon, Anne Murray, if you're sending flowers — insists he will not be in the job long. He bet $500 yesterday, payable to the* Star's *Christmas fund for kids, that he will be out of the job by Christmas Day.*

He paid up and, as always, added significantly more to the cheque for charity. Generosity is one of his permanent traits. Of almost immediate significance, Beeston put the red maple leaf back on the Jays' uniform and installed young Montrealer Alex Anthopoulos as general manager.

Anthopoulos presided over a rebuilding job, not aided at all by the talent-poor farm system left behind by his predecessor, Ricciardi. He made big trades that didn't pay off, but by 2015, the results of the Beeston-Anthopoulos partnership together showed up on the field in a big way. Except Beeston, nearing 70, had been stabbed in the back and replaced on the direction of Rogers' son Edward, a rich man's son who somehow decided that inheriting his father's fortune was some kind of indication of his own greatness. The Jays' shabby treatment of Beeston will be an enduring disgrace that stains the younger Rogers forever.

The one job Beeston had always coveted was the one job he never got, namely running the Toronto Maple Leafs. No surprise there, because there seldom was an occasion the Maple Leafs, certainly in my time around the team, ever hired the right man.

CHAPTER THIRTEEN

Match Play

I mentioned that I attended 10 Ryder and Presidents Cups and these were outstanding events, usually packed with drama and fun to write, although most Presidents Cups tended to be one-sided. Because I angled most stories from the International side of the Presidents Cup, for the obvious reason that Mike Weir was there on behalf of Canada and unfailingly giving an excellent account of himself, I tended to lean the Europeans' way in the Ryder Cup, as well.

The 1999 Cup at Brookline, outside Boston, was a spectacular but ugly affair, marked by the monster U.S. comeback in Sunday's singles that led to a premature celebration on the green after Justin Leonard famously holed that long putt. The week had been marked by the torrents of vile abuse handed out to Colin Montgomerie, the sour Scot who was a Ryder Cup standout. As I suggested after the first day:

> *Most of the Americans looked stiff and grim-faced, like young investment bankers going to work, while the Euros looked as if they were out whacking it with their mates and playing for pints instead of points.*
>
> *It was like this all week in practice and, aside from Colin Montgomerie, the greatly talented and combative sourball, barking at mouthy dolts in the galleries, it was this way when they played for keeps.*
>
> *If the rest of the weekend is like this, it could be the greatest Ryder Cup of them all. This day the Europeans were simply more brilliant than the Americans. This doesn't mean they will win the Cup, despite the lush lead. Few people with good golf sense expected them to take Samuel Ryder's bowling trophy home with them again. Not with seven rookies.*

That's how it worked out eventually, although the die was cast for more bad blood in future Ryder Cups because of the U.S. line dance across the green, after Leonard's putt, while José María Olazábal still had a 22-footer to halve the decisive hole. When he missed it, the Europeans were spitting mad — some of them are still that way — although no one ever seemed to mention that Olazábal had been four holes ahead with seven to play and got himself tracked down for the biggest point of the competition. The Europeans commenced kicking U.S. tail in the Ryder Cup from then on, though, winning five of the next six.

It was a different story in the Presidents Cup, where things were much more friendly, but the Internationals seldom made a game of it. There were some good times, though. I recall a press conference with four Australians and K.J. Choi sharing the podium, K.J. taking his information through a translator. The Aussies, as usual, were goofing on each other, talking about sheep-shagging and carnal relations with other barnyard animals. This kind of talk, filtered through the translator, seemed a huge mystery to Choi, whose face took on an ever greater look of bemusement. It was lots of fun, actually.

The Americans, who had Jack Nicklaus as captain a few times, went with Ken Venturi in the 2000 competition in Virginia and that, too, was a hoot. I referred to Venturi as "the Casey Stengel of golf" because of his rambling, disjointed answers to even the simplest questions. For example, when someone asked if the Robert Trent Jones Golf Club course suited Tiger Woods's game, here was Venturi's response, verbatim:

> *"I think the golf course leads for Tiger because of the dog legs and bunkering. The first hole is a perfect example. I watched him yesterday. He was practising and [my assistant] and I went out to follow him around and he made a very good statement this morning, is that this is coming in October rather than when we went down to Australia, it was the end of the year for us."*

Wow. This from a guy who was a long-time TV commentator.

The subject had been Woods, and we might just as well tackle it here, because this was the guy who dominated golf coverage, for both the right and wrong reasons, almost all of the time I covered the game. For all the people who hated Woods and said they didn't want to watch him or read about him, the facts told a different story; numbers were off the charts for anything to do with him.

I was there at Augusta National in 1997, when he was starting his run at Nicklaus's total of 18 professional majors, and attended 13 of the 14 he ended up winning through the 2008 U.S. Open, missing only the 2000 PGA Championship because it got in the way of preparations for the Sydney Olympics. That 2008 victory, accomplished on a decided limp, marked the start of his serious physical decline. He has had at least five significant surgeries. Worse, possibly, his mental advantage over his competition seemed to depart. No longer was everyone scared of him, the way they had been for years. The next generation of golfers, now headed by Rory McIlroy, Jordan Spieth, Jason Day and others who grew up watching Woods close out victories when he had the chance, were not intimidated by him at all. They took their cues from him in that regard.

When he arrived as a professional in 1996, in a blaze of hype and money, he began changing golf almost immediately. He was as resented as he was welcomed within the industry. Even before the Masters in 1997, I saw him in action at Bay Hill that March and detected some of what was ahead:

> *The argyle sweater crowd, patting their forepaws in appreciation of a soothingly struck 7-iron, are getting crowded out by Tiger's Troops. This vast brigade of (it seems) golf newcomers is different. They often wear shirts and shorts that do not match, they come to root strictly for Tiger and those of legal age want to have a beer and enjoy themselves. Just like real sports fans.*
>
> *Imagine that, though. Staid old golf having to deal with these vulgarians taking an interest in their game. Why, some of them do not even belong to private clubs.*
>
> *Tiger has reintroduced superstar power to the golf tour and when he is playing, people come out, usually in record numbers, to see him. Many of the other pros,*

who could not sell 10 tickets, are downright jealous of Woods for his popularity, talent and youth.

Battle lines have been drawn in golf. You're one of the Woods people or you're not.

This, essentially, still was true 15 years later, after he had gone through the vast public humiliation of the exposure of his infidelity and seeing his marriage collapse. I was a Woods guy, I suppose, because he was always a pretty good story, even though he never said much. He was an ordinary guy as a young man; his idea of a good time seemed to be to hang with his buddies at Hooters, checking out the waitresses, a pastime he no longer could enjoy when he became Beatle-sized. He loved dirty jokes; I got a chance to tell him one, in a parking lot one day. He liked it. I probably sat in a press room with him 200 times, but I never sat down with him one-on-one. In South Africa, three or four of us chatted informally with him for a few minutes before an official press conference. I mentioned that later that day they were going to announce Royal Montreal, a course he didn't much like, as the site of the 2007 Presidents Cup.

"You've got to be fucking kidding me," he said. "There's better courses in Canada."

An hour later, when he was asked about Royal Montreal officially, he was slightly more diplomatic.

He played a Canadian Open at Royal Montreal in 2001, his fourth appearance in Canada in six years. His win in 2000 at Glen Abbey was sealed with a 72nd-hole bunker shot across a pond that every hacker tries to replicate to this day. He returned to defend at Royal Montreal, but (I always believed) he was chased away to stay by Jean Chrétien, the country's prime minister at the time.

Woods, in the few events where he was required to play a

pro-am on the Wednesday, always wanted the day's first tee time. That was his routine and tournament organizers were happy to provide the leadoff slot as a cost of getting him into their field. That year, Chrétien decided two days before that he wanted to play with Woods on the Wednesday. The tee time was delayed until late morning so Chrétien could get there. This did not sit well with Woods, a strict creature of golf habit. It's surely not a coincidence that he's never been back, although as a reason this became moot; when the Canadian Open moved into the week behind the British Open, that also excused him. He doesn't play the week after a major. Now, given the deterioration in his game, it hardly matters.

Woods made plenty of enemies in his career. Much of the criticism of him that came through my inbox was race-based, without question. (I got the letters and emails. I know how much vile stuff I read.) But there was plenty of legitimate criticism, too, and when his personal life leapt to the front page in sordid detail, school was out forever on that subject. I consider myself fortunate that most of my golf writing happened in the Woods era, for the simple reason that whether people liked him or loathed him, they wanted to read about him. Every word, too.

CHAPTER FOURTEEN

Round and Round

Because my father liked a trotting race and a small wager now and then, I well knew the location of Greenwood, the historic trotting track not far from downtown Toronto. Directions to Woodbine were well-known, too.

If that knowledge cost me a few dollars over the years, as it likely did and as I would know if I had bothered to keep a lifetime balance sheet, it also provided more laughs, stories and good times that any other set of arenas. An apprenticeship served partly at the track was part of the newspaper business, but that was long ago. As I've said for years, more sportswriters these days have been to Lamaze class than to Woodbine.

That's because horse racing has become a tiny fraction of what it used to be. The sporting calendar simply got clogged. In Toronto alone, at one point in the early 1970s, hockey was the dominant No. 1 beat, the CFL was No. 2 and horse racing, primarily thoroughbred with harness racing a poor little brother, was the third-best beat on the sports pages. Then the Blue Jays arrived. Then the Raptors. Golf and tennis got bigger. Even pro soccer finally made it. TV brought us a huge diet of major worldwide sporting events. Racing, which needed to scrap for any and all media coverage, not only never kept up, it never even tried to. Worse, it lost its monopoly on gambling

Driving a pacer (whose name I forget) at the old Greenwood Raceway in a media race, about 1976. I was in three of them, winning two.
PHOTO COURTESY OF MICHAEL BURNS.

as lotteries arrived, then scratch-off games. The government became the biggest bookmaker in town. Horse racing became what it is now, which is basically an afterthought. That's a pity because racing always contained some of the very best stories. It featured people who were stars in their game if they could win one out of five tries and therefore knew how to lose. Pound for pound, my favourite folks to deal with came from racing and from the side that sometimes had the shit on their shoes.

The Ontario Jockey Club? That's another matter. Most racetracks, including the OJC's thoroughbred and harness tracks, were old boys' clubs run mostly for the benefit of the old boys. You usually needed a stuffed shirt or a rich father to be admitted to their little club. The directors fancied themselves some kind of royalty, or something. They tended to call themselves Lt. Col. or the Right Honourable and so on. At one time, I think the OJC featured two Viscounts and a Baron on its board. Or perhaps it was the other way around.

One of the first races I ever covered, for the *Globe and Mail*, was won by one of the trustee's horses. (We called them house horses in those days.) I went to the winner's circle with the other reporters, where the owner, Lt. Col. Charles Baker — Bud to his friends, of which I was not one — decided I should be banished immediately because I was not wearing a necktie in his presence. Neither were most of the other reporters, but Bud decided that as a newcomer, I needed to be taught a lesson. When I got back to the *Globe* and reported my failings, sports editor Jim Vipond picked up the telephone, called somebody at the OJC and reamed them out. After that, Baker considered me a troublemaker. I tried not to disappoint him.

The OJC had a trustee named Baron von Richthofen, who was a descendant of the World War One German flying ace. The reasons for the insult have long since misted over, but I suggested, in print, that certain members had attended the board meeting sporting a $1 haircut — 25 cents a corner. Couldn't get away with that today.

I was more of a harness fan than a thoroughbred guy, even though my good friend Dan Loiselle spent decades as the track announcer at Woodbine. (Dan got his start on the harness side, working in the race office there, a few years before I started covering the game.) Southern Ontario was the hotbed for talent, both four-legged and, especially, two-legged, on the harness side. Many of the best trainers and drivers were born in this part of the world and they didn't necessarily rebel at the idea of a newspaper guy calling to chat. For instance, when Ontario native John Campbell was the biggest star in the sport, leading driver at The Meadowlands in New Jersey, I could call him at home to ask about certain horses or big races and he was always happy to help. (There are not many pro athletes you can call at home without setting off a rocket — and that's if you can get their number.) Campbell's counterpart on the thoroughbred side was Sandy Hawley, Canada's greatest horsebacker, who works for Woodbine and has since become one of racing's finest ambassadors. At the peak of his career, I didn't deal often with Hawley, who left for California and dominated there for a few years, but after his return to Woodbine, and since his retirement from riding, he has been nothing but gracious and a true gentleman. He's a giant in Canadian sport and one of my prouder professional moments was when I was given the Sandy Hawley Award, from the Ontario Sports Hall of Fame, for some charity work a few years back. There's no greater name to have on a Canadian plaque than his.

Back to the horses, where no matter how accomplished an animal might have been, horsemen seldom liked to brag on them. They always knew it was too easy to lose, for something to go wrong, for illness or unsoundness or bad racing luck to arrive at any moment. They tended to leave the hyperbole to the typists and we tended to accommodate.

Was there larceny at the track? Sure there was, and the further back you look for it, the more you can find. No more than what's practised every day in business by the sons of inherited wealth in the trustees' lounge, I'll bet, but there were traces of it. But after purses, aided by the revenues from slots machines, began to grow into six and seven figures for the biggest events, science and technology played an ever greater part: advances in equipment, nutrition, medication, training procedures and breeding produced ever faster animals and eased suspicions of choreographed races. Even with that, I always thought part of the attraction for some racegoers was seeking out and believing rumours that not only had the fifth race been tampered with, but that they could find their way to the correct side of the result.

I liked to bet and I saw no problem in betting on a race that I was writing about, because I had nothing to do with the outcome. (Hell, I always had a bet on Super Bowls I covered, too. Who didn't?) Matter of fact, I didn't trust a race writer who didn't bet, because that meant he or she didn't quite understand what the game was about and what motivated its fans. For a few years around 1980, a couple of us at the *Star*, race fans all, owned a few cheap horses in a small-time stable, although given my situation, doing the handicaps for the paper, I could see a conflict there. So I got clearance from the paper and my wife at the time got herself licensed as the owner. Other than a little claiming horse named Kickback Dick that got hot one winter and won a bunch of races, we didn't have much luck — and I mean both the racing stable and that marriage.

I wasn't a big bettor; $100 usually would make my hand shake. Biggest bet I ever made on one horse — about $2,300 — I lost and it wasn't even close. Most I ever made on one race was $9,500, when I loaded up on a longshot that came in. I went out and bought a Buick Riviera with the proceeds.

(Life was simpler then.) Once, for the 2005 Queen's Plate, the nation's leading 3-year-old thoroughbred race, I liked a horse a lot. It was a well-meant horse named Wild Desert, owned by a syndicate that included Yankee manager Joe Torre. The horse showed very little beyond 10 weeks of official idleness, but based solely on backstretch rumours and how he looked in the walking ring, I bet everything I had in my pocket and then, for the first and only time in my life, borrowed money and bet that, too. The next day's *Star*:

> *All credit to the connections of Wild Desert. Whoever they might be. Because it doesn't pay to ask. No one in the after-telling seemed to be exactly sure who owns him, or how much, and no one was exactly sure who trains him and the owners' spokesman wasn't certain who had saddled the horse. Nobody knew anything except they were going to win — and win big. This was as well-meant as a horse can be.*
>
> *A principal owner named Daniel Borislow, who overcame the urge to be modest and referred to himself as the biggest gambler in America, let slip that the raiding party, mostly from New York, took out more than $100,000 in bets cashed. The $600,000 winner's share from the $1 million purse, even in Canadian money, is the stuff they pay taxes on.*
>
> *There was no reason for the horse to be bet down to next to nothing — he paid $8.30 for $2 — except that somebody knew something. Somebody knew a lot, actually. But no one can say he or she wasn't warned. The advance word here was that the connections, including the suspended trainer of record, were trying to sneak a live one past us rubes.*

The Woodbine people held an investigation and later tried to keep the trainer off the grounds, but it all petered out eventually. They almost always do.

The best standardbred racehorses I ever saw were Niatross, Cam Fella and Somebeachsomewhere. Because their careers reached 30 years from front to back, from the late 1970s to 2009, I can't begin to guess which would have handled which had they ever met. Beach was probably the fastest, Cam Fella was the toughest and the best racehorse. Niatross was a ground breaker, a classic story. He was owned by a little old lady loyal to a cagey veteran trainer named Clint Galbraith, never one of the big names but a terrific guy. They caught lightning (almost literally) in a bottle with this horse. When the big money moved in and wanted to both buy and manage the horse, things got ugly. A New Jerseyan named Lou Guida tried to take control of the horse after investing and when Niatross suffered a shock defeat at Saratoga, New York, when he spooked and jumped over the rail, Guida went to court to have him retired. Didn't succeed, though.

That fall in Lexington, Kentucky, where the horses go as fast as they ever do in time trials, Niatross "went against the clock," as the time trials were called. The fastest mile ever paced to that point had been 1 minute and 52 seconds. When Niatross stopped the teletimer in 1 minute, 49 1/5 seconds, the place went crazy. No one in racing had ever seen anything like it and the colt's value immediately stretched to millions of dollars. After Lou Guida went out to get his picture taken, I asked him if he still wished he had been able to have the horse retired months previously. He did not respond kindly. Perhaps it was not the wisest opening question.

Such was the relaxed atmosphere of the races back then that

you could wander around to Galbraith's stable — any big trainer, really — and pull up a chair a few feet from the horse, crack open a beverage and shoot the breeze. Nowadays, it might be easier to get a mortar on to an airliner than to get a wandering scribbler through backstretch security and up to a champion's stall door.

To compare, Somebeachsomewhere eventually went more than two seconds faster than Niatross, albeit in a different and much faster era. He was trained by a friendly Maritimer named Brent MacGrath, who had his wonderful colt watched by 24/7 security cameras linked to a website and had a nationwide relay of friends and relatives who would monitor the website at all hours, just to be safe.

Cam Fella was a sensation, a locally owned horse, not the most fancifully bred, that went everywhere and simply outraced all his competition, winning his final 28 races. Busloads of his fans would travel to his races in the U.S. or Canada, which made for a terrific travelling party. There was a documentary-type movie made about him, which I wrote. (Somehow it failed to win an Oscar.) Initially, Cam drew zero interest as a stallion, yet ended up becoming one of the greatest standardbred sires of them all. His two years of dominant racing marked the most fun I ever had around the racetrack.

I used to like getting out in the morning and jog horses now and then. It was great relaxation, sitting in the jogging cart knowing there was no telephone to ring. A terrific trainer named Stew Firlotte, who has since passed on, was always friendly and had a great 3-year-old one year named Ralph Hanover, driven by the local record-breaking reinsman Ron Waples. Ralph was worth, minimum, $6 or $8 million. One morning at Greenwood, Stew let me drive Ralph a few laps around the racetrack, just jogging, so I could write a story on what it was like to sit behind so valuable an animal. I know Stew was more nervous than I was. Luckily, Ralph's opinion was not known.

I was friendly with a trainer named Dr. John Hayes, a veterinarian who was extremely helpful in explaining terms and practices and helping with my racing education. Plus, he would let me drive a few horses for him in the mornings when I dropped in on his farm. His father, John G. Hayes, was a plain-speaking, cantankerous and opinionated horseman who loved the action and didn't care on whose toes he stepped, especially verbally. Highlight of his career was winning the precious Little Brown Jug in Delaware, Ohio, with his own colt named Strike Out. His signature line was always, "I'd rather win the Jug than go to heaven" and in 1972 he took care of the first part of that statement. Back then, ABC's *Wide World of Sports* covered the race and Chris Schenkel, the famed U.S. sportscaster, interviewed Hayes before the race and asked him about his chances. "I didn't come down here to run for senator," Hayes answered, thereby earning the nickname Senator for the rest of his life. Others called him Rip, because his other nickname, for his driving style, had been inspired by Jack the Ripper. No one used that one to his face.

Hayes loved to make bets, sometimes the goofier the better. There was a nice 3-year-old race at Flamboro Downs outside Hamilton, Ontario, called the Confederation Cup. The standout favourite one year was named Hot Hitter. Hayes asked a companion in the dining room how much he thought Hot Hitter would pay. The man said something like $2.50 for $2. Hayes offered to bet him everything he had in his pocket — about $80, if I recall right — that the payoff would be even more meager, and once they shook on it, Hayes pulled out several thousand in cash and bet Hot Hitter down to the point he paid $2.20 or something close. The idea, of course, was getting that $80, which meant more to him than the couple of thousand he made through the mutuels. That was the Senator.

On the thoroughbred side, the highlight was the 1996 Breeders Cup coming to Woodbine, which was kind of the end of the era of huge thoroughbred race days. Slots machines soon moved in under a deal negotiated with the provincial Conservative government, which recognized it was cheaper to put the inevitable machines in places already built and zoned for gambling. Meanwhile, the Ontario Jockey Club became the Woodbine Entertainment Group under the direction of head man David Willmot and began to modernize and become less of an old boys' club. Revenues climbed for about a decade, at least until the Ontario government, now under Liberal control, misguidedly cut off that revenue stream in 2013 by revoking the deal on slots revenues, thereby crippling racing. I wrote numerous columns banging on the government for its short-sighted stupidity in damaging an old and honourable game. It was like pissing into the wind, of course. The thrust behind it was to shutter the racetracks — a few closed — and swing the gambling emphasis to bingo halls, many of which had been recently purchased by Liberal party big-shots. It was a disastrous move and ended up costing thousands of people their jobs in horse racing, to say nothing of the millions of dollars lost by taxpayers in the overall picture. At one point in the proceedings, when new Premier Kathleen Wynne was making an ever larger mess of things, I wrote that there was more honour and honesty on any backstretch in Ontario than there was at Queen's Park. I doubt if I ever wrote truer words.

Anyway, back to that '96 Breeders Cup, when I bet a horse

named Swain, ridden by Frankie Dettori, and Frankie got him beat single-handedly with a poor ride. Four years later, when Frankie showed up to ride a horse named Mutafaweq in the Canadian International, I still hadn't forgiven him. As I wrote:

> *Frankie Dettori owes me money.*
>
> *Every bettor remembers Frankie riding a horse named Swain in the Breeders Cup. Swain was much the best that day, poised to gallop away at the head of the stretch and make a bundle of people, me included, rich. Or at least racetrack-rich, which is that bullet-proof feeling that comes from a day of cashing tickets.*
>
> *Except Dettori commenced hitting Swain with his left hand and Swain, which looked like a winner under any kind of sane urging, began running right to get away from the smacking. Muhammad Ali never got hit with as many left hands and as Frankie ge-stick-ulated, Swain began running a circle route that would have made Jerry Rice proud. Bobsleds have gone straighter to the finish line than Swain, which, naturally, lost the race.*
>
> *When it comes to Frankie, we still blame him. But come this Sunday at Woodbine, he has a chance to pay me back.*

After that buildup, I am happy to report that Mutafaweq did indeed win the International, by a tiny little nose, and paid almost $11 to win while doing it. But guess which idiot talked himself out of betting the horse. Right. I switched off at the last minute, then had to pretend that I had written a bang-up advance and steered everyone else to such an obvious winner.

One last thing about that '96 Breeders Cup, which included

a nag named Ricks Natural Star. He was a nothing horse, a cheap claimer that had earned $44 that year and $6,000 lifetime, but was entered in the $2 million Turf as someone's idea of a joke.

> *In short, he is a horse with no upside whatsoever. Mind you, Cliff Fletcher might trade a 2-year-old stakes winner for him, but, really, it's just a lark. Someone is out to pop the buttons on a few stuffed shirts.*

That was all true, but he raced and was beaten about an eighth of a mile. Still, somewhat unbelievably:

> *There was a rather incredible $60,529 in win-place-show money bet on the nonsensical Ricks Natural Star. This, once and for all, ends the argument: People do have more money than brains. There no longer is any doubt. At the finish, the nag was moving so slowly you'd think he was playing for the Leaf defence.*

This, by the way, also shows how poorly the Maple Leafs were doing in those days. Two zings at them in two days in horse-racing columns. Good thing that changes were coming, eh? Wait. What?

CHAPTER FIFTEEN

Shaking Up the Corpse

The gross mismanagement of the Toronto Maple Leafs began long before my time as a scribbler, when Harold Ballard was the owner. He and Stafford Smythe, son of the Leafs original architect, Conn Smythe, presided over the collapse of the team, from Stanley Cup champion (four times in the 1960s) to national laughingstock. On the way to that status, Ballard went to jail for theft. Smythe would have joined him in the crowbar hotel, but died before he could face the legal music.

The great hockey writer Frank Orr, who had a long and distinguished career with the *Star*, always told a story he got from a Maple Leaf Gardens confidant. The night before Smythe's funeral, as he was laid out in a coffin at centre ice at the Gardens, a boozy Ballard wandered down from his apartment within the Gardens itself and began screaming and shaking the corpse of his partner in crime. According to Orr's source, who helped break it up and get Ballard back upstairs, Harold was yelling at the body for letting him, Harold, face the fraud charges and take the rap all by himself. Frank Orr was not the kind of guy to make anything up and I always believed it; years later, I had the story confirmed by a Ballard acquaintance, who reaffirmed what we all knew: that Harold was capable of anything distasteful.

It was when Ballard died, though, in 1990, that the fun level around the Gardens was ramped up. A man named Steve Stavro, who was a worshipper of Alexander the Great, ran a grocery chain called Knob Hill Farms and was active for years in local soccer and horse racing, was Ballard's buddy and was named executor of his estate.

Now, Stavro was as crooked as cat shit. He attempted to have the hockey team and arena officially evaluated to a minimum worth, then tried to buy everything for himself at this greatly reduced rate. The money, Ballard had stipulated, would go to several charities, so by acting as both buyer and seller and depressing the price, Stavro was in effect trying to screw the charities out of what rightfully should have been a lot more money.

The fly shit in the pepper was a relative handful of outstanding shares in the company, some of them owned by a man named Harry Ornest, who lived in Los Angeles and owned other sports teams, including the NHL's St. Louis Blues and, for a while, the Toronto Argonauts of the CFL. Ornest, who despised Stavro, knew his shares were being undervalued so Stavro could grab everything for himself at a bargain rate. Ornest raised holy hell, naturally. We were in regular conversation and Harry was a willing source of terrific information.

It took years to play out, but the public trustee finally figured Stavro — whom I had taken to calling the Honest Grocer in my columns — had stiffed the charities by more than $50 million and he was forced to pay up to stay out of jail.

This, of course, was the kind of owner the hockey team had — a man who would openly screw charities. Because of the money he needed to come up with — and his grocery stores went broke and there was some question as to what happened to the pension funds for employees there — the Honest Grocer always seemed to have a case of the shorts. When the Leafs had a chance to sign Wayne Gretzky at the end of his career, with an eye toward getting him into the top executive suite after his playing days ceased, it was the Grocer who nixed the deal as too expensive.

Ultimately this left him vulnerable to those with more money. The Ontario Teachers' Pension Plan arrived, as did Larry Tanenbaum, who had an eye for basketball, and eventually the Grocer, who was dead set against anything to do with basketball, was squeezed out. Before he departed, he was part of one of the most shameful incidents in Canadian history, a dirty pedophilia scandal that had begun in the Ballard years.

As the story broke in its sickening detail, Stavro went underground. There were dozens if not hundreds of victims of one or more sexual predators operating behind the drawing power of the Maple Leaf logo, but all the Leafs did for the victims who emerged was question their integrity and try to cast doubt on them. Stavro let chief underling Brian Bellmore do the dirty work in public, as my *Star* column laid out in February 1997:

> *Steve Stavro did not have the sand to show up yesterday to try to put out the sexual abuse fire at Maple Leaf Gardens.*
>
> *He left the job to Brian Bellmore, one of his trained cobras, who displayed nothing but arrogance and contempt for the alleged victims of abuse — dozens and perhaps, ultimately, hundreds of victims*

— he further suggested may not even exist. He said he'll let the courts decide whether anyone was abused at Maple Leaf Gardens and until then, the organization's official position is that nothin' happened to nobody and if it did, it's news to us.

Bellmore said he still doubts whether Martin Kruze, to whom the Leafs paid $60,000 in hush money after Kruze approached the Leafs with charges of sexual abuse suffered years before, really had a legit case. "Investigations were conducted on our behalf and revealed no evidence of any such conduct," Bellmore said.

Yeah, that's their story and they're sticking to it. They only paid off Kruze because it was cheaper than fighting charges and they still maintain it was up to Kruze to call the cops, not them.

The Leafs, in other words, just don't get it. They have no clue. Victims are coming forward tearfully and the Leafs still are pretending that somebody tried to shake them down for a batch of cash.

The sad postscript to all this is that they put private detectives on Kruze, hounding him, and the young man, who hated the publicity from the case, eventually jumped off a bridge.

The Leafs looked consistently pathetic during the pedophilia scandal. The hockey team wasn't much good, either. Ultimately, to escape the shadow of the former and, in theory, do something about the latter, they hired Ken Dryden, the Hall of Fame former goaltender, the eloquent and cerebral (but supremely long-winded) national conscience of hockey, to be president of the organization. As it said in the *Star* when the announcement was made in July 1997:

A small double funeral was held at Maple Leaf Gardens Friday morning. Services were said for the souls of the short, direct answer and its life partner, the declarative sentence. We may never see their like again; Ken Dryden is in a position of authority now.

He was hired, as everyone knows, to be the Maple Leafs' titular hockey honcho, the ultimate voice to speak on hockey matters. He therefore fills at least one job requirement because his is a voice made for hearing.

Talk? The man could talk a glacier through a peaceful valley.

All those pucks he stopped all those years? Few seemed to have hit him in the throat.

This is not necessarily a bad thing, by the way. Here comes an obviously erudite, thoughtful buffer to insert himself between non-rights-holding media nasties and the high sheriffs of the woebegone franchise, some of whom have mastered the grunt.

Dryden is one of those guys, you ask him the time and he tells you Einstein's theory of relativity. The fact he understands it is only part of it; he deals in $8 words and seldom makes much change.

The other major issue running on parallel tracks at this point was the impending birth of the Toronto Raptors of the National Basketball Association, a team that had been awarded to a group headed by John Bitove Jr., who later in life gained some fame as the head of the Toronto 2008 Olympic bid. Among other things, Bitove also was Steve Stavro's second cousin. The Bitoves and the Stavros had mutual relatives buried under the same headstone in Toronto's Mount Pleasant Cemetery, but the two cousins hated each other.

Bitove's crew got the jump on a new arena, which enraged the Maple Leaf people, who now included Larry Tanenbaum as a director. Tanenbaum had been on the group that lost out to Bitove when the NBA franchise was awarded to Toronto in 1993. It made sense to everyone that the basketball and hockey people get together on one nice new arena, with Maple Leaf Gardens aging and incapable of providing the expensive private boxes that are a lifeblood of modern professional revenue streams.

Stavro, still the principal owner of the Leafs, would have none of it and the Leafs kept floating hare-brained arena schemes, hoping to head off the basketball arena with a project of their own. Taxpayers would be allowed to contribute substantially, naturally, to projects located downtown, on the waterfront, on top of the railroad station or wherever the next dreamy drawing indicated. I was among those not buying the bullshit and occasionally even our elected officials identified the prevailing aroma, such as the time the Leafs tried to halt Bitove's rejuvenation of an old postal building that would become the Air Canada Centre in order to build their own playpen:

> *Congratulations to Toronto's city council for rejecting the snake-oil salesmen from Maple Leaf Gardens. They seemed to recognize a taxpayer fleecing before it actually happened and took steps to prevent it. Perhaps they actually remember what happened with the SkyDome.*
>
> *This burg will somehow need to live without the "most spectacular arena in North America, if not the world." Somehow it will, too.*
>
> *That description is what Larry Tanenbaum, in the team's snivelling news release distributed after the pols turned down the Leafs' so-called best offer for*

> *the site, called the whimsical flight of fancy that some people, including some who should know better, actually pretended was viable.*
>
> *They tried to throw a monkey wrench into the Air Canada Centre, nom de net of the Raptors arena. They wanted to slow that project down before it got too far along.*

Unsuccessful that time, they came back six months later with a plan for an arena at the Canadian National Exhibition grounds, one that set aside space for the politicians. This time they struck gold, at least at the committee level.

> *It was so cold out yesterday, I saw some city politicians with their hands in their own pockets.*
>
> *None of them, though, seems to be associated with the Metro financial priorities committee, the latest bunch trying to give away the municipal farm to the Honest Grocer and his happy hockey team.*
>
> *That committee . . . quickly approved the latest flavour-of-the-month arena deal in principle while asking that the Leafs throw in a private box "for the express use of city officials, politicians and their guests."*
>
> *Right out there in the open, isn't it? Apparently, some people are willing to do business for a couple of pairs of reds.*

Eventually, Tanenbaum and the Teachers' Pension Plan, who had big money into the team, recognized that Stavro's way of doing business wasn't going to fly. His hatred for his cousin led to constant commitments to building a hockey-only arena, at the same time a basketball structure was under construction. It made no sense whatsoever and helped lead to his eventual ouster from the Leafs. As I phrased it in the *Star*:

> *[Stavro's] entire business philosophy seems based on what happened in Macedonia between some cousins a generation or two back. Plus, he also makes decisions based on who co-operated with the public trustee when that one questioned his ultimately discredited practice of being both buyer and, as executor of Harold Ballard's estate, seller of Gardens stock.*
>
> *In other words, he won't have anything to do with anyone who can even spell the word NBA.*
>
> *Fair enough. If it were only him, go ahead and make a hash of everything. But it's not only him. Tanenbaum didn't get where he is by riding around with a wild man at the wheel who appears to be out to settle personal scores.*
>
> *And what about the teachers? Is there no one watching their money who wonders whether it's best used for doing battle with the Raptors while the (hockey) team continues to flounder around in the tank?*

A couple more notes about Stavro, who seemed to like being called the Honest Grocer, both in person and in print, but still wished to see his name mentioned, too. One time he sent me a $1,000 cheque when I was running the Jim Proudfoot Corner, an annual Christmas charity operated for more than a century by the *Star*. I acknowledged all money received by name and there it was: a G note from the Steve and Sally Stavro Foundation. The day it appeared in the paper, he called to needle me that he had sneaked his name into my column.

As much of a nudging as I gave him, from time to time, the only time he ever got truly angry at me — started calling me words with Ks in them — was when I was teasing him about his hero, Alexander the Great. The Grocer had a good-looking 3-year-old thoroughbred named Leonnatus Anteas that was one of the favourites for the Queen's Plate. I did some research and discovered the horse was named for one of Alexander the Great's personal guards — and a guy history suggests might have been one of Alex's homosexual lovers. Now, I was just discovering that ATG was gay, or at least bisexual, although who cares? Well, Stavro cared. When I asked him whether it was true his hero was a little light in the sandals, as historians seem to agree, Stavro went nuts. He started yelling that I couldn't say such a thing — didn't dare repeat such a filthy lie — and while he didn't give a shit what I called him I'd better not ever say this to him again or there would be serious trouble. When I would protest that no one really cared and it didn't make old Alex a bad person and so on, he just got more and more revved up. It was the angriest I ever encountered him. Go figure.

The last time I spoke to Stavro, shortly before he died in 2006, he called to tell me I had written a column he liked, one that took a small poke at his successors. In his time there, the Leafs had operated their top farm team in St. John's, Newfoundland, in a spiffy new arena built specifically for the team. Later on, after Stavro was out of the picture, the Leafs yanked the team out of Newfoundland and installed it in a newly refurbished arena — renovations paid for by taxpayers, of course — at the CNE. This was a disgrace, to leave the St. John's people high and dry after they had spent so much money to build a new arena, and I carved the idea.

Lo and behold, the Grocer agreed. He called me and was livid about the situation. He said, "It's terrible the way they're fucking those people in Newfoundland. We had a good deal. Great people, love their hockey. It's just terrible." I said to him, "Grocer, with your track record, it must really be something if you think somebody is fucking somebody else." He snarled something nasty and hung up. It was an appropriate final conversation.

When Maple Leaf Sports and Entertainment was assembled, in all its financial glory, Richard Peddie was installed as president, moving up from his position overseeing the new arena. Peddie's hiring represented one of my great mistakes in the business. He had previously been in charge of the SkyDome and one night when the Raptors were playing at the dome while the MLSE search committee was doing its hunting, I asked Richard who they might come up with. He told me it was going to be him. I laughed. I honestly thought he was kidding. I had never pegged Richard as that kind of guy. Three days later, when he was announced, I was stunned. At the press conference, he looked at me and gave it the palms-up shrug, like asking me what happened. My bad, that's all.

Over the years, neither the Maple Leafs nor the Raptors were much good competitively on Peddie's watch, as both featured a constant parade of coaches and general managers and endless rebuilding plans. The soccer team, Toronto FC, when it was hatched in 2006, was a competitive embarrassment for several years, exasperating loyal fans' patience. Peddie absorbed a lot of abuse for meddling. His claims to be hands off tended to fall on deaf ears. What is indisputable is that MLSE has made a lot of terrible choices to run its sports franchises.

On the other hand, Peddie presided over gobs of profits and several facilities pried out of taxpayers. Once, I wrote — and he mentioned the next day I had it correct — that the MLSE types at least deserved credit for thinking big. While other sports organizations were trying to sell T-shirts and coffee mugs and key chains, MLSE was selling multi-million-dollar condominium developments and a restaurant chain based on the public's never-ending loyalty to the logo. How much money MLSE left on the table because of terrible teams will remain forever unknowable.

CHAPTER SIXTEEN

Butterbeans?

I don't want this to sound like one of those interminable and unrecognizable Oscar speeches, when someone you never heard of goes on thanking several more people you never heard of. But a guy who travelled extensively — meaning 120 nights a year in baseball and Olympics years, average of 90 nights a year otherwise — came to rely on a few of the fellow travellers for pleasant company and to maintain sanity, if nothing else. Not only press types, either.

All those years doing baseball with the Blue Jays, it was the non-uniformed personnel we were closest to, rather than players. Howard Starkman, king of baseball's public relations types and a long-time Blue Jay stalwart, having come over from the Maple Leafs after a sentence working for Harold Ballard, was always a sensible guy, easy to get along with and a great pro. Clubhouse man Kevin Malloy, then as now, had the best sense of humour on the team and many is the line he muttered that starving writers would borrow for their next column. Equipment manager Jeff Ross, a terrific golfer himself, organized the golf games on the road and always was happy to add a writer's clubs to the team equipment truck. Matter of fact, when Jimy Williams was manager, players were not supposed to golf on the road, but he had no problem with writers' clubs making the trip. That led, a few times, to my handing out spare bag tags, with my name on them, to a prominent pitcher and catcher who loved to hit the small ball. They would slap my tag on their golf bag, play their round, then deposit the clubs with the hotel concierge. I would pick them up and return "my" clubs to the truck when it was time to change cities. No harm, no foul.

One of the other regulars was trainer Tommy Craig, a screamingly funny Southerner with a thick accent and a down-home way of talking that, we used to say, required subtitles, if not outright translation. Tommy had no time for his hypochondriacs, the players who would constantly be in the trainer's room looking for relief from tiny or imagined aches and pains. One night, someone got nicked by a pitch or something and came out of the game. Afterward, we would ask the manager about the absence, because this was the pecking order on injuries: you asked the manager and if they didn't want you to know, he would tell you basically that. Otherwise, if it was insignificant or required a more detailed explanation, he would steer us to Tommy. So we would troop over to the trainer and say, "What about so-and-so?"

This night, Tommy got a disgusted look on his face, and said, "He's got a contusion." By that he meant bruise. "It's 'bout the size of a butterbean."

We reporters looked at each other and the great Bob Elliott said, "Tommy, ferchrissakes, what the hell is a butterbean?"

Tommy held up his thumb and forefinger a half inch apart and said, "Y'll got no butterbeans up here?"

One time, George Bell imagined himself to have a shoulder issue that could be treated by taping tiny magnets to himself, front and back. He got them from a friend and said they made him feel better.

The trainer just rolled his eyes at what he called "Chinese magnetic hocus-pocus" but added, "If they make him feel better, that's fine with me. I could tape an Aspirin to his shoulder and it would do as much good."

One constant visitor to his training room was always met with skepticism. Officially, Tommy would bite his tongue, but in unguarded moments he would let slip that the individual "wants a friggin' purple heart every time he plays."

Tommy liked to play golf and could hit the ball nine miles, but was wild off the tee. Incredibly wild. He could hit a ball not one fairway over, but two. He would lose golf balls at a record rate and once, partnered with Cito Gaston, whom he always called "Dad," he lost all his golf balls early in the round. He began borrowing balls from Gaston and losing them, too. Finally, Gaston was out of ammunition as well, at which point Tommy gave him hell for not bringing enough golf balls. Cito still mentions that.

Usually, there were plenty of golf balls, because Jeff Ross would get a supply from equipment manufacturers he dealt with. One year, he had a case of balls made by AMF-Voit. They were all stamped the same, with a logo and AMF. Tommy Craig, once again out of golf balls, asked if anyone had a spare. Someone tossed him one of the AMF pellets. Craig eyed it as he put it on the tee.

"AMF, huh?" he said, beginning his backswing. "Well, then: adios, motherfucker."

One of the golfers at every stop was the late, great Tom Cheek, original Blue Jays broadcaster and long-time partner of Jerry Howarth, who came aboard a few years into the team's journey. Howarth was the livelier, more exuberant of the pair, who did not always get along so famously in their off-air moments. Two vastly different people, to be sure, who spent their days differently. Jerry studied and read and visited with friends. Tom played golf.

Cheek was, I always said, a museum-quality guy, a military brat with a highly cultivated sense of humour and an old-fashioned, down-to-earth way about him that people enjoyed. He was one of those guys who would burst into song for no apparent reason, favouring a tune on a busload of coaches and writers (because the players, without families, had their own bus). Once, leaving the old Comiskey Park in Chicago, the bus driver had turned out the vehicle's interior lights because, lately, someone from the upper stories of a nearby apartment project had taken to lobbing a bullet or two in the general direction of a lighted vehicle. No one ever got hit, but no one was taking chances, either. Everyone kind of huddled quietly in the dark, waiting to get past the caution area, but Cheek decided it was time for a song and bellowed out a couple of bars of "Shrimp Boat's A Comin'." Broke up the tension perfectly.

He had his sayings. A chilly morning would be described as "colder than old Billy Hell." When someone would lament the ravages of aging, among them the occasional bout of constipation, Cheek would laugh and say not him. "I'm as regular as a Navy clock," he would insist.

He was a poor sleeper who travelled with black tape, in order to seal off curtains that let cracks of light into his hotel room. He also would tape over the glowing numbers on a clock radio, seeking total darkness. He knew the floor plan of every hotel in the league and never once (when I was watching) picked up his room key without glancing at it, saying, "Nope," and heading to the front desk to change it. Once, in Milwaukee, he switched sides of the hotel because one side of the structure, he insisted, would transmit vibrations from the newspaper office a block up the street when they started the printing presses after midnight.

Cheek loved to gamble on golf, although if 10 dollars changed hands it was a monumental upset. Once, when an off-day opened up on the schedule in Chicago, a handful of the Jays' travelling party threw out the idea for a tournament, which would be called the Tom Cheek Open. They would organize the participants, book the course and the transportation. Cheek's job was to collect the handicaps of the players involved, determine teams and opponents, match up the games, assign the strokes and set the stakes. He took this job very seriously. Several foursomes, their clubs stowed underneath, boarded the bus in the morning and it set off for the course. Cheek, double-checking his handicaps and assigning the pairings, scarcely noticed as the bus headed not out to green suburbs but deeper and deeper into the city. Once, he lifted his head, saw a stretch of boarded-up buildings and used car lots and muttered, "Where the hell are we?" but someone drew him back to his assignment and he began renegotiating strokes with the sandbaggers.

Finally, the bus pulled up and disgorged its passengers in a questionable part of town in front of an old putt-putt miniature golf course, one that featured a nice new banner, "Welcome to the Tom Cheek Open." Cheek, naturally, laughed harder than anyone.

It became something of a game, among his friends, to get Cheek whipped up about something the rest of us would barely notice. For instance, one morning I flew to Minneapolis for a Blue Jay series. The team had flown in the night before from Texas or someplace. As I checked in to the hotel around lunchtime, I saw a friend and asked if anything was happening. He said not really, but Cheek had been quizzing the flight attendant last night about how much rice they were using. Said you used to see more potatoes and vegetables, but now all you see is rice everywhere on the dinner plate. Tom's assumption: it's another sign the world is running out of food.

I kind of laughed it off and went upstairs. Couple of hours later, I went down to get on the bus to the ballpark. On it was Cheek, who asked where I had come from. "Just flew in from Toronto," I answered. "I'm damned hungry, too. Airplane food was lousy. Too much rice, if you ask me. I don't know what's going on."

Then I looked out the window, biting my tongue. A minute later, I felt a tap on my knee. It was Cheek, leaning in and saying, conspiratorially, "I've been worried about the same thing about this rice business." From the look on my face and the eventual tears of laughter, he knew he'd been had. Didn't bother him, though. He laughed it off and went looking for the next windmill to tilt.

In Florida one time, at spring training, we had a nice game of golf at his club there, East Lake Woodlands. It was a delightful day, and we pulled up behind four very attractive, early middle-aged ladies, out having a game of their own. We watched as all four, stylishly dressed, tanned and fit, hit perfect little tee shots across a pond and onto the green at a par-three hole. Four chances for birdie. They brushed past us, all looking good, on their way to their carts, and wished us a good day and smiled and drove away. The four of us, naturally smitten, watched them go, looked at each other and then looked back at them and their four coming birdie putts. We all sighed. Cheek broke the silence and got right to his personal nub of the matter, as only he could: "I bet they have dirty houses," he said.

Cheek, as every fan knows, never missed a game for years and years, running his streak to 4,306 in a row, through bad times and good. He finally missed a game after his father, a war hero, passed away, and not long after that he was diagnosed with the brain cancer that took him away about a year later. I visited him and his great lady, Shirley, a couple of times at their Florida home and he came up to Toronto in his final summer to see friends and admirers, of which he had many. The morning he passed, Shirley called me and the news, while not unexpected, still was numbing. I wrote a front-page obituary and could only think of the good times he had provided, in the broadcast booth and on the buses and golf courses and around countless pre-game dinner tables.

He told a story I led with, of how he used to get letters from fans and dutifully responded. One troubled soul, in particular, began to accelerate the correspondence and each letter got progressively stranger. Uh-oh, Cheek used to say, I've got a live one here. The weirdness intensified until one day he opened the letter, with the now recognizable handwriting, and all it said was, "You know what they've done to Petula Clark." Cheek thought hard about the 1960s pop icon, but he couldn't remember any significant worldwide plots she was involved in. He used to laugh and say, "At least now I've got the title for my book." Sadly for all of us, he never did get to write it.

A year before Tom passed, the shock of shocks was delivered when John Cerutti, a one-time Blue Jay pitcher, broadcaster and golf companion, died suddenly in his SkyDome hotel room of some kind of mysterious heart ailment. He was only 44 and much fitter than most men that age and had stopped in to the press box the day before to chat about a golf game we had planned for a few days later. We often would run out to a course, after summer Saturday afternoon games, and play as many holes as we could before it got dark, but this day he had his family up from Albany, N.Y.

The next morning, a season-ending Sunday, when he didn't show up to call the game, those who knew him were worried immediately. No possible way John was the kind to grab a girl and a bottle and lose track of everything else. It was a miserable moment, when the word spread. In my early days around the ball team, Cerutti had been a workman-like, friendly and quotable pitcher, a good guy to put a day's results, win or lose, into perspective. He got the most out of his ability in a seven-year big-league career before eventually turning to the broadcast booth. He was learning that game pretty well when he left us. Great golfer, too; he once got to the second stage of U.S. Open qualifying, a significant achievement for an amateur.

Not to get too down here, but there's one other lefty who died too young who was a particular favourite here, namely Mike Flanagan. He was an honoured veteran when he came over to the Jays from Baltimore in 1987, a former Cy Young Memorial Award winner who was a great student, and explainer, of the game. Jimmy Key was my favourite Blue Jays pitcher, both to watch and cover, but Flanagan was a walking, talking pitching seminar. He loved to talk pitching and would sit on a barstool, smoke his cigarettes and discuss the game he had just watched. It was, vaguely, the same game I had just watched from the press box and then written about, but Flanagan would explain it from his perspective, how one pitch in this at-bat led to a certain result in the next at-bat and so on and so forth. It was an invaluable lesson for someone who was interested enough in the game to want to learn (like myself). Flanny, as everyone called him, spent a couple more years in Toronto and I always said he and Paul Molitor, who was a fantastic interpreter of the game, not only knew baseball better than anyone else I ever dealt with, but they could explain it better.

It was with great sadness I learned Flanagan killed himself in 2011, after taking to heart and becoming despondent over vicious internet comments from Orioles fans who felt entitled to rip apart his job as general manager of the team. He was another guy who deserved much better than he got.

CHAPTER SEVENTEEN

I'm Positive I'll Shut Up Now

A favourite subject of sports fans in every bar, and on every call-in show, is answering the unanswerable question: Which sports record is the most unbreakable?

There are dozens of candidates and depending on the persuasions of the opinion involved, the responses could begin with a half-dozen Gretzky standards, or Cal Ripken's 2,632-game run or Joe DiMaggio's 56 game hit-streak or Cy Young's 511 wins or Glenn Hall's 502 consecutive games in an NHL goal. We could go on for pages, but while we're up, how about Byron Nelson's 18 PGA Tour tournament victories in 1945, including 11 in a row? Do we think anyone will ever get close again to either of those accomplishments? Hell, the top guys barely play 18 times a year these days; they're too busy taking the private jet over to the Middle East for a million-dollar Nassau with the oil guys.

Byron's feat arises — as well it should — because yours truly once spent a nice moment with the gentleman, back when they were opening his exhibit at the World Golf Hall of Fame outside St. Augustine, Florida. Before the PGA Tour changed its schedule around, the Players Championship, a few miles from St. Augustine, was held the week after Arnold Palmer's Bay Hill event, which always drew a first-rate field and was a great place to pick up information for Masters previews a few weeks hence. On the Monday of Players week, the World Golf Hall of Fame tended to launch its new exhibits and in order to drum up some publicity, officials there would invite the golfing press, who would then drive two and a half hours from Bay Hill to TPC Sawgrass. We would play golf (naturally) and have a nice lunch and sit around and chat somewhat informally with the guest of honour, who would then lead us through the memorabilia included in his exhibit. Very civilized. A wonderful day not to be missed — and in other years the guests of honour had been Gary Player, Jack Nicklaus, Arnold and so on. No lightweights.

Byron Nelson, on this day, was 92 or 93 and while that is an age at which no one would buy many green bananas, he still had a couple of years to go. He was hale and sharp. Very sharp.

After lunch I plunked down beside him and introduced myself and mentioned where I was from and that I was a big fan of Thornhill Golf Club in Toronto, a beautiful layout that was one of the loveliest green jewels laid out by Stanley Thompson, the greatest of all Canadian course designers. Back in 1945, a tournament in Montreal had been Nelson's 10th in a row and the Canadian Open, that year played at Thornhill, had been the 11th consecutive win in his phenomenal streak. I gently asked Byron if he had any memories of his experience at Thornhill.

"Sure, I loved that course," he said, flipping the mental Rolodex on a layout he had played nearly 60 years before. "I liked that tee shot off the top of the hill, then you crossed the creek and went up a little hill. Then there was that sharp dogleg . . ."

He went on like this, describing several holes. He had them bang on, too, and think about that. He had played — what? — thousands of golf courses in his life, but here he was, 60 years later, replaying a course in his mind. I thought to myself, *Yikes. I can't remember what I had for dinner last night and here's this guy in his 90s rattling off golf holes from 60 years ago.*

I expressed my amazement and noted that Thornhill was a Stanley Thompson design and did he have any thoughts on any other Thompson courses?

"Well, son, I knew Stanley Thompson. We often talked about golf courses," he said, then started talking about Stanley Thompson, who had been dead about 50 years at that point. I thought to myself, *Better shut up now. You're overmatched.* Someone else moved in to ask Byron about something or other. I thanked him for his time and left pretty much in shock. What an experience. Wonderful gentleman. Wonderful mind.

This all leads me to another Stanley Thompson moment, from Nick Faldo, a not-so-wonderful guy when it came to Stanley.

Faldo, like many golfers when their prime is past, had ideas about becoming at least a part-time course designer. It needs to happen quickly to capitalize on their name recognition because the next guy will be along soon.

Some of them are good at it and some of them have growing pains. As an aside, I recall Mark O'Meara laying out a course named Grandview in Muskoka, about 100 miles north of Toronto. It's an area of very rugged and beautiful terrain with some terrific golf courses. But sometimes there are some clunkers, too, and Grandview was not everyone's idea of a good time. I went up for a press day or the official opening or something, where O'Meara hit the ceremonial first shot and then played a few holes. I was standing close behind him at one tee and heard O'Meara, after looking out from the tee box, lean over to an assistant and say, "Tell me again what I was thinking here?"

Anyway, I was writing a column for the *Toronto Star* and got a call telling me Faldo was coming in next week to do some preliminary layout work on his new course. Would I like to go up, ride around with him for the day and pick his brain?

This sounded like a great idea, totally different from the usual access we would get to golfers. I wrapped up a couple of sandwiches and put on some thick boots and drove to the middle of nowhere, where I encountered Faldo, a set of plans and a few guys with axes and some spray paint. The course was in its baby steps, and it was autumn and the bugs weren't too bad. But what seemed like a good day had one snag: Faldo knew nothing of my arrival and wasn't too happy to see me. He hadn't received any messages. He grudgingly said I could ride around in the truck with him and his crew as long as I kept quiet. It was a marginally better offer than turning around and driving home.

I didn't get much to use for a column, but when we stopped for lunch to eat our chicken salad sandwiches, Faldo talked a little bit about golf courses and design and how he had never seen so much natural stone and loved the way he could shape holes around rock faces and such. I asked him if he was familiar with Stanley Thompson, the best Canadian designer, who worked with every surface and type of land in the country. Faldo had never heard of him and didn't seem to care about my descriptions.

So, fast-forward to the next summer's Open Championship. Knowing I would see Faldo there, I had called the Stanley Thompson Society, a group of Thompson aficionados. There had been a good little biography written about Thompson and they had a copy they could sell me. So I bought it and took it to the Open. I went into the players' locker room and found Faldo on the Tuesday of Open week, 48 hours before tournament play began. He didn't remember me, but I spoke about his course and Stanley Thompson and so on and jogged his memory. Then I gave him the book and said, "You can read it in one plane ride, maybe pick up some of his ideas and his thoughts on Canadian topography and weather and so on. It can't hurt." He took the book, offered a lukewarm thanks and put it in his locker.

Three days later, I needed to speak to Mike Weir about something, so I went back into the locker room. The cut had come and gone and Faldo had missed it. I got what I needed from Weir and headed out, walking past Faldo's now-empty locker. Close to it was a trash can and there, on top of whatever refuse had been discarded, sat the Stanley Thompson book. I'm guessing Faldo never even opened it before he tossed it, but perhaps he should have. His course was pretty much a flop.

That tiny piece of trauma aside, the giants of golf with whom I dealt were invariably gentlemanly and generous with their time and memories. Some of the current guys are like mini-corporations, trained to avoid the press or else be monosyllabic whenever possible. But the legends, for the most part, would do everything but take your notes for you. Like Byron Nelson, they all had abilities to amaze.

For instance, Gary Player, who undoubtedly flew more miles in his lifetime than anyone who is neither a pilot nor an astronaut, was always friendly and chatty and might have been the fittest little bugger anyone ever saw. On the year his World Golf Hall of Fame exhibit opened, he rode one of his horses around the grounds, greeting the press. He also showed up just as my group was teeing off on a par-three hole, a nice little

155-yarder with the pin at the back of a kidney-shaped green, tucked behind a bunker. Well, for some reason, I hit about the best 7-iron of my life, drawing it right over the flag and stopping it dead, perhaps 10 feet from the pin. Player gushed appreciatively and said, "Well, I see what you can do with a 7-iron. But can you do this with it?"

At that point — and feel free to try this at home — he extended his right arm, palm down. He inserted the club between his index and second fingers, at the end of the grip so the entire club was sticking straight up. Then he began rolling his wrist from side to side so that the club went from horizon to horizon, 180 degrees back and forth. He was, if I remember correctly, 73 years old at the time and was rolling this club back and forth with his two fingers like it was a pencil. We all tried and none of us could do it once. Impressive? No kidding.

A year or two later, a couple of days before another Open Championship, a course in the west of Scotland named Dundonald was being officially opened. It was a rainy, miserable day, but having been invited, and living up to the golfing press's reputation of going any distance in any condition to play somewhere for free, a few of us headed over to check out the place. (One reason the Open Championship is so popular is that because of the time difference, you could play golf every day, still get to the course at noon and have many hours to catch up on whatever had transpired, without ever threatening your deadline. And, yes, I suspect Twitter and 24/7 internet demands have ruined that part of it for those still working. My sympathies.)

So there we are at Dundonald, soaking wet and bedraggled after golf. I go into the men's room for a wash up and a squirt and am standing at the urinal. Up to the next urinal pulls Gary Player. On the other side of him is Prince Andrew, the Queen's son. I'm not much on the royals, but I recognize this as the guy who married Fergie, the big redhead, at least briefly. He's a golf nut and he and Player had been out there knocking it around at the opening, same as the rest of us.

With all of us still standing at the urinals, Player looks at me and says something like, "Hello, David. Nice to see you again. Not a great day, but hope you enjoyed the course. May I present His Royal Highness Prince Andrew?"

Well, that was slightly awkward. I finished off and stepped back and mumbled something about how I was honoured but this was not necessarily the proper place to shake hands. They both laughed, at least.

No kidding, but two days later, I was sitting at the back of the press room on the telephone, speaking to my wife, who is a lot more tuned in to the world of royalty than I am. Who wanders by, with a couple of security types, but Prince Andrew. He seemed to show some vague sense of recognition and nodded to me as I cheerily waved and said, "Hey, Prince." My wife asked me who I was talking to and I said, "Oh, that's just my buddy, Prince Andrew. You know. The Queen's son." To this day I don't think she believed me.

To get back to the dimpled legends, there never was a better guy in the press room than Jack Nicklaus, who would sit and talk and tell stories and entertain like no one else. He had a sense of humour and either cared, or pretended to care, about someone else's opinions. He knew I was from Toronto and he had a great friend in Dick Grimm, the long-time director of the Canadian Open and a grand man who sadly passed on not long ago. Nicklaus would invariably ask me if I'd seen Dick lately (we went out for lunch now and then to catch up on the talk of the day) and how he looked and so on. Jack also went into my bag of clubs one day and hefted my putter and left me with a story.

Once again back at the World Golf Hall of Fame and this year it was Nicklaus being honoured with an exhibit. Same deal. Again, a bunch of us played golf before we had lunch with the honoree and shot the breeze and so on. I was a very good putter in those days and I used (and still do) a Jack Nicklaus Response model putter, a big old version of the brick on a stick with which he had won the Masters in 1986. I played that day with Alex Miceli and won the money, if memory serves, by holing everything in sight. As we rolled in from the 18th green, there was Nicklaus, welcoming everyone and joking and such. Alex jokingly said to him, jabbing his thumb at me, "Jack, this guy putts better with that old Response than you did."

Nicklaus laughed and walked over to our cart, then picked out my putter. "Where did you get this? How long have you owned it? Did you buy it at a store?" He sounded really interested.

I told him I had bought it, still in the plastic, at a golf shop in Dunedin, Florida, at spring training 1987. I told him it had been the best club in my bag since I figured out how to use it and it had won me a little money over the years.

He smiled approvingly and said he was glad of all that, but it wasn't the club he was looking for. He even pointed out the club's serial number to me and said he knew when it was made, etc.

It turns out, Nicklaus had lost the putter with which he won the '86 Masters and had been looking for it for 15 years. Whenever he saw an original Response, like mine, he checked the serial number. I asked him if he had any other missing clubs of historic value and he told a story. He said a middle-aged guy had approached him not long before, asking if an old driver was, indeed, Jack's. It was the driver with which he had won the 1980 U.S. Open and the man offering it turned out to be a college roommate of one of Jack's sons. It was easy to figure out what happened and the club had been in the man's garage for years, it turns out, before finding its way back to its rightful owner.

I can't say enough about Nicklaus, how outstanding he was to deal with over the years, how generous with his time and how interested he was in every aspect not only of golf, but also of the people associated with golf. I have plenty of sports-associated memorabilia, picked up over the years, but I can honestly state I have asked sports figures to sign something for me only three times. The first was running in to Sadaharu Oh, the great Japanese home-run hitter, at a spring training ballpark and asking him to sign a page in my notebook — in Japanese. He did, too, writing the Japanese characters, then helpfully adding it in English underneath. The second time was when I met Muhammad Ali in the middle of a Las Vegas casino. I asked him to sign something; instead he handed me a pamphlet, entitled Concept of God in Islam, which he was distributing. He had autographed every pamphlet.

The third was Jack Nicklaus, although it wasn't for me. As a long-time sports columnist I often was asked to donate items to charity auctions and always tried to help out. I would ask athletes for old equipment to turn over to a good cause and always tried to follow up, to let them know how much their old batting glove or pitching wedge or whatever had sold for. A few years ago, the Bank of Scotland hired Nicklaus as a spokesman and somehow arranged to put his picture on five-pound notes. They were released during Open Championship week and a friend in Scotland got me a handful of fresh new notes. I put them in an envelope and later on, when Nicklaus was captain of the Presidents Cup team, I asked him to sign a few for charity purposes. He was more than gracious and signed every one I had. I handed them out to a few auctions and they were always popular items that drew sizeable bids.

Now, those who know me have heard my favourite Jack Nicklaus story and if you're easily shocked, go on to the next chapter now. But it stemmed from Nicklaus's last U.S. Open appearance, which happened to be at Pebble Beach in 2000, the year Tiger Woods ran away with everything. Jack missed the cut, but came into the press room and talked and talked and told stories. Larry Guest, formerly a columnist in Orlando, knew Nicklaus well and

Teeing off on the 18th hole at Pebble Beach, circa 1988.
Hooked it into the Pacific Ocean, of course.

primed the pump for some of his best old stories, and one of them concerned Jack's first time at Augusta National, when he was 19 years old and an outstanding amateur. In those days, golfers were required to use an Augusta caddie and Nicklaus, feeling like most 19-year-olds confident in their own abilities, told his caddie he liked to read his own putts, thanks. But it didn't take him long to realize he had bitten off too much; Augusta's greens, then as now, were treacherous, demanding and required knowledge and experience.

A few holes in, conscious of what he had said earlier but recognizing the situation, Nicklaus turned to his caddie and suggested he could use a little help. "I see this two balls outside left," he said of the particular putt that awaited him. The caddie bent down, took a look and shook his head. "Two balls outside right." Nicklaus looked again and asked, "Outside right? Are you positive?"

The caddie said simply, "Mr. Jack. I've been positive once in my life. First time I ever jacked off, I was positive I was going to do that again."

Nicklaus said when he stopped laughing, it was indeed two balls outside to the right. He apparently learned about the greens, too. There's no other way to win six green jackets.

CHAPTER EIGHTEEN

Disorder on the Court

The National Basketball Association, which arrived in Toronto in 1995, did something that was extremely intelligent. It directed that the sports media, or at least most of us, be seated courtside.

Toronto, as both its supporters and detractors would acknowledge, was and is a trendy and moneyed place. That applies to sports and popular culture, to say nothing of real estate. The most expensive seats tend to be the first ones to sell out at any event. Perhaps the same situation exists everywhere, but it is emphatically so in Toronto. So the conglomerate eventually known as Maple Leaf Sports and Entertainment could have enriched itself substantially by selling those courtside locations, at a few hundred dollars a pop, rather than turn them over to several dozen newspaper, radio and television types. But it didn't. At least not for many years.

Why not? What was in it for the owners? This: Almost

never does someone sit courtside and report what a boring game just took place. The excitement level, when chroniclers are that close and hear the sounds and smell the smells and absorb the vibrations when these giants thump into each other, tends to eliminate any sense of tedium. The reporting reflects that. Peter Bavasi, one of the original drum-beaters for the Blue Jays, spoke famously of selling the sizzle when he had no steaks to offer. For an expansion NBA team, particularly one denied for five years the opportunity to draft No. 1 overall, it was all about the sizzle. The media, especially from its close-up perch, helped sell.

Yes, you could get lousy games and the wrong results, particularly with a new team that seldom got itself sorted out, but the entertainment and amazement level tended to be high when viewed close-up, simply because of the size, speed and pure physicality of the athletes. Believe me, it is much easier to dismiss any game as (appearing) cement-shoed and safely station-to-station when one is perched high above it, viewing from a distance. There's a built-in disconnect that way.

One early example of the sizzle involved a Michael Jordan appearance in 1996 when more than 36,000 fans packed the SkyDome, as the Rogers Centre was originally known. To many of the spectators, the basketball was a distant dot, yet their reaction immediately marked them as different from the hockey crowd:

> *Many hockey fans routinely boo Wayne Gretzky at Maple Leaf Gardens, the same way, over the decades, many booed Gordie Howe, Bobby Hull and Bobby Orr, among the game's ultra-elite. Then they chanted "We Want Shack."*
>
> *This is how they got to be known as the most discerning and knowledgeable fans in hockey.*

> *The basketball customers, by comparison, mainly come to worship at the altar of excellence, in this case Michael Jordan, and they did it again last night at the SkyDome. They came to marvel at the world's No. 1 sporting icon and they cheered him madly upon introduction. Good thing, too, because they couldn't have cheered him after it. Jordan had one of his worst scoring games as a pro. He did not score in the second half, totalling a season-low 13 points in . . . a 97–89 Raptor win.*
>
> *Not one Bull type, not the coach or the PR man, could recall a specific game in which Jordan didn't score in a half. Someone suggested it might have been in high school. Himself was not talking afterward.*

Naturally, the basketball dynamic changed. The team, particularly upon the arrival of Vince Carter, who was downright spectacular in the first half of his career, cultivated a knowledgeable and passionate fan base. It took a while, but by 2014, when the team controlled the top of a historically weak division, the fan base was one of the league's more loud and proud collections. Social media, which put a revved-up fan in immediate contact with hundreds of like-minded rooters, cultivated all passions.

Myself, I was always a pretty good NBA fan in the distant days when Canadian television stations broadcast games one at a time and usually in pieces. In my college days, I loved watching a game a week, which was pretty much all we got before the playoffs. The first sports story I ever wrote for the *Ryersonian*, back in 1971, was on a basketball player named Rick Mount, who arrived with his Indiana Pacers teammates for an American Basketball Association game at Maple Leaf Gardens. Almost no one remembers ABA games in Toronto, but the league of Dr. J and the red-white-and-blue ball played games wherever it could sell a few tickets before the merger with the NBA. Likewise, the Buffalo Braves played a few "home" games in Toronto in the early 1970s, and I covered a couple of them in my infant days at the *Globe and Mail*. Years later, when someone on the Raptors was disputing a point about something I had written that day by asking how much basketball I had actually seen, I responded that, hell, I had covered Wilt Chamberlain before you were born. This was mildly true; the Lakers had been one of the "TorBuff" Braves' opponents, and one night thirty-some years before, I had dutifully scrambled into the tiny dressing room to scratch out a few quotes from the giant himself. I also interviewed New York Knicks all-star Walt Frazier in his hotel room one game-day afternoon, while he lay under the covers watching soap operas, keeping one eye on the TV set while answering questions. Access then was, shall we say, different from the tightly controlled and monitored scrums that reporters deal with today. With a couple of exceptions among the travelling beat men, no one in the media really gets close enough for long enough to know the players personally.

(One of those exceptions, in a famously unprinted story, was a beat man, unmarried, who had a strong preference for Asian women. One of the Raptors at the time shared a similar preference and on a Christmas-week trip, the player, in a magnanimous gesture, ordered up an Asian hooker to arrive at the reporter's hotel room. Merry Christmas. One problem: there had been a mix-up in the media room lists and the working girl arrived at a *Star* reporter's door. A female reporter, if you're counting. Oh, well. It's the thought that counts.)

I was happy to see the NBA arrive in Toronto and not only because I never considered myself much of a hockey guy. Toronto was changing its face and Raptors crowds, even in the early days, contained more colour and more young people and far, far fewer of the corporate types who controlled (and could afford) the precious gems known as Maple Leaf tickets. To this day, Raptor crowds look a lot more like modern Toronto than do Leaf crowds.

Anyway, the NBA was a good gig to cover. You sat courtside, the game lasted a little over two hours — they're a lot longer these days thanks to increased TV commercials and seemingly endless timeouts — and the players usually were nicely quotable. A lot of basketball is based on at least the perception of trying to intimidate the other side and post-game quotes tended to echo that philosophy. Even with a 10 p.m. deadline, you could watch a 7:10 start, hustle a quote or two and file a column that didn't need to be replaced by an updated version in later editions of the paper. For a columnist, those were good times. The fewer rewrites for the subsequent editions of the paper, the better. At the *Star*, I always worked with Doug Smith, the best in the basketball-writing business. There was never anyone easier to work beside; he knew which angles he would use and which he wouldn't and how my column would dovetail with his game story. Plus, he worked as fast or faster than me and there was always time to go for a beer or two. A real pro all the way.

In the very early days of the NBA franchise in Toronto, when John Bitove's group had won the expansion team nod (over a consortium headed by Larry Tanenbaum, another basketball enthusiast), things looked promising. The great Detroit Piston Isaiah Thomas, his playing career freshly ended by a torn Achilles tendon, was hired to run the team, a bold move. I was sports editor at the *Star* at that point and I went out to lunch with Bitove and Thomas. They had a question: They were going to hire an American to run their PR operation. Would it be a one-day shitstorm or would there be lingering local resentment? I suggested the former. I must have guessed correctly because it soon was no issue.

Thomas, stamped like Bitove with an Indiana University tattoo, drafted promisingly, starting with Damon Stoudamire and, in the second year, Marcus Camby. The first-year team won the expected 21 games (61 losses), and Stoudamire was rookie of the year. Except he had some knee issues and Brendan Malone, the head coach, was fired for, management decided, riding the rookie point guard too hard. They called it "philosophical differences" when they rinsed him.

That was the first flake of the avalanche. The disastrous Darrell Walker was hired as coach. Co-owner Allan Slaight worked the infamous "shotgun clause" to buy out Bitove, shortly before ground was broken for the new arena. Richard Peddie came on as team president. By November 1997, Thomas was out, Slaight buying his 9 percent of ownership. Maple Leaf Gardens Ltd., the company that owned the hockey team and the outmoded building it played in, bought the basketball team from Slaight in February 1998 and fired Walker as coach the next day, replacing him with Butch Carter, who later went goofy on everyone, commencing a play to expand his powers within the organization, a stunt that eventually got him fired. But that was a couple of years in the future. Central to the 1998 takeover by the new ownership group, Peddie was named Raptors president and the head man for the arena, which by now was well under construction. By July 1998, the new conglomerate was called Maple Leaf Sports and Entertainment and there was nowhere to go but up after the Raptors' pathetic 16-66 season. Crowds were so sparse that a crazy promotion was tried for a game against Washington, prompting the following:

This coming Friday, when the Raptors play host to the Washington Wizards, anyone named Dorothy will be admitted free of charge. Wizards. Dorothy. Get it?

Along these lines, then, the Raptors are sure to get a heart . . . a brain . . . the nerve. All they lacked last night, in a 107–89 loss to the Atlanta Hawks, in other words.

They do, however, already possess the bricks, yellow and otherwise. Plus a little dog.

The Vancouver Grizzlies, who entered the NBA at the same time as the Raptors, didn't last long out in British Columbia and moved to Memphis. Crowds and interest dwindled in Toronto, beyond the impact of opening the spiffy new arena named the Air Canada Centre — which I always called the House that Bitove Built. The mood turned almost immediately with the arrival of Vince Carter, who soon won the NBA's dunk contest — a silly competition that seems to carry far more importance than it should — was voted to the all-star team, and for a couple of years, was as big a star as the NBA had.

His cousin, Tracy McGrady, had no wish to play second fiddle and steamrolled his way out of town at first opportunity. He cited the usual Canadian-themed problems, such as going through customs on every trip and the lack of ESPN on local cable TV. His exit plan was obvious, even though his preferred destination, Orlando, was curious, at least to me, because a first fiddle already was in place there, too:

. . . What McGrady wants — and he wants it more than ESPN on his TV set and don't laugh because that stuff matters — is to be out from under the long shadow cast by the bright lights on his cousin Vince.

> *Somebody got it into McGrady's head that Carter is the 40-minute, 24-shot man and always will be and McGrady is 30 minutes and 15 shots in perpetuity. Without knowing whether that turns out to be right or wrong, because this is sports and things always, always change, doesn't that scenario figure to be similar to what he'll face playing with Grant Hill in Orlando?*

McGrady left, but the Raps added some expensive talent and the future seemed brighter in early 2002, especially when the federal government was making noises about removing the handcuffs on marijuana, the recreational drug of choice for many NBA players:

> *If things aren't already looking up for the Raptors, they soon might be. The federal government seems to be edging toward decriminalizing marijuana and imagine the NBA free-agent bait if that happy piece of social engineering takes hold.*
>
> *As GM Glen Grunwald said, only partly kidding, when told the news, "Geez, we could be the hot spot of the league."*
>
> *Yes, and Keon Clark might come back on his hands and knees.*

(The gangly Clark, a one-time Raptor, was well-known to enjoy the odd spliff. Alas, the rumoured pot legislation never arrived in those days, although it seemed possible as 2016 dawned. As a columnist, I appreciated the idea regardless.)

Even without the lure of legal salad, GM Grunwald one summer spent a quarter-billion dollars locking up some names

— Hakeem Olajuwon and Antonio Davis for starters — but the franchise was never rewarded with more than one single lonely playoff-series win. One night in Philadelphia in 2001, they came within a missed Carter jumpshot of going to the Eastern Conference final at the Game 7 buzzer. Carter was always scorched for missing that shot, having attended his university graduation earlier in the day. I never figured out how the two were related and always thought that was a misguided piece of criticism; for a fit athlete in his 20s, taking a one-hour ride on a private jet is not exactly enervating. If he had been out at a strip club at 3 a.m. the previous morning, no one would have said a thing, right?

Carter, who was always an easy guy to get along with and had a decent sense of humour, had two issues. He wasn't very tough — he did the fake-tough-guy act pretty poorly, too — and his mother Michelle was always hanging around, inserting herself into situations that made her son look like the mama's boy he essentially was. At one point, teammate Charles Oakley, who always played the Grumpy Old Man and didn't think much of Carter, was loudly calling out Vince during a playoff run, one in which neither one of them did much:

> *[Oakley] is yapping and moaning about "these young guys" who don't know how to play properly, don't respect the game and so yawn. He's been doing it for a couple of years here and one way or another he's complaining, indirectly but unmistakably, about the attention Vince Carter, and Tracy McGrady before him, receive. Now he's even making snide references to Carter's TV commercials.*
>
> *Put him in an old folks' home. Let him go down to Washington and play on that God's-waiting-room*

> *team with Michael Jordan and Charles Barkley. They can all sit there and dump on the younger generation together and remember how they had to walk through 10 miles of snow, uphill both ways, to get to school.*
>
> *As Oakley throws his darts at Carter and challenges him to "be a man" and such nonsense, how neatly he sidesteps his own pitiful contribution to this series.*

Oakley's chirping prompted Michelle Carter to fire back at Oakley and, well, you couldn't make this kind of stuff up. When you needed something to write about, the Raps provided generously.

Things naturally fell apart. Olajuwon was a disaster. Davis constantly grumbled about things, such as his children being taught the metric system in school and being told to stand for the Canadian anthem — and imagine those hardships. One night, when Davis and a couple of other veterans had been benched for an extended period by Lenny Wilkens, the ancient and worn-out coach who was playing out the string in Toronto, Davis's wife Kendra was in the main hallway underneath the Air Canada Centre stands loudly and strongly suggesting her man had had enough of this place and would be departing soon enough. This, naturally, sounded like news. Davis started backpedalling and swearing when approached, more than once, to discuss his wife's outburst. I wrote it anyway, however gently:

> *Kendra Davis, wandering past reporters under the stands, suggested that her husband will demand a trade in another week and even if she was simply making a point — and she clearly was — there was no chance to bounce the theory off Davis. He dressed in a heartbeat and fled the locker room, blew off*

> *trailing reporters with a quiet but emphatic no comment and asked that they remove themselves from his face. Hard to know if he was upset at sitting so long . . . (or) if he's fed up with all the losing or with his personal situation.*

The next day at practice, Davis started yelling at me for quoting his wife. I yelled back. We went at it and I was actually following him as he departed the practice gym, telling him to stop and talk like a man and such. Security was in between us as he got into an elevator and departed, but at some point I thought, *All right. The guy is 6-foot-10 and fit and is 20 years younger and not very smart and you're yelling at him and telling him to be a man? Are you nuts?* Davis left town not long afterward and we never did talk. His wife went on the radio and accused me of "stalking" her, although she had been loudly yapping in front of reporters in a hallway right outside the press room and I happened to be there at that moment. The only people who couldn't hear her were deaf. If that's stalking, I'm Sarah Palin. Like all these things, it blew over in a couple of days, but, because there was video of Davis grandstanding at practice, the whole sorry mess will stand as the most public "confrontation" I ever had in my career.

For various well-documented reasons, the fans' love affair with Carter waned and there were fears that, like the Vancouver Grizzlies of a few years before, the NBA's remaining Canadian content might hit the highway. Such talk was widely encouraged by much of the town's hockey media; the hockey people always hated basketball, if for nothing else than for crowding their game.

As Carter's time in Toronto sped through the hourglass, Grizzlies vice-president and general manager Dick Versace, a former NBA coach and television talking-head, suggested that basketball could never fly in a hockey town and the Raps soon would follow the Grizzlies' lead on emigration. To which I led off a column, referencing a famous celebrity murder:

> *Did Andrew Cunanan go after the wrong Versace, or what?*
>
> *The first mate of Vancouver's sinking ship was running his mouth about Toronto soon to follow Vancouver down the swirl of the NBA drain. Hey, when did Dick Versace become a hockey guy?*
>
> *While Versace was correct about the team being in a tough spot when Carter leaves . . . he made one major mistake in comparing the two situations: In Vancouver, the latest owner was a tenant in a market that was bad from the start and draws about half the paying customers Toronto does. But the owners of the basketball team here also own the arena in which the team plays. When you own the building you want the team there and you want it popular.*

There were a lot of snotty emails about that first sentence, naturally. Yes, Cunanan, a nutbar, had stalked and murdered the designer Gianni Versace, but that had been a couple of years before and it seemed like reasonably fair game. It's another of those things that would have set off a forest fire in the current Twittersphere. But I thought it was funny and as the man said, screw 'em if they can't take a joke.

There was, naturally, a divide between a middle-aged Canadian white guy writing sports and the young, mostly black and mostly American athletes, any of whom had far less on their mortgage than I did at the time. Occasionally, the subject matter was a circus freak such as Dennis Rodman, who was on the same wavelength with exactly nobody, regardless of background. Such individuals, of course, are a columnist's main course and Rodman, especially after he had married a TV personality named Carmen Electra, was something of a buffet:

> *The thing is, Dennis Rodman gets drunk in Vegas and marries a babe with a balcony you could do Shakespeare off. So? He's not the first to go there.*
>
> *Is it just me, or for the first time maybe ever does Rodman look something like a normal guy?*
>
> *Other than wanting to know what kind of gown the groom was wearing — they say it was a police uniform — and how many of his WrestleMania friends were in attendance and what could she possibly be thinking, what's the big deal?*
>
> *Some guys have a few too many and, two weeks later, wake up in Mexico with a full beard and a tattoo. Rodman, who already has the tattoos, wakes up in his suite at the Hard Rock Hotel and he's married to a TV star with what even Bulls coach Phil Jackson admitted are "distracting" qualities.*
>
> *Rodman's problem — if that is the right word here — reminds us of a tee shot that veers into the woods, hits a tree and returns to the middle of the fairway. It is what is known as a good miss.*

Rodman capers aside, as much as I enjoyed dealing with the NBA players, because they generally were quotable types, most discussions tended to remain strictly on the basketball levels because we didn't have a lot in common outside our working relationships. The major exception here was when

Sam Mitchell coached the Raptors from 2004 to 2009, because Sam was a golf nut and every time I would come back from a tournament, particularly a major, Sam wanted to know all about it and soak up the gossip and so on. He loved to needle, both give and take, and was a very good listener when it came to golf stories. Sports in general but golf in particular. Once, discussing practice habits, both good and bad, I told him a story Jack Nicklaus had relayed once. I forget where Jack first said it, to tell you the truth, because I was lucky enough to sit in on several extended chats with Nicklaus, but I clearly remember the thrust of it, which was this: Nicklaus, at every major when he was in his prime, always walked slowly to the far end of the practice tee, greeting friends but checking every player out and noting what they were working on. After practice, he would walk back in the same way. He said he worried more about the guys hitting the poorest shots, because anybody working on his weakness, in public, was dedicated and committed to improving and therefore potentially dangerous. The players hitting perfect rainbows, he didn't worry so much about. His point was that it's easy to practise what you're already good at, but tougher to put the effort into what needs the most help.

Mitchell told me later that the next day he interrupted practice to relay the message to his team in a bid to get the players to practise their damned free-throw shooting. I asked him if I could get a day's wages for assistant coach. He laughed at that. I wish he'd stuck around longer.

CHAPTER NINETEEN

In the Press Box

The best first sentence these eyes ever read in a newspaper story was penned by the late Rex MacLeod and kicked off his 1990 obituary of Harold Ballard, the prickly and ridiculous owner of the Toronto Maple Leafs and a long-time sparring partner of not only MacLeod, but most scribblers in town.

"The fat is in the fire," Rex wrote in a sensational opening salvo.

Alas, a couple of squeamish editors at the *Toronto Star* pulled the plug on that memorable line, plus a follow-up assertion that Ballard's last act ideally would have been to sell advertising on the side of his casket. They mumbled something about respecting "good taste," although nothing in his lifetime would ever have equated Harold Ballard with those two words. The gatekeepers grudgingly let through MacLeod's finishing touch, which was that Ballard had been predeceased by his hockey team. A quarter century later, it still isn't wrong.

Rex's lovely opener eventually saw print a few years later, unfortunately as a part of his own obit, included as an example of his craft that ranks on the top shelf of those with whom I was fortunate enough to share press boxes over the years.

MacLeod, whose son Rob followed him into the same corner of the business at the *Globe and Mail*, was the best deadline writer I ever encountered. When I broke into the newspaper business, at the *Globe* in 1973, he covered the Leafs. He had a well-trained eye for the game and knew it extremely well. His post-game questions were to the point and his ability to craft sharp, authoritative and highly literate game stories was unmatched, in this opinion. When I worked on the copy desk, it was a pleasure to be handed his stuff; you did more admiring than editing.

That *Globe* sports staff was an all-star collection when I arrived in 1973. Hockey chronicler Scott Young, father of singer Neil, was there briefly but our paths did not cross long; he quit in a huff because the *Globe* ran a piece about a Maple Leaf player harassing a stewardess on a commercial flight. Young, very much of the old school, thought such stories were off limits.

Christie Blatchford, a year ahead of me at Ryerson, already had begun making her name with some lively features at the *Globe*. Larry Millson handled the thoroughbreds and James Golla did the standardbreds, back when horse racing was a significant beat at every paper. (Millson, by the way, is still active as a sportswriter, always understands what he is seeing and possesses one of the greatest bullshit detectors in the business.) Dick Beddoes, the flamboyant cape- and fedora-wearing wordsmith, was the lead columnist and a very good one. Matter of fact, a situation with Dick got me into a jackpot, the only time anyone ever accused me of stealing a line. Except it was my line originally.

The 1973 Grey Cup was in Toronto and while working part-time at the *Globe*, I still attended Ryerson. I drew the journalism school's credential and assignment to cover the championship of the Canadian Football League. I wrote the advances for the school paper and included a prediction: Ottawa 22, Edmonton 18. When that assertion was chopped off the bottom of the story, I shrugged; sometimes you get edited.

The game wasn't the greatest, but there I was, sharing a press box with the best writers in Canada. Out of my league, for sure. The game ended — Ottawa 22, Edmonton 18, by the way, for my one and only correct score prediction in four decades of trying. (Alas, because it had been edited out, no one ever believed me and probably still won't.) I worked the dressing room to collect quotes and angles, then hustled to the *Globe* to start my Sunday shift. Shortly thereafter, in came Beddoes. We talked about the game, in which penalties played a large part, and agreed it hadn't been the best. "I don't like those games where the referee is the leading ground-gainer," I said. Beddoes laughed and said that was a good line. Did I mind if he borrowed it?

Did I mind? Hell, no. I would be honoured. Somewhere in his copy, he dropped in a version of it.

During supper break, I wrote my own Grey Cup story for the *Ryersonian*. Next morning I trotted into school and dropped off my story on the game. Hours later, I was being summoned to the journalism chairman and ordered to explain why, in my report, I had used the same line as Dick Beddoes in that very morning's *Globe*. Did I not understand the severity of stealing someone else's work?

I tried to explain how it was my line and Dick had asked permission to use it. Nobody seemed to buy it initially, but, to his credit after I explained the situation, Beddoes, who hadn't known I would be writing my own report, called the school and backed my story.

One other Beddoes story: When Rex MacLeod left the *Globe* for the *Star*, the *Globe* didn't fight to keep him. Rex was no favourite of managing editor Clark Davey; in fact they hated each other. We had a boozy going-away for Rex, and Davey showed up. Beddoes, who did not drink, gave the keynote address and jabbed a finger at Davey and blamed him for driving the best sportswriter in the country to the opposition. There was substantial truth in what Beddoes said, but Davey, who clearly did not appreciate the public harangue, was not the sort of enemy one cultivated lightly. I always thought Dick was incredibly brave to make that speech.

Beddoes, MacLeod and the rest of the *Globe* crew drove into me what I have always called the first rule of sportswriting and one I tried to follow for 40 years: Watch the damned game you are covering. Watch each play. Write notes at breaks, but pay attention. It sounds simple enough, but it surely is about the last rule to be observed in modern-day press boxes. It's a different world now; many, if not most, reporters are there to Tweet endlessly and to post website updates, and they tend to have their heads in their computers and phones. Many do more writing than watching, snapping their heads up at the roar of the crowd and relying on replays for details. This is a dangerous practice and much of a game's subtleties are missed because of it. Stories tend to reflect that, at least to me. There are, of course, a few throwbacks who pay attention and both know and understand what happened and can question players and coaches afterward. They are rare animals.

There also are times, usually when deadlines are approaching quickly, when it is necessary to both write and watch at the same time. For instance, the first time the Blue Jays won the World Series, in Atlanta, we had eight minutes from final out of the game to first-edition deadline, which had been held by the paper at enormous cost. (The tall foreheads quite rightly figured there was no point in trying to sell a paper the next day that didn't contain the result of the Jays game.) You can only write (and send) so much in eight minutes, so a column constantly rewritten to include game developments, then topped in the first few seconds after a decision is reached, is the only possibility.

I left the *Globe* in 1977 for the *Toronto Star*, although not without incident. The *Star* had added a Sunday paper and printing seven days a week required more staff. I was sick of working 6 p.m. to 2 a.m. at the *Globe* and a *Star* offer of permanent overnight desk shifts — midnight to 7 a.m. — was preferable. It would leave evenings free to go to the racetrack and part of the *Star* deal was doing the harness racing handicaps and writing a weekly racing column on a freelance basis. It was a good deal and I jumped at it.

But there was a silly complication. I had played for the *Globe* team for three or four years in the press fastball league — decent calibre and highly competitive softball. The *Star* had a team whose pitcher was the legendary president and publisher, Martin Goodman. Marty took softball seriously; he would get his pitching arm rubbed down at the Cambridge Club before games. (Years later, when he was battling the cancer that ultimately took him but he still wanted to pitch, he made sure he took his chemotherapy treatments through his left arm so that he could still use that right one to pitch.)

In 1977, Marty still was a pretty good pitcher, but I could often hit him well. There was no love lost between the *Star* and *Globe* and some of the games got wild. One Saturday morning, I hit home runs my first two times up against Goodman, and the third time, he drilled me with a pitch. There we were chirping and cursing each other and, as usually happens in these things, a crowd gathered and there was a lot of yapping and F-bombs lobbed, but no punches. The nonsense died down, the game went on and that was the end of it.

For a while, I had been negotiating with the *Star* and eventually agreed to accept their offer. I gave my notice at the *Globe* on a Friday night — about 14 hours before I got into the squawk with Goodman. Monday morning the phone rang. It was Ken McKee, assistant sports editor at the *Star* and the man with whom I had negotiated, telling me not to quit my *Globe* job. He had heard I had been in a fight with the *Star* president and there was some question now whether they could hire me.

Great, I thought. *I've already quit the* Globe. *Now what?*

Luckily, Goodman couldn't have cared less about Saturday's situation; he apparently said something like, "We need another righthanded hitter with power. Hire him." So I not only switched papers, I switched fastball teams and ended up as a teammate of Goodman's for a few years, catching him for three of them before he left us. Not that it adds anything to the story, but a quarter century later my son and Marty's grandson ended up teammates on the same rep baseball team.

When I got to the *Star*, there were giants in place. Milt Dunnell was already retired from full-time duties at age 70, but still wrote a brilliant, literate column that would continue regularly for another 17 years. Jim Proudfoot was the sports editor and main columnist. Frank Orr was the hockey writer. Neil MacCarl handled baseball. Allan Ryan and Garth Wooley were the young guys filling in here and there and Rick Matsumoto handled football.

I worked my overnights, laying out the section while supplying the harness coverage in what was a 30-man department that seemed to run on momentum. With seven-day publication and the staffing that required, there was a lot of juggling of beats and manpower, to say nothing of travel issues. Luckily, I was paying attention to all of it, although I wouldn't become sports editor myself for anther 16 years.

Jobs changed over time. Gerry Hall and Phil Bingley took over as sports editors. Bob McKenzie arrived to write hockey, then Damien Cox and Paul Hunter. Mark Zwolinski filled in on several beats. Eventually, when basketball arrived years later, Mike Clarkson, followed by hoops lifer Doug Smith, covered the roundball, with Chris Young, a long-time friend and terrific writer, jumping in from the column side. The *Star* always had a huge crew of both reporters and editors and it never dropped below the 30 men in place when I arrived there.

I should correct that to at least 29 men and Alison Gordon and now's the time to mention women and sportswriting. The 1970s were the time almost every paper figured out that women could be, and should be, writing sports. When I was at the *Globe*, Blatchford was working her way in. A very nice woman named Mary Trueman, who was a good reporter but knew nothing whatsoever about sports, was drafted to become a football writer. She was done a great disservice by an editor trying to make a statement. Part of the reason many women were successful writing sports was their desire to do the job, to shoulder through sometimes outrageous abuse and mostly indifferent support from male colleagues.

Alison Gordon was a baseball nut and a good writer. She was willing to put up with a lot of shit in the Blue Jays' early days: The lack of respect . . . the sexual innuendo . . . the resentment from a few players' wives who mistakenly assumed she was there to bed their husbands . . . the loads of abuse from readers who didn't want women — any woman — trying to tell them about sport. All that, and more, was very real.

She was a pioneer in her field, no question, and surely made it easier for the women who followed — not that it was ever easy. In my time at the *Star*, plenty of women moved into the press box after Gordon, including Blatchford (Christie always moved from paper to paper), Mary Ormsby, Rosie DiManno and Jennifer Quinn, to list the high-profile writers who have gone on to great things. Mary had a long career while raising four kids with sportswriter husband Paul Hunter, Rosie still churns out high-grade columns at an unmatched pace for both the city side and sports, and Jennifer, after a stint in the diplomatic world in London, returned to the *Star* and became its first female sports editor in late 2013.

Likewise, the electronic types, meaning radio and TV, began hiring females and assigning them to sports. It was a big deal 40 years ago, but nobody even notices any longer, which is the way it should be. As I look back I would like to think I was supportive of most of them, but I doubt that I was as much of an ally as I could have been. I did get into it once with a Blue Jays player who was waving his penis at a woman reporter across the clubhouse. I told him to grow up, that it might be his own daughter doing that job some day and to act accordingly. The team asked the woman if she cared to pursue the matter and she did not. All she wanted was to do her job without a big issue.

I did recognize one aspect of women covering sports, though, that was true then and is true now: Unlike some males — certainly not all or even many, but some — no woman reporter ever secretly thought it should have been her out there on the power play, or playing third base, except for that damned old knee injury. No woman I worked beside ever thought that.

Newspapers were a world I understood much better than TV or radio, certainly, although if I go back all the way to my high school years, TV-radio was what I was working toward when I finished grade 13. I had applied to Ryerson's Radio and Television Arts School and was given an interview. I long ago forgot the name of the individual who talked to me when I was 17 and hoping to get in front of a camera or microphone, but he did me a huge favour. He told me I didn't have the looks for TV or the voice for radio and that I should get into print. This is not what every 17-year-old wants to hear, of course. If it happened today, there would be a lawsuit and a sprint to the psychiatrist's couch. But I trusted what he said and switched to journalism. It all worked out pretty well and not only because I ended up seeing the world on someone else's dime. I saw some historic sporting events and made some terrific friends along the way, most of them in press boxes and, later in the evening, on the next barstool.

Steve Milton of the *Hamilton Spectator* was a constant companion on the baseball and Olympic roads and for sheer miles travelled, Cam Cole, now turning out his must-read columns from his base in Vancouver, shared more destinations with me than I can begin to name. Plenty of *Sun*, *Globe* and *Post* guys were great company on the road. In no particular order, good times were shared with the likes of Stephen Brunt, Larry Millson, Michael Grange, Scotty Morrison, Steve Buffery, Bill Lankhoff, the great baseball Hall of Famer Bob Elliott, Ken Fidlin, Mike Zeisberger, Frank Ziccarelli, Steve Simmons, Rob Longley, John Lott and Shi Davidi. Canadian Press, the national wire service, employed terrific journalists who became great travelling companions, including Neil Stevens, Lori Ewing, Julie Scott, Donna Spencer, Chris Johnston and Jim Morris, among others. Friendships were cultivated across the country, including Robin Short in St. John's, Dave Stubbs and Pat Hickey in Montreal, Tim Campbell in Winnipeg, Terry Jones in Edmonton, Vicki Hall in Calgary and Ed Willes in Vancouver, among front-line journalists from coast to coast.

Among the *Star* crew, Tom Slater and I spent years together on the desk, then handling baseball. He was the beat man when I was the columnist and after I moved on to be sports editor, Richard Griffin eventually took over the baseball columnist's job, a position he still holds. Rich had been PR director for the Montreal Expos when I hired him as my replacement as baseball columnist. I also can't forget the late, great Randy Starkman, our amateur sports enthusiast who made covering Olympics a breeze. Starks, who made a name for himself — and got himself a job at the *Star* — with his excellent coverage of Ben Johnson's steroid bust at the 1988 Games in Seoul, was passionate about amateur athletes and their games and knew many if not most of the athletes as friends. At any Olympics, when we divided assignments, Starkman mapped out his day to put himself and his unmatched background information to best use, then (if asked) would hand over to the rest of us his files on other athletes or provide background information and different story angles the rest of us could rely on.

Once, after Starkman had done some groundbreaking and important work on the lack of safety of hockey helmets, he was eligible for a $10,000 prize put up by an institute devoted to head safety. He asked me to write a nomination letter. I did. He won. I suggested, semi-seriously, that he peel off the outside part of that 10 grand and we take our wives away for a sunny week in the middle of winter. He just looked at me sadly and pretended I was joking; he had already donated every cent to his favourite charity. He was always doing work for charity and whenever a hat was passed in the office for whatever cause (flowers, going-away gifts or whatever), his was the first hand that went into his pocket. When he caught some kind of terrible infection while on assignment in the spring of 2012, we thought it was merely a setback he would overcome. We were all shocked into despair when it kept worsening and took him away. Several athletes dedicated medal-winning performances to Randy at the 2012 Summer Olympics, not long after. Terrific journalist. Better guy.

Earlier, I mentioned Milt Dunnell, the man we called the "sports editor of the country" and a man with whom I became friendly late in his life. Along with Brian Williams, the best (and best-known) TV sports guy in Canada and another close friend, I delivered the *Star*'s card and birthday wishes when Milt turned 100 in 2007; he put off a trip to the casino that day in order to hang around and wait for well-wishers. Dunnell died a week after his 102nd birthday, by the way — about 14 years after he retired once and for all, on my watch as sports editor, I am sorry to say.

At that point, in 1995, Milt wrote a column each Saturday for the *Star*. Regularly each Friday evening, a cab would arrive with his meticulous copy. One Friday night it didn't. The slotman called Milt's home and was told, essentially, "Milt no longer works for the *Star*. Why are you phoning here?"

Clearly, something was up. They phoned the sports editor at home. I phoned Milt. He was kind enough to say he no longer worked for the *Star* and if I did not know why not, then please phone publisher John Honderich for further information. So I called Honderich at home and he said, "Oh, is that happening this weekend? I guess I forgot. He won't be writing again. I'll explain it all Monday."

We shouldered on and Monday morning I marched into Honderich's office to get the story. It turns out that one year before, Milt had a beef with my predecessor and had quit over some editing of his column with which he disagreed. At his age, he figured, why did he need this? Honderich had gone to Milt's home to beg him to change his mind. Milt agreed, but under one condition: if they opened a permanent staff job for a certain young reporter Milt thought was deserving, he would write for one more year, then disappear with zero official sendoff. Plus, Honderich couldn't say Word One to the sports editor. Those were Dunnell's terms. The *Star* agreed, hired the person Milt recommended — a young woman on the news side, by the way — and he resumed his columns. No one knew a thing including, it turns out, the new sports editor who had taken over the job a few months before. That would be me.

Powerless to change Milt's decision, I nonetheless altered the deal: a week later, I wrote a sendoff column for the greatest columnist this paper, if not this city and this country, had ever produced. I figured we owed that much to the readers, at least. Milt sent me back a thank-you note. I still have it.

There are a million Dunnell stories but one always stood out here. It was in the old Metrodome, an hour or so before the first game of the 1987 World Series. He and I were in the upper deck, in the auxiliary press box. He was a kid then; a few months shy of 80. A handful of baseball writers were hanging around, eating the boxed-lunch sandwiches, and someone asked each of us to identify the signature of the first World Series we covered. This Series would be mine. Somebody else spoke of the We-Are-Famalee Pirates. Then the Big Red Machine. The Miracle Mets. One of the veterans mentioned Bill Mazeroski hitting his home run, so now we were back to 1960. Milt hadn't said a word and someone prodded him.

"Well," Milt said, "Cincinnati's Paul Derringer . . ."

He never got to finish his sentence because everyone else

was groaning and throwing up their hands and carrying on. Milt had taken us back to 1940. He clearly had won this one by stretching nearly five decades. Five and six years later, Milt was in the press box when the Blue Jays reached the World Series. If you're counting, those put him past five decades there.

That's just baseball, too. In hockey he covered Howie Morenz as a junior player and went right through the Wayne Gretzky era, plus wrote close-up about every heavyweight champion from Joe Louis through Mike Tyson. He saw more Queen's Plate winners than just about anyone. Next to the great Dan Jenkins covering more than 240 major golf championships — they play only four a year, so do the arithmetic — Milt's run is as great as they come in this business.

A few years before Dunnell died, Muhammad Ali was honoured by the Toronto Argonauts, and Brian Williams was the master of ceremonies. Williams huddled briefly with Ali before the ceremony and Williams passed on a hello from Milt. "You know Milt Dunnell?" Ali asked Williams, brightening. "Man, you a lucky guy to know Milt."

An awful lot of us thought that way.

Personally, I'd throw quite a few more names of press-box pals into that category, too.

CHAPTER TWENTY

One Hard Bounce Away

I mentioned being fortunate enough to cover 58 golf majors. That's in addition to probably another 150 regular tournaments, a few women's events, some minor tour fixtures around Toronto and 10 Ryder and/or Presidents Cups. They were almost all a pleasure to attend, to varying degree, but if I needed to pick one event, in any sport, that was my favourite annual event, it would be the Open Championship. There was just something about being in Britain, even with the (usually) attendant lousy weather and questionable plumbing, that was exhilarating. I loved the golf courses, loved the style of play, very much enjoyed the fans, who also played and appreciated the game. For most Open Championship fans, particularly in Scotland, there was a sense that the circus had come to town and we were all able to get into the main tent.

The greatest of all my Opens, from 1996 to 2013, was Turnberry in 2009, when beloved five-time Open champion Tom Watson, aged 59, came within one hole of pulling off (in this estimation) the greatest achievement in the history of golf. That he lost to Stewart Cink, a talented professional incapable of moving the excitement needle either then or now, somewhat diminished the week. But what a week, as Watson's early competence turned from a delightful curiosity into a cause worth openly rooting for. Right to the end, he was enjoying it, the fans were beside themselves and other golfers were shaking their heads in disbelief.

After Watson's tee shot at the 72nd hole, as he led by one stroke, I hustled out to the green, anxious to see this much history in person. From the middle of the fairway, he needed par to replace Old Tom Morris in the books as the oldest man ever to win the Open; Old Tom had been 46 back in 1867, 13 years younger than Watson was at this point. Watson lofted a high, soft iron to the 18th green that looked almost perfect. It soared on a line straight toward me, but landed hard. Too hard. It took too much of a hop and bounced off the green. It seemed to me he had hit the one hard spot on an otherwise soft green. He could have gotten up and down for par to win, but he hit a mediocre chip. His shoulders sagged. The crowd urged him, but his eight-footer to win never had a chance and he made bogey. In the playoff, the younger, stronger Cink destroyed the suddenly older and worn-out Watson. After four days of turning back the clock, the clock turned on him with a vengeance:

> *Old Tom Morris will stay in the record books — and possibly forever. Old Tom Watson will live on in another way, though. What the 59-year-old did here this past week will become a part of golf — even*

sporting — lore, an inspiration to anyone who ever thinks, "I'm too old to beat these kids."

But Watson and his ultimate defeat in the 138th Open Championship, a one-sided playoff loss to veteran Stewart Cink, whose late-afternoon brilliance will be an underplayed part of the story, ultimately did prove that sentiment. Watson, alas, was too old to come through, which means there will be too much pain, the pain of reality, associated with this very special week. With the opportunity right there in his hands, an eight-foot putt at the final hole, Watson displayed the shaky, tired stroke you might expect from most 59-year-olds, finally worn down under the increasing pressure of the world's greatest golf tournament.

Suddenly the air was out of the place; the tension, wound ever tighter through a day of not-great but still fascinating golf, disappeared. Cink was by far the better man in the playoff; Watson, now in full dodder, knowing how close he had come to perhaps the greatest achievement in the history of golf, had nothing left to give.

"It would have been a hell of a story, wouldn't it?" Watson asked later. "It wasn't meant to be. And, yes, it's a great disappointment. It tears at your gut, as it has always torn at my gut. It's not easy to take."

The choice of that 2009 Open as my favourite tournament doubtless will make people wonder if I've forgotten Mike Weir's 2003 Masters triumph. The short answer, naturally, is that it's not possible to.

But for a newspaper guy covering what we call "a local," it's a very different gig trying to keep the home crowd happy. For starters, once Weir was thickly in contention and a win seemed possible, I started receiving all kinds of "help" from the home office. Editors who had never set foot in Georgia, much less at Augusta National, were suddenly suggesting how I should go out and cover the final round and phoning with explicit instructions for sidebars and front-page stories and what questions to ask and such — so explicit they would change five minutes later. At one point, while the leaders were entering Amen Corner, one of the editors at the *Star* decided to send me an email requesting I go out to the golf shop and buy him a nice shirt as a souvenir. Yeah, sure, I had time to do that. The only way to deal with all this back-home idiocy, of course, was to ignore all emails, switch off the cell phone and do what I normally do at a big tournament. Which is what I did. Once it was over, I sent a list of what I had planned and told them they would have it all in 45 minutes. Which they did.

Weir was — still is — a fine guy. I walked a lot of holes over the years beside his father, Rich, and his brothers Jim and Craig and his (now-ex) wife Bricia and always enjoyed the time spent there. Good people. Weir was never what we called a good quote; he wasn't glib or particularly insightful in his comments and never controversial, but he was invariably friendly and usually accessible, although you needed to step lightly if he'd had a bad round. That he was a big sports fan and loved to talk Blue Jays or NHL or whatever, helped us get closer. He also had a terrific caddie named Brennan Little who got to know all the newspaper guys and wasn't scared to share a joke with them.

Weir was a tremendously hard-working and stubborn individual who got the most out of his ability. He got up to No. 4 in the world, which is pretty amazing considering he was giving away 30 or 40 yards off the tee to most players and sometimes more after the golf technology boom hit. That he won eight PGA Tour tournaments, including some big ones such as the Tour Championship and a World Golf Championship event, was a tribute to his work ethic. Sometimes I used to think, in racetrack jargon, that he was overtrained, that he pushed himself too hard sometimes when things weren't going well, but I always chalked that up to his stubbornness. When he set his mind to something, there was no talking him out of it.

That weekend at Augusta in 2003 had been the one Martha Burk held court. It also rained on and off and heavily, breaking up the tournament rounds into multi-day affairs. It was difficult to piece together an accurate leader board until the final round began, since somebody was always several holes ahead of or behind someone else. But when they turned for home and Weir was in the best spot, the Canadians in the press room were quietly but firmly rooting for him; we all knew how much it meant to him and to Canada. The first rule in the press box is no cheering, but it's permissible to root for the story and for us, this was by far the best story.

When Weir came to the 18th hole tied with Len Mattiace, he needed a par to force a sudden-death playoff. I went out to the press stand overlooking the 18th green — best press viewing spot in sports, I used to say — and watched Weir hit a good drive but a short approach. He had about 40 feet for birdie and hit a poor putt, leaving about seven feet for par. I was sitting beside Rick Reilly of *Sports Illustrated* and Rick murmured, "Choke stroke." At that point, I thought how miserable an assignment it would be to chronicle a three-putt that handed the Masters to Mattiace, and, far worse, how crushing it would be to Weir to fail so publicly. This was a life-changing moment few of us could ever comprehend. I was proud of Weir when he knocked in that par, forcing the playoff. His win kept me hopping for a while. At times like this, when something memorable has happened and you're on the scene, the phone calls and emails start from radio stations wanting you to drop whatever insignificant thing you're doing and go on the air live to share with their listeners. Those requests would get the same consideration as the 4 p.m. shirt guy.

While Weir was going well, which was pretty much for six or seven years, from late 1998 through 2004, he was a fixture at the biggest events, including the Presidents Cup. He's the reason three papers (but only three) from North America — the *Star*, *Sun* and *National Post* — covered the Presidents Cup in South Africa in 2003. I also covered a World Cup in Buenos Aires in 2000, mostly because Weir was there representing Canada and golf fans couldn't get enough of him, although it didn't hurt that Tiger Woods was playing for the U.S. and in those days you couldn't write enough about Woods, either.

That Buenos Aires event, by the way, was wild. Weir, who was under the weather, was 50-50 on coming or cancelling until the final day. (Let me say how nervous I was, down there in B.A., having sold the trip to my editor and now facing the prospect of Canada pulling out of the damned thing. Thankfully, he showed up to partner Glen Hnatiuk and they played reasonably well.) I mentioned how boisterous the fans were:

> *Wild? Cattle have been herded with far greater ease than the marshals and crowd-control rent-a-cops were accomplishing yesterday. There were fans on tee boxes, running across fairways, roaring and cheering and jumping up and down and doing the crazed-soccer-fan thing — everything except peeing on the person in front of them.*

That event also was memorable for a Woods moment, when Argentine journalists, in their first crack at him, tried to pin him down on such diverse subjects as soccer, marriage, travel and whether he would like to meet Maradona, the former national hero lately very publicly dealing with substance-abuse issues:

> *This last elicited a response so political it suggested [Woods] could run for office some day. He said both he and Maradona were busy, but — getting to the corporate nut, as he often does — "we both represent Nike and hopefully, one day down the road, our paths will cross."*
>
> *What? Is Tiger going into rehab?*

It was a joke. Hey, who knew what was several years in the future?

Back to Weir, whose most painful moment was missing a couple of short putts and losing the 2004 Canadian Open, eventually in a playoff, to Vijay Singh. This may be on the level of cocktail-party psychology, but I don't think Weir ever quite recovered completely from that disappointment. When he dunked his final approach into Glen Abbey's green-front pond at the 18th hole, thereby sealing his fate in that playoff with Singh, I turned to hobble back to the press room. (I had damaged a knee doing something or other and was moving very slowly.) It was a long way to the press room, through the parking lot, and during my journey, a large black SUV pulled up beside me and offered me a ride. I hopped in and found myself sitting next to Weir, who was being driven to the press room. His eyes still had red rims; this one had hurt and hurt badly. I expressed my thanks for the lift, but I didn't say much else. It was a sad finish and every year that goes past without a Canadian winner, I think of that afternoon. No doubt Mike does, too.

The one performance spike he had, as his career declined, was a sensational win over Woods in the 2007 Presidents Cup at Royal Montreal. He also won a late-season tournament a year or two later, but injuries took their toll. He changed his swing, changed his coaches, changed equipment, ultimately changed his caddie and then, the final stage in the progression, split with his wife. Along the way, much of the Canadian public seemed to have turned against him; Cam Cole, Lorne Rubenstein and I used to discuss this, how snarky and hateful emails would clog the inbox whenever any of us wrote anything about Weir, no matter how innocent or innocuous. None of us could figure it out; he wasn't hurting a team, he wasn't dragging anyone else down. We never understood the reason so many people turned against him. We just shrugged as email after email commanded him to retire and go away and stop embarrassing everyone. And those were the polite ones. Weird stuff.

Weir, a stubborn cuss, never stopped working on trying to hone his game, to get it back into some kind of shape, even as his world ranking sank into four figures. As I wrote at the Masters in 2013:

> *Go offer this deal to any 27-year-old on any ham-and-egg pro golf tour: He will make $26 million playing the game, win eight PGA Tour tournaments including a major, get as high as No. 4 in the world, take private jets to all the big events and have Tiger Woods on speed-dial.*
>
> *The catch is, it will all be over for him by age 40.*
>
> *Guaranteed, 100 percent would sign for the best*

deal since the one Faust got. Yet that is definitely not how Mike Weir looks at things, even though the description fits.

Weir never did get his game back, certainly. He will have to settle for knowing he ended up getting every bit of the best he could out of his own ability. I hope it eventually will be enough comfort to him.

Which brings us to Stephen Ames, a smart, talented golfer who definitely didn't get the most out of his abilities and simply didn't work hard enough on his craft, in this opinion. He also complained about everything, complained incessantly. In his early days on the tour, he would holler misquote when his yapping doubled back on him. When presented with electronic proof he had been quoted accurately, he would often play the out-of-context card. (A career note-taker, I began carrying a tape recorder strictly because of Stephen. I always had to make sure of exactly what he said.) He was from Trinidad and Tobago, married a lovely Canadian girl and eventually settled in Calgary and obtained Canadian citizenship. Remained outspoken and quotable, too, which is good for us.

He seemed to hate almost every golf course he ever played, including many historic and revered British Open tracks. He didn't like most tournaments. Didn't like Mike Weir and how much attention he got. Ditto for Tiger Woods. He complained about the Canadian Open being played too often at Glen Abbey — he was not the only one — but when they took it to beautiful old Shaughnessy in Vancouver, even though he was the only Canadian to make the cut, he still was banging away on the course to the extent that I led off the next day thusly:

Memo to travel agent. Please book next golfing vacation to Trinidad and Tobago. Apparently the courses there are perfect beyond belief.

Stephen Ames, who is One Of Us now, spread the same day-old slander about Shaughnessy Golf and Country Club and its "horrendous" greenside rough, which only proves a guy can shoot 64, tie the course record, move into contention in the Bell Canadian Open and still insist on having the last word.

Ames gets the last word on things Canadian this week by default as the only Habitant still standing from the 16 who began the tiff. Credit him for embracing the role of national standard-bearer.

"It would be awesome. Everybody is rooting for me," he said, perhaps forgetting Shaughnessy members.

He didn't win that weekend, but he had won some big ones. He took the Western Open in 2004 and then hammered the field to win the Players Championship, fifth-best tournament in the world, in 2006. Even then he shocked everyone, having played his way into the Masters with the triumph, by suggesting he probably wouldn't bother with the Masters a couple of weeks later. "I'd rather go on vacation, to be truthful. I have no plans of playing Augusta. My kids have come down here for spring break and we had plans to go somewhere else. [Augusta] wasn't on my schedule," he said.

This sent chroniclers scurrying for cold compresses for their aching foreheads, but it was simply the way Ames conducted himself. His wife, Jodi, had been through a cancer ordeal and this was his way of saying he would check with her first. And she, of course, told him to go to Augusta. Which he did. And where he complained about the size of the field and how it really wasn't a major with so few good golfers around and so on. Sigh. That was Stephen Ames. Never a dull moment.

The other accomplished Canadian pro of the era was Lorie Kane, the ever-cheerful Maritimer who had a terrible time breaking through for her first win, which finally came in 2000 and was thoroughly welcomed by every Canadian, particularly the golf writers. The year before, I had been in Las Vegas, covering a Lennox Lewis fight, and Lorie was co-leader through three rounds of the LPGA Tour Championship being played in Vegas. So I stuck around on the Sunday. Perhaps this would be the time.

Alas, she made two late bogeys, fell to fifth place and was extremely upset, as in crying. This marked her fourth year on the LPGA Tour, and 100th tournament, without a win. A couple of us stood outside the scorer's tent, wishing we were in New Jersey and wondering what to ask this time. Out she came from the scorer's tent and immediately her caddie was consoling her, Se Ri Pak, who had just won the tournament, was consoling her and LPGA officials were hugging her and trying to say comforting things. Before she had gotten near us, fans were yelling at us to leave her alone and to stop hounding her and to get away from her and calling us jackals and vultures and words with Ks in them. To Lorie's credit, she shushed the fans and pointed at us and said, "It's not their fault." Then we tossed her a couple of gentle questions, collected her responses and fled as quickly as possible. I wrote as straightforward a story as I could, with an oh-poor-Lorie angle, suggesting that when the cork finally vacated the bottle, probably next year, the wins would arrive in bunches. Then I flew home. The next day, there were the usual angry how-dare-you emails and a real you-prick-you zinger from Anne Murray. Yes, that Anne Murray, whom I knew to be a nice golfer at a private Toronto club I much admired. I responded that I possibly did need straightening out and educating when it came to golf and if she would only invite me out to her club one afternoon for 18 holes of attitude adjustment, I am sure she could change my mind as to what constituted a proper report. I got a slightly warm response back with what I thought was a nibble, but never heard from her again.

Thankfully for all concerned, Kane won a tournament the next summer and, as I suspected, a couple more followed in a hurry. I always got along nicely with Lorie Kane in our few meetings after that, and when they played the Canadian Women's Open at Angus Glen outside Toronto, a club where I played regularly, I happily covered the event. Karrie Webb was there, nearing the height of her powers, and was a complete misery to deal with. In the next day's paper I referred to her as Nurse Ratched Webb. I was walking into the press room when Kane ran over to me, trying to put on a disapproving face, but failing. She said all the girls in the locker room were giggling at my description and began giggling herself. Amazingly enough, Webb herself was not enthralled.

CHAPTER TWENTY-ONE

Lighting Up

Unlike some common frustrations that once were described as having the power to drive a man to drink, the Atlanta Summer Olympic Games literally drove myself, and more than a few colleagues, to smoke. At least temporarily.

Now, before embarking on this particular five-ringed path, let me say I was a big fan of Olympic Games and by that I mean the competitions themselves. They always produced riveting moments and superb feats and the athletes, on the whole, were compelling and provided some of the very best stories of the year. Pound for pound, the "amateur" athletes found at each Olympics, the ones largely ignored by fans, press and sponsors in the intervening four years, were the most admirable group of sporting labourers.

That said, there was much about covering an Olympics to detest, almost all of which was outside the lines: the commercialism and rampant jingoism, overbearing omnipresent sponsors, the International Olympic Committee stuffed shirts — not all of them, certainly, but many of them — and self-important puffed-up sports officials could make the Olympics a chore to be around. Make no mistake, the Olympics represent a mammoth worldwide business opportunity, first and foremost. In the so-called modern era, which seems to have begun with the 1984 Los Angeles Games and really ramped up starting about 1992 with the appearance of the biggest names in professional basketball, the U.S. "Dream Team," the athletes and competitions essentially became a way for the IOC to make ungodly amounts of money every two years. Looking back, I suppose the glut of great stories that emerged from every Games outweighed the bad, but it seldom felt that way at the time.

Of the 10 Olympics (six winter and four summer) that I covered for the *Toronto Star*, the absolute worst, in terms of organization, were those 1996 summer squabbles in Atlanta. At least until the homegrown terrorist bomb went off, resulting in the death of two innocents and deepening the stain of terrorism first made at Munich in 1972, the Games themselves were going to be widely remembered not only for the breakaway commercialism and worst-ever organization, but for the stunning visuals of Muhammad Ali lighting the Olympic cauldron at the end of the opening ceremonies. They also are recalled here for a different kind of lighting up.

Granted, Atlanta had a difficult act to follow, coming two years after the best of them on this scorecard, namely the 1994 Lillehammer Winter Games. Those were a dream. Atlanta was a nightmare.

My media village was at a dormitory at Clark Atlanta University, a small, leafy, comfortable campus a reasonable bus ride from the media centre and Olympic bus depot in downtown Atlanta. Buses left regularly for the bus hub and took a route that drove basically right past the main media building, nerve centre for any Olympics. But the bus did not stop there. Instead it bumped through traffic another 10 minutes to the bus centre, at which point we needed to get off our bus, line up for another bus and then ride back basically the same route we had just traversed to an official stop near the media centre. This silliness would add perhaps a half-hour to what should have been no more than a 10-minute journey. This doesn't sound like a lot, but the last thing a group of grumpy journalists needs is pointless delay, especially when they are already committed to 14- and 16-hour working days and the full assortment of lineups and hurry-up-and-wait moments that define any Olympics.

First day, as the bus neared the media centre, a few of us asked the driver to please let us off at the next stoplight and we would walk the short distance, maybe 100 yards, to our destination.

"Can't do it," the driver said. "We can only let you off at the official stops."

After a couple of days of this, one of the Brits figured it out. As the bus neared the point closest to the media centre, he fired up a cigarette. Several of us then would exclaim, "Hey, bussy. This guy's smoking."

The poor driver would immediately stop the bus, march back to the offending puffer and order him off the bus, which obviously was intended to be non-smoking. As he opened the doors to let the smoker off, we all would pile out. After that, many of us bought cigarettes and carried them for bus emergencies.

Ridiculous? Juvenile? Of course it was. But a half-hour is a half-hour and effective time management, so vital at an Olympics, comes in different forms.

This also absolves the bus drivers from blame here. They were following orders and they were very poorly managed. They groused constantly about the way they were used — and with good reason. For instance, drivers reported being given different assignments, meaning different routes to different venues, every day. They would say that as professional drivers, brought in from all around the country and usually unfamiliar with Atlanta's layout, what they needed was a chance. Give them a few days on the same route and they would figure the traffic patterns and know when the proper turns were arriving and so on. Instead, they were faced with a new and, usually, unfamiliar route most days. Tales of buses lost all over Georgia, and athletes and officials arriving late to events, were common. Steve Redgrave, the great English rower, hijacked a bus and forced it to get to his venue in time for his event. There were other documented bus hijackings and as someone clearly brilliant wrote in the *Star*, "Getting from A to B seems to involve a lot of F words."

Not to get too bogged down in Atlanta misery stories, but add this one to the file on transport chaos. About an hour in traffic outside the main Olympic hub, near Stone Mountain, Georgia, sat two venues, the velodrome and archery. It was great to see everyone pedalling and firing those arrows under the watchful, bas-relief gaze of Robert E. Lee, Jefferson Davis and Stonewall Jackson, who adorn the side of the enormous monolith. (You ask me, half the people down there are still fighting that war, or at least wish they were. But that's another story.)

One afternoon, I was out covering cycling — always a gas; velodrome events are very cool — and once it was over, I had time to hop to the next venue and cover a local who was about to shoot some arrows. (A local, by the way, is what reporters call someone who lives anywhere our paper is delivered.) So I headed over to the archery venue, which was separated from cycling by a chain-link fence. There was a gate and a guard and I showed my credential and then was stopped dead.

"You can't arrive on foot," he said. "Media must arrive on an official vehicle." (Naturally, he pronounced it vee-hick-ull.)

The way to get on an official vehicle? Take the cycling bus back to downtown Atlanta, wait for an archery bus and then ride it back to Stone Mountain. That would be, minimum, two and a half hours. Instead of walking perhaps 100 feet to the archery pit.

No amount of arguing would work. Common sense refused to arrive. The guardian of the gate was, as was almost always the case in Atlanta, friendly and polite and kept insisting we all have a good day, but he had his instructions and his instructions apparently included not allowing any walking media member through his gate. Officials and volunteers and members of the "Olympic family" passed through with a cheery wave and smile, but no press. This time cigarettes didn't work. All those archery fans were probably wondering why the *Star* shortchanged them in the next day's paper.

This was the way it was in Atlanta. Plenty of small, avoidable stupidities that made the place much worse than it needed to be — and already it resembled a heavily guarded rib fest and T-shirt sale rather than a gathering of the world's athletic elite. This, remember, was five years before 9/11 and the subsequent ramping up of overwrought security that marks almost every large sporting event. Atlanta, though, was kind of a template, with 30,000 security and military personnel eyeballing everyone and everything and, to their credit, getting it right on the backpack bomb and clearing the crowd as well as they did before the explosion.

Yours truly had suggested to readers, pre-Games, that if this many military had been ready for General Sherman during the

U.S. Civil War, history might have been greatly different. For instance, we wouldn't have had a book or a movie named *Gone with the Wind*, which probably means *Wuthering Heights* would have won the Oscar for best picture in 1939. (That joke had a limited audience, but I always liked it.)

A week in to the Games, insulting Atlanta had become the new national pastime, at least for me. I had called it "Mayberry on steroids" and my midpoint Games column included the suggestion, considering all the stupidity on display, that *Forrest Gump was a documentary . . . Come to think of it, Forrest might enjoy these Games; he can run from event to event. There's no other way to get there.*

Naturally, this was not fondly received everywhere in the Deep South. I became something of a target for local media and the next morning I was snapped out of sleep very early by the ringing of the telephone in my room. It was two local shock-jocks, morning radio types who had been given my dorm-room phone number. (By whom I could only guess.) Years and the grogginess of sleep render what follows as approximate, but they said something like, "Hey, Dave Perkins! You're the man who doesn't like Atlanta! You're live on the air with So-and-so and Such-and-such."

At that moment, I channelled my inner Jim Proudfoot, a much-respected colleague who knew how to avoid such ambushes, and grunted "No, I'm not" and both hung up and disconnected the phone. Not surprisingly, I had no difficulty returning to sleep.

Everyone who went near Atlanta that year has a horror story, but think of the great moments, particularly for a Canadian scribbler. Marnie McBean, who later became an admired friend, won a gold medal with her sculling partner,

Kathleen Heddle, on the same day Donovan Bailey earned the title of world's fastest man by winning the 100-metre dash. (I'll always remember heading into the stadium for that race and running into Johnnie Cochran, O. J. Simpson's defender, a man I had accused in print of being able to talk the spots off a Dalmatian. Cochran, dressed to the nines in impeccable suit-and-tie despite the searing heat, was posing for pictures with fans and volunteers and signing autographs. Not far away, Chief Noc-A-Homa, the Atlanta Braves' dreadfully racist mascot, was doing the same thing. You had to be there, but the juxtaposition certainly said Atlanta to me.)

As magnificent as Bailey's win was in the 100, a week later the story somehow grew even larger when he, Bruny Surin, Glenroy Gilbert and Robert Esmie kicked the hell out of everyone, especially the yappy Americans, in the 4 × 100-metre relay. NBC had been lobbying for the odious Carl Lewis to run for the Americans, who had never been beaten to the wire in Olympic history (their only loss coming on a disqualification). Lewis didn't run and it wouldn't have mattered; he'd have never gotten close to what could have been a record 10th Olympic gold medal. The Canadians, who justifiably had felt mightily disrespected by being all but ignored in NBC's pre-race buildup, crushed them by several metres, and I must confess, I pocketed a large amount of wagering money from some of my U.S. press-box friends on that result. (I felt somewhat badly about admitting that, but the feeling passed quickly.)

All told, Canada won 22 medals in Atlanta, although only three of them gold. Those three stand out in this memory, though. Just like the bus mayhem and the overall horrible nature of the Games. Other Games had been — and would be — much better.

ALBERTVILLE 1992

They were my first Olympic Games and such were the Olympics in those pre-internet years, particularly a Games held in Europe with its lovely six-hour time cushion, that only two *Star* reporters were required. In later years, when the internet was requiring the kind of often slapdash, 24/7 breathlessness that now passes for reporting, the paper was sending six or eight or 10 people when it could — and/or when it could afford to.

Things were more relaxed in 1992, particularly from a staffing perspective, and that meant myself and veteran columnist Jim Proudfoot would make it to France. Everyone called him Chester, for reasons that were obvious at the time, although might be mystifying today (Chester Proudfoot was a character in the long-running TV series *Gunsmoke*), and Chester provided one of the greatest memories of an interesting Olympics.

Now, Chester was a terrific and elegant writer, very cultured and well read. He was a slow, painstaking columnist who crafted his thoughts and words carefully and was equally fastidious in his personal upkeep. Chester was the kind of guy who travelled with a robe and slippers. He also was afflicted with Bell's palsy, had a slight droop in his face, spoke slowly and deliberately and had a quiet little heh-heh-heh chuckle. Plenty of wiseasses in Canadian press boxes would do a little Chester impression, but he was a hugely respected guy in the business and a tremendous companion on the road.

We stayed at a brand new little hotel in Albertville. It was a chain that featured tiny rooms with no closets and walls made out of cardboard, or so it seemed. You could easily hear every word of a phone conversation from the next room. Not a great place to sleep, in other words.

One night, the two of us met for a late dinner or a drink

— Chester probably had a snifter of kir, or something — then walked back to our hotel. I had covered short-track speed skating and Chester had been to hockey, I believe. At short-track, a South Korean skater had won a bronze medal, the country's first medal in any Winter Olympics. At the time, I thought, *Good for them, but who really cares?* Except that the South Korean media also was staying at our hotel and it was party time. Any number of robust (mostly) young men were celebrating and carrying on and drinking heavily. But this was an Olympics; long days always stretched ahead. Sleep, at least a little of it, was necessary, but try sleeping in this place, right?

I got my head down and tried to grab a few hours and was just drifting off in the din when I heard a voice, in English, hollering out in the hall. It was Chester. I bolted out and there he was, in his slippers and dressing gown, berating a large group of drunks.

"Shut the hell up! There are decent people trying to sleep and you're acting like a bunch of fucking savages," Chester was yelling. "It's a fucking bronze medal. It's short-track speed skating. No one cares. Shut up! Go to bed! Let decent people sleep."

With that he turned, went back to his room and slammed the door. The party quickly broke up.

Seven hours later, I was in the breakfast room, inhaling the jet fuel they pass off as coffee. A table of six or eight gruesomely hungover Koreans was nearby. They were silent, clearly in pain. In strolled Chester, looking refreshed. Every Korean at the table jumped to his feet, turned toward the approaching Proudfoot and bowed deeply from the waist. Chester never broke stride, casually waved his right hand toward them and said, "At ease, men." He sat down and ordered his breakfast. No one like him.

While we're on Chester, fast-forward two years and we're flying to Oslo, Norway, for the next Winter Games, held in Lillehammer. We changed planes in London and somehow Chester was seated next to Queen Sonja of Norway for the flight. She was a handsome woman of, well, regal carriage, and Chester no doubt was at his most charming — and Jim could be extremely charming. I was a few rows back and couldn't hear their conversation and by the time the plane unloaded she was long gone, swept away by handlers. When I caught Chester at the baggage claim, he was clearly smitten. I jokingly asked him if he'd been able to get her phone number and I'll never forget his response: "No, but she favoured me with a twinkly eye." Only Proudfoot could phrase it like that.

Back to Albertville, where, by the grace of sheer beginner's luck, I happened to be in the right place at the right time for every one of Canada's seven medals, including Kerrin Lee-Gartner's downhill skiing gold medal, the only downhill gold Canada has ever won. It also was Lee-Gartner's only career downhill victory and such was the tepid buildup that there were only a handful of Canadian reporters at the bottom of the hill. We crowded around her and absorbed her excitement; she had turned in the race of her life when it mattered most and was overjoyed simply by that fact, as well she should have been. But as her time stood up through the inevitable Austrian and Swiss attempts to better it, the realization sank in deeper on all of us that this was becoming something enormous. Canadian Olympic officials arrived to whisk her away shortly before taxicabs began pulling up, dispensing more Canadian journalists. By the time her victory was official, every Canadian with a notepad and a microphone had arrived. There were no pictures to tweet in those days.

Something all together similar happened a few days later

when Myriam Bédard, the biathlon maverick, won her first medal — the first in this demanding sport's history by a North American. The biathlon course was up the mountains in a charming little town called Les Saisies. It was a harrowing bus ride to get there, a terrifying thrill ride of hairpin turns and switchbacks. My friend Dave Anderson of the *New York Times* correctly labelled the bus ride itself "the 44-man bobsled," and I suggested there certainly was no French word for "guardrail" simply because there never were any guardrails.

Four of us braved the journey that day to see Bédard and the field go 15 kilometres. I remember the others — Michael Farber of the *Montreal Gazette*, Neil A. Campbell of the *Globe and Mail* and Toronto radio guy Chris Mayberry — because of what followed.

Bédard won her medal about 11 a.m. and we did our interviews and so on. But it turned out the medal ceremony wouldn't be held until the evening. Normally, no one hangs around for a medal ceremony except TV guys who need the video. But at some point early in the afternoon, we had been tipped off that Bédard, who later in life would become known for some bizarre behaviour, was demanding that instead of the Canadian flag, she wanted the Quebec fleurs-de-lis flown at the ceremony.

What a story. No one would confirm or deny officially and Bédard had been squirreled away by the Canadian Olympic Association (now Committee). Now we had to wait hours for the ceremony to find out for ourselves. So the four of us did what any self-respecting reporters would do in those pre-internet days. We found a great restaurant, had a fine lunch and a few drinks and thought, "Lunch in the French Alps, great food and great wine and the sun is shining. We're sitting on a great story. Life is not so bad."

With a couple of drinks in us, the four of us formed the

Canadian Biathlon Writers' Association and were in the process of writing out our constitution and electing our officers when Bédard walked past the patio, with a COA mandarin named Walter Sieber, who was the Chef de Mission at these Games. That job description tends to refer to the person who holds the bail money; in Wally's case, his best trick appeared to be materializing for photo opportunities with medal winners. Anyway, off we went after Myriam. Sieber saw us coming and grabbed Bédard by the hand and took off on a sprint. I am sure the locals were intrigued; here were two people, in Canadian Olympic outfits, being pursued down the street by four scruffy looking, shouting maniacs, three of whom were quite large guys (only Farber was average sized). When they slowed to get into a COA car, we caught up. Bédard was in the back seat and Sieber spread himself across the door, shouting, "No, no. Get away," or something equally as gallant.

Naturally, we persisted and brushed aside Sieber and queried Myriam about the flag issue. Naturally, too, she had no idea what we were talking about. It had been a bum steer and the medal ceremony eventually went off as uneventfully as they always do. Sadly, too, the Canadian Biathlon Writers' Association never held another meeting.

At Albertville, a small arena held figure skating and short-track speed skating on alternate nights. Most nights, after a day chasing down skiers or biathletes or long-track speed skaters — their events still held on an outdoor track at those Games — a clutch of Canadian reporters ended up at the arena. Canadians were usually strong in figure skating, which is a wonderful sport to both watch and cover, by the way, and in short-track, a relatively new Olympic sport in which Canadians were among the pioneers. (Asians have long since caught up and become dominant.)

The Albertville arena afforded several wagering possibilities, as well. For instance, there were 10 little girls from a local skating club charged with entering the ice after each skater's performance. While the athletes awaited their marks from the judges, one or two of the young ladies would skate around picking up the bundles of flowers or teddy bears or whatever junk had been thrown on to the ice in appreciation of the skater. For the big-name skaters, six or eight of the girls were needed and they would return with armloads. Because the girls wore different coloured outfits, it led to the following suggestion: "I bet you 20 francs the little red elf picks up her load and gets off the ice quicker than the purple one."

You can see where this led. Bored Canadians were picking their favourite colours, throwing their money into the pot and then cheering wildly. The practice grew until we settled on this for a grand finale: Ten contestants, each drawing for a different colour, put 50 francs each into the pot, which totalled something like $130 in Canadian dollars. Last elf left on the ice gets all the money. It would all be riding on beloved French ice dancers Isabelle and Paul Duchesnay, a 10-elf pairing for sure, when they competed in the dance final. One rule: any elf that fell down (and many did) was disqualified.

The Duchesnays, skating last, achieved the usual rapturous reception and were greeted by an avalanche of stuff from the stands. Out went the urchins. Up went 10 Canadian reporters, beseeching their charges and rooting against the opposition. "Go back, blue! You missed some flowers!" "No, green. There are more balloons coming your way. Stay out there." "Trip, orange! Lose your balance!" That kind of thing.

Long after the cheers and applause for the skaters had ceased, as they awaited their scores, a small pocket of lunatics in the press tribune was up screeching. For what, of course, only they knew.

Ultimately, in a very tight finish, my pal Christie Blatchford, who was then working for the *Globe* or *Toronto Sun* in those days — Christie went back and forth a lot — won all the money in a photo finish. If I remember right, red nosed out yellow at the exit gate. Yellow was at the door, ready to depart, but was gracious enough to usher the other kid off first. Blatchford, being a great Canadian, threw her winnings into the middle of the table at the local bar later that evening and we drank it and then, possibly, some more. And that, friends, is how to cover figure skating.

The other great wagering opportunity arose from the short track, which is an action-packed roller derby on ice, but can get pretty tedious in the early rounds when numerous eliminations boil down a couple of dozen skaters into the four or six who are truly good and medal contenders. The *Toronto Sun*'s Steve Buffery — Beezer to his friends and he has plenty of them — and I would sit there watching the preliminary rounds and soon were betting horse for horse at 10 francs. I would pick, say, the Dutchman in his heat and Buff would go for the Korean. Whoever finished higher won the 10 francs and the loser picked first the next race.

We did all this while munching Mars bars and there's a story here, too. The food available at Olympic venues — yes, even in the land of cordon bleu and heavy cream sauces — was generally horrible. This is not uncommon for an Olympics, where the sandwiches always taste as if they were made in New Jersey two weeks ago and then sent over in a container. The highlight of the Albertville menu seemed to be a ham-and-cheese arrangement on an inevitably stale baguette known as a "croque monsieur." Now, I have had a proper croque monsieur, with the luscious, velvety béchamel oozing out over the succulent ham. These were not those. One bite and someone early on correctly diagnosed that yes, it tasted like a dead French guy.

Our hunger pangs therefore were combatted with Mars bars, the epitome of trustworthy nourishment sold at the arenas. Buffery and I would sit there in the press tribune, eating our candy, cheering for no-hope skaters and handing 10-franc pieces back and forth. Eventually, someone with a thick European accent asked what in hell we were doing and Buffery responded that this was a widespread Canadian tradition, that every Saturday night the entire nation would sit around the TV set, eat Mars bars and bet on short-track speed skating. I almost think the guy believed him.

Two more wonderfully silly moments linger from Albertville. Since it was my first Olympics, I figured it was worth getting the entire experience, which therefore included attending the opening ceremonies. Like all OCs, which I soon came to avoid strenuously, on the grounds that they tended to be long, boring and took themselves much too seriously, this one was based on the usual blue-skies speeches — how the children are our future and how the glory of sport helps shape all mankind and so on — but began with the spectacular arrival, down the long valley, of three French fighter jets spewing red, white and blue smoke. Jet flybys are de rigueur at big sporting events now, but it was new enough to be borderline exciting back in 1992. As they roared overhead, the *Hamilton Spectator*'s Steve Milton, a treasured companion on the baseball-beat road for a few years and one of the more erudite and clever of the travelling gang, pointed to the direction from which they had arrived.

"That means the war is over there," he deadpanned.

The entertainment part of the ceremonies included some pretty terrific performance art with a French flavour: there were spectacular acrobatics and mimes in giant Plexiglas balls and dancers on swaying poles and bungee jumpers and so on. It was vastly entertaining, in this opinion, and worth sitting in the cold for four hours to see. Later on, at a Canadian Olympic function, I was opining as much in a group that included the mayor (or perhaps former mayor) of Calgary and his wife. Calgary, of course, had been host city to the previous Winter Games, in 1988, so it was no surprise when the lady sniffed at my assessment. "Acrobats and mimes. Buncha crap. How does that mean anything to an Olympics?" she said.

In jumped Milton again: "You mean like chuckwagons do?" he asked her, bringing down at least part of the house.

LILLEHAMMER 1994

"Norwegians are more fun than people."

That was a line I had written at the end of the Albertville Games, with an eye toward Lillehammer in 1994, after exposure to the wild, sports-loving fans who had made the trek south to France. The International Olympic Committee, in an effort to "build the brand," as they say, had switched off the traditional format of holding a Winter and Summer Games in the same year. They began staggering them so there was a Games every two years. Much more effective for selling sponsorships, they figured.

So the Winter Games reconvened two years later, instead of the four it had always been before (minus the wartime interruptions) and has been since. This time, we headed for Lillehammer, a nice little town in a spectacular and beautiful natural area a couple of hours from Oslo.

Having been exposed to the Norwegian fans at Albertville, I had some idea of what to expect. Generalizing, obviously, the hosts were genial, fit, good-looking people who seemed to know every word to every rock 'n' roll song ever written

All dressed up for the opening ceremonies of the 1994 Lillehammer Winter Olympics. That hat has been around a few Games.

and sang at all times, even if the words came out phonetically. *Toronto Sun* columnist Steve Simmons always enjoyed telling of a karaoke kind of place on the Storgata, the action-packed main street of the town, where several locals in full throat were belting out, in honour of the Beatles, the line "Yo-Yo left his home in Tuck-son, Arizona."

One prominent Storgata pedestrian was the Condom Man, a young, good-looking guy wearing a sandwich board advertising and selling condoms. He had the style and price printed on his board and carried strips of each. They say he sold out his stock every night.

Several things stand out from these great Games, starting with the wonderful fans going bonkers at every competition and — this is different from every other Olympics — rooting like mad for every athlete, regardless of his or her uniform. We knew things were different from the very first big event, the men's downhill skiing, when American Tommy Moe flashed down the hill to defeat Norwegian hero Kjetil André Aamodt, the big favourite in the race. That turn of events briefly stunned the crowd into silence, but they soon returned to their vocal ways and, it being Moe's birthday, the thousands at the finish area then serenaded Moe with a chorus of "Happy Birthday to You." Cynical reporters eyed each other, wondering, "Really? What's going on here?"

The other tent pole to these Games, of course, was the figure skating saga involving Tonya Harding and Nancy Kerrigan, an irresistibly tawdry soap opera that was easily the biggest story in the world at the time, and no, not simply the biggest sports story. The short background is that Harding, a gritty but mildly talented skater, had essentially hired a goon named Jeff Gillooly to break Kerrigan's leg a month earlier. Kerrigan, a much more elegant and slightly better skater than Harding, was the beautiful ice princess in this one. The United States Figure Skating Association held its pre-Games press conference, as most organizations do, exposing the athletes to a kind of boilerplate press experience before cocooning them away until their competitions. This was standard practice, but far from standard was the size of the skating palaver. There were several hundred reporters clamouring to get in. The venue was switched to a large auditorium and there was the world's press, hundreds of lead columnists — many of whom who didn't know a Salchow from a dish of coleslaw — itching for a Tonya-Nancy cat fight. And if they couldn't get a proper cat fight, the least they needed was someone getting a saucer of milk.

What they got instead was a USFSA dope essentially saying we would not talk about the alleged incident and all questions should be limited to asking about the skaters' routine and training and so on.

Naturally, several hundred reporters muttered variations of "Uh, no," either under their breath or out loud. No one was going to let this story get away without a fight. The skaters, peppered with questions they had been assured would be blocked, looked shocked and terrorized and mumbled inanities, saying things like "I'm only focused on my routine and what my coaches tell me" and such. Clearly, the beast of the press was not properly fed by those tepid responses. The story spread to every other skater at the Olympics; every single interview sought out an opinion on the kneecapping, and skaters who truly were in a bubble, thinking only of their next Lutz, were suddenly pondering the results of being hit with a steel rod. What fun it was.

For years since, this was exhibit A (at least to me) in how not to handle a crisis. You can't make a bad story go away by trying to ignore it and pretending it never happened. If you are smart, you get out in front of it. Faced with about two Super Bowls' worth of press coverage and worldwide interest, someone should have crafted a neutrally worded statement, read it out and handed it out, and told the skaters, when questioned, to parrot the statement. That's thin soup to a ravenous media horde, sure, but it's much better than what transpired. The lesson when something goes wrong, witnessed a hundred times since and only exacerbated by the outbreak of an unstructured and uncontrolled social media, is easy: either you drive the bus or the press will and if you let the press drive, you're going over a cliff. I never met a good PR man or woman who did not understand that getting in front of a train wreck is better than trying to pretend it didn't happen.

Now back to the figure skating, which, Tonya and Nancy aside, was not such a big deal in Lillehammer. Host countries aim to sell tickets, of course, and plan their venues accordingly. So Norway, which is mad about all sports but completely insane for ski jumping and cross-country skiing, built enormous stadiums for those two, seating 30,000 and 40,000. Indeed, the cross-country ski races drew upward of 100,000 spectators, counting those who wedged into the stadium and who camped out in the woods along the route of the longer races. This, essentially, to see people walking by on skis, right? Fantastic athletes, no question, but here they come and there they go and each one essentially looks like the one ahead and the one behind. But that is what turned local cranks, so good for them.

Figure skating, not so much. The arena, a cedar-panelled bowl we called the hot tub, held no more than 5,000 paying customers. Elvis Stojko, the great world champion, surveyed the size of the house at one of his early practice sessions and figured he had skated before larger crowds at Ontario regional meets.

The joint was beyond jammed when Harding and Kerrigan

skated and therein lies another story. Press tickets for high-demand events, like hockey and figure skating were allocated by country. Canada would get X number, but it would never be enough because every Canadian journalist wanted to attend figure skating. That's because Canadians are good at it and, back home, love to watch it. Plus, that year, the Tonya-Nancy showdown was not to be missed. We at the *Toronto Star* needed another ticket, so I said not to worry, I'd go stand in line for the returns. (Every Olympic country gets a press-ticket allocation and many of the warmer-weather countries, say, do not need them and turn them back in.)

The press office was outside the hot tub, at a kindergarten next door, and when the time came to disperse the extra tickets there were a couple of dozen reporters crammed up against a counter, awaiting their distribution. A young lady arrived with a fistful of tickets and had no idea how to distribute them. Finding no equitable way, she simply tossed them up into the air over the crowd. As you might guess, all hell broke loose as tickets fluttered down. I turned to reach for one of them — being six-foot-two may not work on an airplane, but it came in handy then — and broadsided a small Asian woman who I am pretty sure was Kristi Yamaguchi, the 1992 Olympic singles champion who had retired and was doing some TV work. Apologizing profusely, I picked her up and fled the mayhem with my prize. It's the only time I ever saw figure skating as a contact sport.

As for the skating, when Harding almost got disqualified for showing up late, we might just as well turn to the *Star*'s man on the scene and no, I don't think I was getting carried away. The next day's column began as follows:

> *Never in doubt.*
>
> *Oksana Baiul may have stolen the Olympic figure*

skating gold medal from Nancy Kerrigan last night — and no jokes about Jeff Gillooly going after the wrong target — but Tonya Harding stole the show.

Of course she did.

Stole it? Well, she has the district attorney at her door on other matters, so let's not put theft on the rap sheet, too. Actually, Tonya didn't need to steal it. She has owned it and controlled it all along. But she was never better than she was last night, when she did everything but take a foreign object out of her trunks. Just when it seemed she wouldn't show up . . . she left the dressing room area, burst through the curtains and charged toward the ice, seconds before her two minutes would be up and she would be disqualified, her little asthma inhaler gamely in hand.

I swear, I thought she would be tearing off a muscle shirt, the way Hulk Hogan used to do it when nobody was better. She wobbled out to centre ice, clad in plum and sequins, having shed the scarlet trapeze-lady's costume she wore during the short program.

She prayed a little prayer, clapped her hands, prayed again, balled her fists. Then she turned up her performance a notch.

She gave up on her very first jump, landing it like a child jumping the last three steps off a stoop. She ankled over to centre ice, burst into tears, then charged the judges' stand to plead her case.

Getting in some practice, some would say.

It went on like this for a while. Harding was, incredibly, given a do-over, allegedly for having a broken skate lace, and began her routine again. She wasn't much better this time and finished eighth, but, once again, she was the one you absolutely needed to write about. CBS was ecstatic about the ratings from this fiasco, certainly. Kerrigan played the part of Good Witch and almost went all the way. The only performer off message turned out to be Baiul who, almost incredibly, had been run into by someone at practice earlier in the week, gashing her lower leg for a few stitches, yet overcame that injury to win gold in a gritty display. To sum up, lower-body trauma met high drama. What a show it was.

Once again, Jim Proudfoot was on the *Star* team at Lillehammer and once again, Chester came through to provide a memory. It concerned our fellow reporters and the unwritten rule that forbids cheering in the press box, which is strictly a North American invention. It's also one that is eroding, I should add.

Now, Chester had covered a lot of international hockey and had no use for the Russians, for various reasons. At Lillehammer, the Finns had hammered the Russians early in the tournament and, a night later, three Russian hockey players, wearing fake press credentials, sneaked into the press tribune at figure skating and commenced cheering on, very loudly, their pairs-skating compatriots.

"No cheering in the press box," growled Proudfoot, who recognized the three as hockey players. When they pretended not to understand, Proudfoot began checking credentials.

"You boys all work for *Pravda*, eh?" he said. "Say, did you hear about that great hockey game last night? Finland 5, Russia 0. What a great game. The Finns clobbered them. The Russians looked like jellyfish."

The Russians turned grumpy, but soon were bellowing again as their pairs took gold and silver.

Undeterred, Proudfoot gestured to the ice and shot one more arrow: "Good thing they can skate because your hockey team sure can't."

On the fields of ice and snow at Lillehammer, Myriam Bédard, last seen sprinting through the French Alps, was Canada's standout, winning two gold medals in biathlon and making the country fall in love with her. She had been battling her sport's mandarins, did everything her own way with a secret coach and so on, and was a great story, her humble parents scrimping and saving nickels and dimes to give her a sliver of opportunity and her doing the rest. She was bright, bilingual and easy on the eyes and could have, as was written at the time, wrapped the country around her trigger finger. She did, briefly, before running into some troubles later in life and saying and doing some bizarre things — including an arrest and conviction for child abduction — that had people suggesting she wore a tinfoil hat. Having been in attendance at all three of her Olympic medals, and seeing what a magnificent, dedicated athlete she was in a sport almost no one on this side of the Atlantic really cares about, her decline to national laughing-stock was a particular sadness to me. Canada has had very few athletes as great as she was in her prime.

One last Lillehammer memory was the wolf urine and not just any wolf urine, but synthetic wolf urine. It was in high demand — not as some kind of exotic performance-enhancing device, but as a deterrent to moose getting themselves smacked by trains.

Moose, you understand, are absolutely everywhere in Norway, including every single buffet table. There was moose meat in varying styles, meaning smoked, boiled, broiled, roasted, made into sausages and ground into burgers, or any other way you could think of, and heaped on the steam tables at every single meal, including breakfast. Salmon was a distant second, although the local McDonald's made their Big Macs with salmon rather than beef.

Besides being a major food source, moose was a major headache to the transport system. Every year, hundreds of moose get whacked by trains and with train travel quadrupled to and from Oslo for the Olympics, a way needed to be found to keep the moose off the tracks. Turned out that wolf urine did it. Every 10 metres or so, a little bag of pseudo wolf urine was hung alongside the tracks. If and when a moose broke through, helicopters were flying the route, ready to warn the engineers.

This sounded like a good story and, in one of those flukes that happen every now and then, it turned out the guy in charge of keeping the railroads moose-free during the Games, once I tracked him down, had spent 12 years driving Canadian trains in the Rockies. He was a big fan of Canada and had plenty of time for the *Toronto Star* and provided an interesting column. Sometimes you need to get lucky on a story.

NAGANO 1998

When Juan Antonio Samaranch's travelling athletic circus touched down in Japan for the snowball fights in 1998, it arrived with several additions. For the first time, women's hockey was contested as a medal sport. Same with curling, both men's and women's. Snowboarding also made its debut and Canada was stacked with medal possibilities there, too. Most meaningfully to most Canadians, though, the best professionals from the

National Hockey League now competed, following the lead of the National Basketball Association's pros nearly six years earlier.

With "real" hockey and curling on board, plus the usual array of figure skaters and both short- and long-track speed skaters, this figured to be a Winter Olympics to keep a Canadian newsman hopping. Canada did indeed win a record number of Winter Games medals, partly by loading up on the new stuff — with one glaring exception. Yet what killed the most trees — and what burned up the newish and ever-growing internet — had to do with smoke. Second-hand smoke, actually. And not from an ordinary cigarette.

A classy Canadian named Mark Fawcett was the world's best in the snowboard, but a cheap little part on his board, one he said you could buy at any hardware store for $2, broke during his run and wiped him out. It was a crushing moment for him, although he handled the disappointment superbly. The attendant gloom and doom among Canadian snowboarders soon disappeared, though, when a Whistler, B.C., boarder named Ross Rebagliati swooped out of eighth place and won the gold medal. It was a welcome shock, given that Rebagliati had been absent from most pre-race handicapping (not that most of us had any idea about this stuff). A couple of days later, after the usual medal hoopla had died down, an even more shocking twist arrived: Rebagliati would forfeit his medal and be disqualified for testing positive — for marijuana.

O Cannabis! All hell broke loose. Canada, in some ways, still was smarting from Ben Johnson's disqualification in Seoul almost 10 years earlier for using anabolic steroids. But a little salad? That's a different thing; marijuana is not performance inducing unless, as I wrote, the athlete had the munchies and someone put out a bowl of Smarties at the finish line.

Compounding the issue was Rebagliati's contention that he

hadn't smoked any weed himself and that he had merely been present when some campers fired up at a going-away party for him back in Whistler. Second-hand smoke, in other words. Further murk was piled on the situation when it was revealed that many sports bodies didn't test or punish for recreational drugs, since they weren't performance enhancing. In other words, one Olympic athlete could be busted for doing something, while his roommate in another sport would, by policy, escape not only punishment, but detection.

Things went back and forth for a few days until common sense prevailed — a rarity considering thc International Olympic Committee was involved — and the medal was restored. By that time, Rebagliati had jetted away to appear on *Letterman*. Other mini-dramas took over, of course.

To start with, let's dispense with the hockey disappointment(s). The Canadian men, with coach Marc Crawford somehow deciding Wayne Gretzky was not to be included in a shootout, not only lost their semi-final game, they then went completely flat and even lost the bronze-medal game to a semi-pro goaltender, complaining about lack of motivation. Naturally, coming home empty-handed set off another anguished round of the finger-pointing and navel-gazing that tends to accompany particularly galling international defeats. It didn't help the nation's wounded puck pride that the Canadian women, in what was essentially a two-team competition — and basically remains that way to this day — had lost to arch-rival United States in the gold-medal game. For once, that obnoxious Nike commercial was correct, the one that says, "You don't win silver, you lose gold."

In more hockey news, a few identified members of the U.S. men's team, after underachieving yet again, broke up part of their Olympic village in a drunken rampage. Talk about embarrassment.

No place was busier during those Games than the figure skating and short-track arena, known as the White Ring. Elvis Stojko, a three-time world champion who, like all the great Canadian male skaters before him had been unable to break through with Olympic gold, put up a sensational effort, skating with a previously unmentioned torn groin muscle. He was all heart, but he couldn't defeat a young Russian named Ilia Kulik, a fabulous skater who dressed like Ronald McDonald's wife. As one of the *Star* descriptions held, "His wardrobe suggests there's no light bulb in his closet."

The typical judging nonsense arrived in the ice dance competition, which was preordained by obviously arranged bloc voting. (I know, I know; stop me if you've heard that one before.) The victims, of course, were our plucky Canucks, Shae-Lynn Bourne and Victor Kraatz, who were doing a routine based on Riverdance, a popular Celtic dance program. It was a program the judges simply didn't buy. Neither, for that matter, did Russian beauty Pasha Grishuk, the gold-medal winner with partner Evgeny Platov. Grishuk and Platov had won Olympic gold in 1994 and something like 20 consecutive competitions and they were no fans of Bourne and Kraatz. At a competition earlier that year, Grishuk was sparring gently with the (mostly Canadian) press and someone mentioned their rivals' Riverdance routine. Grishuk practically spit.

"Ha. Reeverdance," she snorted. "It is notting. Why I could pick anyone and do Reeverdance." Then she looked directly at Steve Buffery of the *Toronto Sun*. Buffery was a wrestler in his day, short and stocky and strong and about as far as possible from the willowy, graceful types who figure skate.

"I could pick even you," she said to Buffery. "We do Reeverdance together and you see how well we do."

This, naturally, broke us all up. Nobody laughed harder

than Buffery and to this day, sneak up beside him and whisper "Reeverdance" and he'll snort with laughter.

One other moment from the White Ring endures as incredibly sad. For most sessions, a beautiful Russian woman sat alone in the stands, her expression never changing as she watched the competitions while fans gawked at her and whispered. It was Ekaterina Gordeeva, who had dominated pairs skating (two Olympic and four world titles) with her husband Sergei Grinkov before he dropped dead of a huge heart attack at age 28 during a practice session in November 1995. It was difficult to see her impassively watching skaters — usually of the type she and her husband regularly clobbered — mount the podium. As it said in my wrap-up column, "You never saw such sadness in a face. It would have made Chekhov write a play then and there."

One more from an ice dancing assignment: Now, ice dancing is one of those phony things that no one but the most devoted skating fan really takes seriously. But Bourne and Kraatz were widely beloved and medal threats, so we needed to cover them intensely. So out I went for the first compulsories, which turned out to be the dreaded paso doble. That's bullfight music, by the way. I got there before the start and saw there were 30 tandems skating. Our kids skated 30th. The good Russians were 29th. This meant, with rink floods and warm-ups and such, about four hours of bullfight music.

Well, there was zero chance of my sitting through that without mayhem ensuing. I had noticed on the bus ride to the White Ring that there was a driving range about a mile back. So I parked my computer at the rink and hiked back to the range, a double-decked beauty. It was the first time I ever hit golf balls that I paid for individually. You hit the ball, tap a button and a little metal arm swings another ball on to your tee. You paid so many yen per ball. I hit balls for about an hour, bought some food from a vending machine, because vending machines in Japan sell absolutely everything including hot soup, and wandered back to the arena. Got there in plenty of time to watch the warm-up and see the main contenders do the bullfight thing. Acted as if I'd been there all day.

For reasons mostly to do with a lack of talent, Canada had zero women competing in the women's figure skating singles. Even South Africa had a representative, but Canada didn't. With the U.S. women going one-two and very nearly sweeping the podium, one of my U.S. friends was sticking in the needle.

"Say, where are all your Canadian women?" she asked, which caused me to respond, "Same place as your men's hockey team, only sober."

The White Ring also was the site of short-track speed skating, and the Chinese were awfully powerful in most events, led by the terrific duo of Yang Yang and Yang Yang. That's right, two skaters each named Yang Yang. In order to differentiate, they were officially known as Yang Yang (A) and Yang Yang (S). You would think perhaps Yang Yang (B) for the second one, but no. Anyway, in the press room we called them Butch and Sundance. I think Sundance was slightly better.

Nagano itself was not a pretty place, but far from ugly. It seemed to be overloaded with Colonel Sanders chicken joints among the many U.S. fast-food chains. The hosts also were nutty about shoes. In the media village, each apartment had three or four bedrooms, with a common kitchen and TV room and washrooms. It also had a rack for shoes near the front door and signs posted saying we were not to put our shoes in our bedrooms. You would think, "Who would possibly care where we put our shoes at night?" but you would be wrong. They cared. Quietly, the shoe police came around with master keys, looking for anyone who left shoes in their bedrooms. The trespassing footwear would be taken out and put into the common shoe rack. After it happened two or three times, I woke up one morning to find a ticket by my bed — a handwritten warning that I was breaking the shoe rules. I started piling stuff in front of my bedroom door so they couldn't get in while I slept.

If that was a mistake, well, it was nothing compared to what happened to the *Star* crew. It was at Nagano that one of the most embarrassing and egregious screw-ups in *Toronto Star* history happened, with yours truly front and centre. There were five or six of us working those Games, and usually, once a day, we would meet for a quick beer somewhere and review our assignments, making sure we had everything covered.

Now, the Alpine skiing events were held about two and a half hours away by bus. Someone needed to get up by 4:30 a.m. to be on a bus in time to be set up at the ski-hill press centre by 8 a.m., when the racing was scheduled to start. Except the weather sucked. It was warm and foggy and the races kept getting postponed. One morning, after the early rise and the long ride, our bus pulled into the ski hill's bus depot to learn the race had already been wiped out for the day. We didn't even get off the bus, simply turned around and went home, a complete waste of five hours.

Because the race was postponed several times, every one of the *Star* people got to endure the wasted time. Life in big-city journalism, we figured. I know I went up to cover the men's downhill twice and never saw them go. Other people went on other days and came away empty.

So, one morning I wandered into the main press centre, on my way to speed skating or something. I sat with a couple of *Star* colleagues, inhaling coffee and jabbering. On the TVs came the men's downhill. Great. They're finally going to run the damned thing. We settled back to watch it for a while. One more *Star* person came in. Then one more. (Still no bulbs were lighted.) We crowded around to watch Brian Stemmle, a very popular Canadian skier, a guy who literally had almost been torn in half in a terrible wreck a few years earlier, take his place in the starting box.

"Who's up there for us?" asked the late Randy Starkman, our amateur sports guy and the country's leading Olympic reporter. We all began looking at each other, then we counted. All of us said, at pretty much the same time, "I thought it was you." The correct answer, of course, was no one; the assignment had fallen through the cracks. We had missed a meeting, or something.

"Holy shit!" we all said, then turned back to the TV set to see Stemmle about a half second ahead of the field at the early interval. "Holy shit!"

Now a half-dozen of us were scrambling to put on jackets and pool our cash, because someone was going to need to charter a taxicab immediately and pay the driver handsomely to get up there as fast as possible. Meanwhile, Stemmle was widening his lead.

We naturally wanted this guy to win — what a great story for a fine guy we all liked — but we also were wondering how we could miss such an enormous story and how we would live it down with our colleagues, to say nothing of our bosses.

Suddenly, within sight of the finish line and while leading by an uncatchable margin, Stemmle hit a rut and spun outside a gate. Disqualified. There's no sense pretending that the heartbreak we all felt for Stem wasn't mixed with just a little relief. We got as lucky as Stemmle was unlucky.

Earlier, curling was mentioned and naturally there was a story involved. The curling was held at a golf resort a short train ride away, before dozens of fans, although the crowd swelled to a couple hundred for the medal games. The late, great Sandra Schmirler won the first Olympic medal contested and Mike Harris's rink took silver for Canada on the men's side.

Now, Sandra and I had a history unlike any other, arising from the Canadian Olympic trials held nearly three months previously in Brandon, Manitoba. It was clear Schmirler's rink was the best, simply because there's never been a better one. But Canada has so many outstanding rinks that any one of the entrants had licence to win. Further, Schmirler had recently given birth to a baby and was still nursing.

The press room at the Brandon arena was located in the maintenance ring under the stands, where the Zambonis were parked and hockey nets stored and all kinds of junk and so on. The press room contained a few curtained-off tables, power cords, phone lines, a TV set and a coffee maker. All we needed. We had quick access to ice level for post-game interviews, but it was otherwise dark and empty beyond the curtain. One afternoon, shortly before a session started, I needed to find a men's room. Somebody said there was one on this level just on the other side of the rink. Walk around the dimly lighted ring and you'll find it, they said. So off I went, barely seeing where I was going in the dim light. I turned past a pole and just about jumped. People! And not just people, but Sandra Schmirler and a couple of her teammates. And not just Sandra but Sandra breastfeeding her baby.

Uhhhhhh, this was sensationally uncomfortable. I mumbled and stammered and turned away and pretty much ran back to the press room. A couple of hours later, Schmirler had beaten somebody and reaffirmed herself as the rink to beat, and so several of us trooped out to the ice to interview her. I am rather taller and larger than most reporters, but I tried to shrink and stand in the back row and keep my head down and ask no questions. I looked up once and found her staring right at me while she talked. Just glaring.

What to do? *Suck it up*, I told myself. *Don't pretend nothing happened.* I waited until the scrum broke up and inched over and said, "Uh, Sandra, listen. I'm real sorry. I was looking for —" and before I could grovel any further, she let out a big laugh and said to forget it. No big deal. She had, of course, recognized how uncomfortable I was and played me a little and she and her rink had enjoyed the stupid and uncomfortable look on my face.

After that, she was, naturally, a delight to deal with in Nagano and any other time I ran into her. Sadly, she contracted cancer not long after the Olympics and passed far too young, leaving a husband and two young daughters. A great lady all the way.

SYDNEY 2000

By the time Sydney arrived, the internet dominated our coverage. No longer were things written according to a newspaper schedule. It was all about speed now and keep piling it in. Somebody back home would sort it out and somebody else would read it. So we were told, from 9,000 miles away.

Given the time difference, half a world behind, work expanded to what felt like a 24/7 arrangement. There were fewer of the convivial, post-work assemblies, less storytelling and laughs with our fellow scribblers. Almost all our social activities now were limited to the media village, which was way the hell out there, up to 45 minutes from downtown, depending on traffic, and built on the site of a former (ahem) insane asylum. It was like a camp, hundreds of cabins in the woods — woods that were crawling with all kinds of deadly snakes and spiders, or so said the signs that warned us to stay on the paths.

Those signs might have been a phony; no bites were recorded. One side of the village was bounded by train tracks, one side by factories and the other two sides by the largest cemetery in the Southern Hemisphere. Not a lot of nearby social life and not a lot to see, then. Except, of course, for the fair-sized pen full of kangaroos in the middle of the village.

In the media village at the 2000 Sydney Olympics with, from left, Steve Brunt, Doug Smith, Chris Young and Randy Starkman.

One of our lot, a plaid-shirted outdoors enthusiast from the Canadian Press wire service, threatened to liberate those kangaroos, and one night, after we had primed ourselves with too much of a local nectar known as Victoria Bitters, a small squadron of us attempted to make his dream come true. Unfortunately, we learned the hard way that the fences were electrified. No kangaroos were harmed. Nor were any freed. You'll be happy to know I was 47 years old at the time. Going on 13, of course.

Those Sydney Olympics were not a great one for Canada. The 22 medals won in Atlanta dwarfed the 14 here, and five of those 14 came in brand new events, as the Olympics added all kinds of sports. The Games, I wrote, now featured four kinds of sports: track and field, swimming, ball games and Cirque de Soleil. One of the newbies, though, was women's pole vault, in which all of the entrants seemed to be stunningly good-looking. We all agreed it would become a weekly circuit, televised by FOX Sports, and called the League of Women Vaulters. Strangely, that did not happen.

Aside from the competitions which, as always, were pretty much outstanding despite some rain here and there, Sydney's accompanying noise often concerned drugs. Canada had an issue with the outstanding equestrian Eric Lamaze, who would miss his second consecutive Olympics because of cocaine issues, but in the bigger picture, the finger-pointing, lecture-prone United States was cruising for a doping bruising and got it.

The Americans had been covering up positive drug tests for years, at least partly to keep NBC's myth-making machinery running full speed. This suited the IOC because U.S. television money kept the Olympic financial pumps primed. But there was a fresh new anti-doping religion afoot in the U.S. (it probably started with baseball) and neither the IOC nor other countries felt like getting a lecture from the planet's biggest doping hypocrites.

Dick Pound, the long-time IOC member from Montreal and mahatma of the new World Anti-Doping Agency (WADA) whispered to me on the first Friday of the Games that the Americans were going to take a big hit any day now. I warned a few of my U.S. press-box friends to be ready, and on

Monday it hit: a failed dope test against world shot-put champion C.J. Hunter was reported in Norway.

That was enormous news, because C.J. Hunter, at the time, was married to Marion Jones, the queen of U.S. — make that world — track and field who was on yet another gold-medal quest in Sydney. Ooops. The circle around Marion was tightening, although it didn't become a noose for several years.

A hastily called press conference was arranged at Nike's local headquarters in Sydney and what a show it was. All a mistake, naturally. Johnnie Cochran, the man who got O.J. off, now was working to get C.J. off. Marion said she knew nothing, although she kissed her man goodbye and fled the scene very early to get to training. Hunter, of course, knew nothing and was shocked and said it had to be a food supplement. By long-distance video, they paraded a UCLA professor who said the science couldn't possibly be correct and, locally, they had a dietician or pharmacist or some kind of expert saying it was all a mistake. The debunker in the room was a man named Victor Conte and somewhere that name rang a distant bell.

Yes, that's it! Victor Conte was a bass guitar player for the great East Bay funk/horn band Tower of Power in the 1970s. One of my favourite bands, to be sure. And now he's a chemist, or something? What an accomplished individual.

Years later, of course, that same Victor Conte turned out to be the master of BALCO Labs, the Bay Area company that was handling the doping rituals for Barry Bonds and, of course, for Marion Jones, who was finally exposed as a massive drug fraud and even went to prison. By the time she entered the crowbar hotel, C.J. Hunter had long been discredited as a serial doper and rinsed as a husband. Conte likewise did a brief jail stint. That morning in Sydney, we knew none of this, and the yarn seems a lot better now than it did then.

One of the great stories that didn't have to do with drugs, however, involved Steve Nash and the Canadian basketball team, which put on a great show and nearly made it to a medal. Nash was brilliant and helped engineer an upset defeat of Australia with a dominating 15-assist game, silencing rowdy fans who had been serenading Canada by singing "Winter Wonderland."

The U.S. won the baseball gold in an upset, with old Blue Jay favourite Pat Borders leading the way. Highlight there was watching old phony Tom Lasorda, managing the U.S., get into it with a Spanish-speaking umpire. Lasorda took along an interpreter, former Blue Jay coach Eddie Rodriguez, and Lasorda would scream and rant and gesticulate at Rodriguez, who then turned around and screamed and ranted and gesticulated at the ump. Good theatre.

Best theatre of all, though, was on local TV every night, where a couple of sharp-tongued and hilarious comedians named Roy and H.G. spoofed on everything Olympian. It was unmissable. They had their own Olympic mascot, named Fatso the Big-Arsed Wombat. So popular did he become that people everywhere gave up on the "official" mascots, which were three sketchy characters that scared many children, and tried to buy Fatso merchandise. Except none existed.

The IOC went nuts, banned Fatso and his image from the Games and requested that Roy and H.G. explain to the world that Fatso was not, and ever would be, part of the festivities. It was wonderful stuff.

Two other things from Sydney. I learned that koala bears really stink and are nasty little bastards, and I got to see more royalty compete. An equestrian turned out to be Princess Haya of Jordan — she was Queen Noor's daughter — and while she did not do great, eliminated early, she became, as I wrote, the first princess in the Olympics since Carl Lewis.

You couldn't make a joke like that now without setting off the gay and lesbian cartel.

SALT LAKE 2002

When the five rings reconvened in 2002 in Salt Lake City — or Camp Fourwives, as I possibly uncharitably called it one day — much had changed in and around the Olympic movement. Juan Antonio the Marquess de Samaranch has turned the IOC reins over to an autocratic but unremarkable Belgian named Jacques Rogge, a man who quickly earned the nickname (at least from me) of Brussels Sprout.

There had been enormous scandal, involving bribes and salacious behaviour among IOC members at several levels concerning the awarding of the Games to Salt Lake. A corner was lifted at least briefly on the cover-up, revealing college tuitions handed out to relatives, ski vacations arranged and boob jobs for girlfriends in addition to the envelopes full of cash that had changed hands. In a city and state dominated and run by Mormons, LDS became an acronym not only for Latter-Day Saints but for Large-Dollar Scams.

Public and media taste for exposing more of the crimes, though, mostly evaporated in the wake of 9/11, the terrible day that certainly turned the focus of these Games, less than six months later, into a patriotic show of force for the United States. Keeping Team Osama off the premises became the main focus and despite (or perhaps because of) the endless security lineups and bomb-sniffing dogs and checks and double-checks and screaming sergeants, that part of it was successful. Other than time wasted for hundreds of thousands of athletes, officials, spectators, press, suppliers etc., all it cost was money. There were no disruptions. Plus the facilities, once you could get into them, were first-rate.

That's not to say everything went smoothly. The latest great figure skating debacle took over immediately. Canadians Jamie Salé and David Pelletier were screwed out of the gold medal in pairs by preordained, i.e. fixed, judging. The culprit was a French judge named Marie-Reine Le Gougne, who was acting on orders from the French skating federation. By cooking votes with the Russians and others, French ice dancers later would take that gold, after Elena Berezhnaya and Anton Sikharulidze won the pairs. Salé and Pelletier messed up the deal by being better and everyone knew it.

The plot, obvious from the get-go, quickly unravelled and the press and public wouldn't let go. Rogge sat by idly, suggesting (correctly) that it was a skating problem and not an IOC problem. But the noise got louder and louder. The rest of the Games were virtually ignored and NBC began getting antsy about trying to televise more skating when so clearly the fix had been in. The public may know in its heart of hearts that certain competitions are rigged, but they want to pretend otherwise and go ahead and root for the fairy tale. Faced with proof that the results are made of cheese, it will turn off the channel in a snit — and, in reality, this is what happened. Figure skating went from years of colossal viewership to merely good numbers after the exposure of this particular fraud.

As it said in the *Star*:

> *Deep within the IOC's bunkers, sports federation heads are putting pressure on [Rogge] to end this fiasco. Rogge cannot be happy that the first Games of his regime is all about cheating and the worst scandal in figure skating*

history, which, granted, is about two ticks this side of being the most fixed wrestling match in history.

Rogge was bombarded with complaints from the presidents of other international sporting federations, whose events were being virtually ignored in Salt Lake. Toronto's Paul Henderson, a Canadian IOC member and president of the World Sailing Federation, had no dog in the fight, since sailing was a Summer Olympic sport, but he was upset by Canadian Olympic Committee's dithering and inactivity on the matter. Henderson sat outside Rogge's office for hours until being granted an audience, at which he stressed the need for immediate action. Finally, the Brussels Sprout was prodded to get involved. He called in skating boss Ottavio Cinquanta and ordered a solution. Cinquanta, knowing his International Skating Union presidency carried with it an IOC membership, hummed and hawed for another couple of days before announcing the awarding of a second gold medal and telling the French judge to put on her mink and go home.

That called off most of the dogs, although it was a joke of a ruling. They pretended the French judge was a lone assassin here — I called her Marie-Reine Lee Harvey Gougne — and that there was no conspiracy. Canada got its gold medal and was happy. The Russians kept their gold and the French did indeed win the ice dance, so no squawks from either. NBC was happy because everyone watched the rest of the skating. The only casualty was truth and honesty.

There were other great memories from Salt Lake, including one of the most flawless free-skating performances in history, by Russia's Alexei Yagudin; double golds from Quebec short-tracker Marc Gagnon; and Beckie Scott winning bronze in cross-country skiing — another joke considering the two Russians who finished ahead of her both failed drug tests. Many months later, lawyers won her the appropriate gold in court.

Salt Lake also was the scene of the most bizarre Olympic event these two eyes ever witnessed, namely the men's 1,000-metre short-track final, and that includes both the final and what led up to it. A funny and quotable Australian named Steven Bradbury, usually an also-ran who was better known as a blade maker for some of the big-name skaters, advanced through the ranks by sheer luck; others fell down and he was so far behind he was able to skate around the pile and move up. He was third in his quarter-final when the top two tangled and fell. Advanced. He got through his semi-final this way, skating fourth of four on the last lap when the first three crashed. Advanced. Amazingly, in the five-man final, essentially the same thing happened. A last-lap crash wiped out the four skaters fighting for the medals within yards of the finish line and here came Bradbury, half a lap behind, weaving through the carnage to claim gold.

"Hang on," he said to himself. "This can't be right. I think I've won."

Later, the verb "to Bradbury" was included in the official Australian slang dictionary — who knew there was such a thing? — and it connotes a spectacularly ridiculous upset happening for reasons beyond comprehension. But good on Bradbury, who, quite correctly, viewed the fluke as some kind of cosmic payback for 12 years of toil and effort. He celebrated that very popular gold with his friends long into the Salt Lake evening at a bar called, fittingly, the Last Lap.

In terms of starting slowly and finishing correctly, the Canadian men's hockey team came through perfectly. Three days after the women won gold, the men's professionals beat the U.S. to return Canada to the Olympic podium — 50 years to the day since the last Canadian men to win hockey gold. The Canadians had struggled early in the competition and caught a huge break when the Swedes, who clobbered Canada 5-2 earlier, were upset in the elimination round by Belarus on a late goal from nearly centre ice that beat goalie Tommy Salo. This led to several cruel jokes, including my year-end suggestion that Salo be nominated for the Lou Marsh Award for having contributed the most to Canadian sporting success in 2002. That was about the mildest thing said to and about poor Salo, who was never the same afterward. (Imagine, too, how his life would have deteriorated in the age of social media.)

One last line lingers from Salt Lake, where it's not always easy to get a drink, but where junk food, particularly endless sweets and candy bars, more than made up the caloric difference. There was so much candy available, even at Olympic facilities, that I suggested Brigham Young must have crossed the desert to get here in a chocolate-covered wagon.

ATHENS 2004

What if they held an Olympics and nobody came? We almost found out in Athens, a Games best remembered, at least here, for drug scandal, whining and litigation and, most of all, empty seats.

To this day, I sort of pity the Greeks for this one. They built wonderful facilities, most of which have gone pretty much unused since the three-week festival, and spent upward of $2 billion on security alone. It turns out, they basically sowed the seeds for eventual national bankruptcy in so doing.

The morning we left Athens, a story in the local paper suggested a baby born that very morning would still be paying for the 2004 Summer Games when it was a pensioner. That didn't seem incorrect then and, given what has transpired since with the country's fiscal meltdown, it still rings true.

What did the Greeks get for their money? Not much. An estimated two million Athenians fled the city for the islands, as is their summer custom, and they were most decidedly not replaced by an influx of tourists. The Greeks' just-in-time delivery of the Games — workmen still were painting in my media village as I checked in and there were no light bulbs in the fixtures — had not inspired confidence in anyone who might have been planning a visit. That unsure status, coupled with the usual price gouging by hoteliers, led to Athens pretty much being a ghost town during the Games. On the other hand, traffic was more than manageable, tables were always available in restaurants and the only lineups were caused by security procedures at venues.

On the eve of the Games, the locals also were humiliated by two of their track stars, Kostas Kenteris and Katerina Thanou, who were forced to surrender their credentials for a shameful and bizarre ballet after three missed doping tests that allegedly involved a motorcycle accident and similarly alleged hospital stay.

For a slew of these reasons, the crowds for many early events seemed to be limited to friends and family. One late night I stopped off at the tennis venue because Venus Williams was playing. I counted the house at 15 fans. Never saw anything like that at any Olympics, before or since.

The wonderful old Panathinaikos Stadium, scene of the 1896 Olympics when the modern Games were resurrected, held archery. It sat in the shadow of the Parthenon and was as spectacular a venue as has ever been assembled for any Games that I saw. And it was virtually empty; crowds didn't exceed 400 when I was there and that was with capacity limited to 6,000 in the curved end of the horseshoe. Sad to see, actually.

Crowds crammed the swimming venue to see the great Ian Thorpe-Michael Phelps freestyle showdown — Thorpe won — and some other events drew well, but crowds were generally embarrassingly sparse until they started stuffing the stands with school children during the second week.

My own personal highlight in Athens, arranged by my pal Paul Henderson, was a day on the bay, or ocean or whatever it was, watching the sailing competition. I went out on a boat with a sophisticated and elegant group that included King Constantine II, the deposed but still tolerated king of Greece, and had a lovely day with my new pal Connie and several more of the blazer brigade, all of whom possessed a net worth several zeros beyond mine.

My sailing knowledge was limited to silently repeating the mantra "Port left, starboard right," but there was so much sailing talk flying around that I absorbed enough to write a story that made some sense when, as it happens, a couple of Canadians won a silver medal in one of the classes a few days later.

Other highlights included seeing kayaker Adam van Koeverden, an athlete I have grown to admire greatly, win his first Olympic gold. Greatest close-miss at Athens was seeing the Canadian baseball team come within one long fly ball that died at the wall of upsetting the mighty Cubans to get to the gold-medal game.

As well, Kyle Shewfelt won gold for Canada in gymnastics and might have won a bronze as well, but was nudged off the podium by a Romanian's artificially high marks as awarded by the judges. When Canada lodged a protest to the International Gymnastics Federation, the official who immediately dismissed the complaint just happened to be Romanian. This, of course, set off a frustrating series of failed appeals and spurred the kind of we-wuz-wobbed whining that marks too many

Olympics for Canada. Countries other than Canada squawked about phony marks as well, though; at one point, over-revved fans at the gymnastics pit carried on so long and loudly that athletes were unable to start their routines.

A few days earlier, out at rowing, a pair of Canadians had clearly come out of their lane late in a race and been disqualified for interference. The Canadian Olympic mandarins fought the referee's (absolutely correct) decision to the limit, appealing and re-appealing and petitioning the Court for Arbitration in Sport and completely wasting everyone's time.

These legal defeats, coupled with some famous flame-outs by Canadian world champions — Perdita Felicien, the men's rowing eights and diver Alexandre Despatie, among others — led to a relatively puny medal count, at least in relation to the past few Olympics, and to some serious complaining from back home. On the other hand, it did make the COA and, in particular, the organizing committee for the 2010 Winter Games, which had been awarded in 2003 to Vancouver, recognize the need to get Canada's competitive act together. When IOC president Jacques Rogge reaffirmed that he intended to journey to Ottawa to stress to Canada the importance of a strong competitive team for a home Games, the thrust for future Olympics had been made clear.

TURIN 2006

In terms of competition, the Turin Winter Games are best remembered by Canadians for Cindy Klassen's dynamic five-medal performance on the long track, and for Brad Gushue, the young Newfoundlander who had added 50-year-old Russ Howard to his rink of three guys half Howard's age, winning the men's curling gold medal and setting off an enduring party on The Rock.

There also were a couple of hockey bombs lobbed just before the start of the Games. The first was a bit of a gambling scandal involving the widely revered Wayne Gretzky. His buddy and assistant coach Rick Tocchet was alleged to have been running a bookmaking ring and one of his customers turned out to be not Gretzky himself but Gretzky's wife Janet Jones, who is alleged to have wagered $5,000 on the coin toss in the Super Bowl among $100,000 worth of action in a month. Things like that.

Naturally, Gretzky's many fans, including many in the media, bought his explanation that it was the wife who was taking a few flutters. Myself, I couldn't really care. Having always been fond of wagering, where possible, I begrudged no one a chance to send a little money for a ride now and then and this guy — I mean, this woman — betting 5K was like a regular stiff betting 20 bucks.

It also has been my experience that one of the most misunderstood aspects about sports, particularly by many members of the media, is gambling. An awful lot of people who should know something about it have no idea about it.

Naturally, and partly for that very reason, there was much hysteria when Gretzky showed up in Turin to watch his hockey team. (I asked, in print, who would be nominated as team croupier.) After a couple of tense days, Gretzky waltzed around the issue and as the tournament wore on and his team struggled, came up with some populist drivel about how all those other countries don't like Canada when it comes to hockey. (Really, Wayne? You think?) Ultimately, he should have stayed home; the team was lousy and finished seventh.

This, of course, turned out to be a good thing for Vancouver 2010. If Canada had won gold in 2002 and again in 2006, it would have brought a grim demand, reiterated for four years, that the nation win a third in a row on home ice — or else. But stinking in 2006, while painful at the time, certainly provided a much more welcome storyline for the intervening period: our plucky lads fighting for redemption on home ice, riding that wave of fan emotion, yada yada. (You know it turned just that way, prompting a national orgasm in 2010.)

The other pre-Games bombshell that dropped came from the wily Dick Pound, who suggested — quite correctly, I thought — that at least one-third of NHL players were using some kind of stimulant that would not pass muster with the World Anti-Doping Agency, which he was happily running from Montreal these days. Pound did not say steroids. He said stimulants. But most of the hockey world heard steroids and reacted with the predictable how-dare-he sputtering. Pound, who had known what was coming regarding C.J. Hunter (and, by close association, Marion Jones) back in Sydney in terms of leaked positive tests, calmly sat back as, within hours, a failed test was reported for Montreal goaltender José Theodore. The offending ingredient was a popular masking agent, which Theodore and his apologists claimed was a hair-growing agent. No one promoting that line of reasoning bothered to notice that Theodore had hair like a rock star.

Hockey shenanigans aside, Canada was getting its Olympic act together with a distant eye on Vancouver, riding success in some of the cool new sports to 24 medals. Jennifer Heil had started the parade wonderfully with an early gold medal in what my old pal Patrick Reusse of the *Minneapolis StarTribune* called "twirlybird skiing." Heil was No. 1 in the world and, as I pointed out at the time, winning when you're expected to win is one of the toughest tasks in sports.

The greater beauty of covering these Games was in the

At the bottom of the ski hill, just outside the mixed zone, at the 2006 Turin Olympics. Notice the same old hat.

city itself: wonderful food and outstanding (and inexpensive) local wines. Volunteers once again were terrific and helpful and while security was everywhere in massive numbers, there seldom was any kind of issue or even long delay. As colleague Rosie DiManno, who speaks Italian, correctly surmised, the cops' main job seemed to be to stand around smoking cigarettes and fiddling with the crease in their pants.

As usual, the tragedy and comedy came thickest at the figure skating rink, where Emanuel Sandhu, the talented but pea-hearted Canadian skater, once again fell apart on the big stage. Sandhu, I suggested, "turned more triples into singles than Vernon Wells." No one was a match for Evgeni Plushenko, who became Russia's fourth consecutive men's singles Olympic champion, but flamboyant American Johnny Weir at least gave a good quote when asked, before the long program, if he thought he would need to include a quad jump he had been practising, in order to move up into the medals. Weir responded it all would be determined by how well he slept. "If I wake up tomorrow looking like Nick Nolte's mug shot, there's no quad," he said.

There wasn't one. Nor was there a medal for Weir, as Jeffrey Buttle, a real gentleman who competed for Canada and a world silver medallist, jumped onto the podium for bronze.

My absolute favourite moment from Turin happened a couple of hours away, in Milan. It was Fashion Week and, in a brilliant idea that I claim as my own, I had suggested a swap. On a quiet day, I would train over and "cover" a couple of fashion shows and our fashion writer would come over on a slow day and "cover" an Olympic event for which we could get him a ticket. We got him into speed skating and he did a nice takeout on the neon-orange outfits of the Dutch, but I had the better end of this deal.

I got up early and took the morning train to Milan. Two

things I needed to see: La Scala, the world's greatest opera house, and the old Esso station, or whatever it has since become, where they strung up Mussolini and Clara Petacci in the waning days of the war. Don't ask why; I just like seeing the scenes of famous events. (I never once went through Dallas without walking over to Dealey Plaza and looking up at the sixth-floor window.)

It worked out nicely, even for a guy who thought every shirt came with a golf course's logo on it and whose sense of proper colour was limited to wearing a brown necktie to complement yellow teeth. I began my piece like this:

> *One prepares for Fashion Week by covering Olympic ice dancing, where it's about feathers, billowy chiffon, sequins and overdone eye makeup. And that's just the guys.*

It went on for a while, ran on the front page and was a big hit, judging by the reaction. If someone put a gun to my head, after 40-plus years in the typing business, I'd have to say it was my favourite piece.

BEIJING 2008

China spent something like $41 billion on this burst onto the world sporting stage and for the first time, at least in my experience, the IOC became strictly a passenger at its own event. The hosts ran the show completely while the IOC sat by, somewhat nervously, with no idea what was coming next.

For instance, the IOC had promised there would be no website censorship by the Chinese government and vowed it would countenance none of it. In reality, China censored websites at will and the IOC, despite its explicit denials, had signed off on the practice and was exposed as being meekly complicit. No one should have been surprised.

When three protestors with a hands-off-Tibet message climbed on a huge Olympic display to unfurl a banner, in full view of and filmed by media, they were hauled down and taken away by troops. At the daily IOC briefing when questions were put about the situation, the answer initially was, "We have no idea what incident you are asking about. We will look into it." That bullshit answer arrived for a couple of days, then morphed into the IOC spokesman saying, "We have already answered that question." Which, of course, they never had. No one ever found out what had happened to the protesters. But we could guess.

When a spectacular opening ceremonies was revealed to have relied on lip-synching kids and fake-fireworks videos, all subsequent queries were dismissed. Distasteful or potentially embarrassing events simply became non-events, officially, and the IOC promoted every charade and sanctioned all official dishonesty.

Late in the competition, a wondrous Chinese gymnast named He Kexin performed amazingly well on the uneven bars to win two gold medals. It turned out she probably was too young to participate in the Games and that officials apparently had fiddled with her birth certificate to make her appear old enough. Those experienced in data archaeology found enough well-buried documents online to raise legitimate questions, before the documents disappeared as well, but by that point, with China closing in on an astounding final total of 51 gold medals, neither the IOC nor the gymnastics federation was interested in handing out any speeding tickets. The IOC, of course, would always look the other way when official blindness suited its purposes.

Despite the beating that truth took almost daily, the Beijing Olympics overall were a delight to experience because of the variety of compelling local stories. For instance, I went out to both badminton and table tennis — and never, under any circumstance, could you call the latter ping-pong without starting trouble. Those were two of the more beloved national pastimes. Both barely register in Canada, of course, but both were played with amazing skill and speed before screeching crowds of appreciative fans in Beijing. It compared to, say, covering cross-country skiing in Norway, where sold-out crowds of enthusiastic locals both understood and celebrated every nuance of the sport. These were memorable assignments, even though I would need to look up who beat whom to win what medal. But I figured I was there for the bells and whistles, not to write the results sheet.

Other rock-star moments for Chinese athletes included boxer Zou Shiming, a world-class light-flyweight who navigated through his opposition all the way to the entirely expected gold medal. Boxing, you might recall, had been closely identified with Western brutality by Mao Tse-tung and banned nearly 50 years before. It had been resurrected only in 1991 and Shiming was the leader of this new, modern national charge. So compelling was this terrific little fighter than even Don King, the ex-con promoter who could make boxing veterans count their fingers after a handshake, stood and waved a small Chinese flag as Shiming entered the ring.

Beyond the numerous Chinese successes at home, Beijing produced the stage for two other world superstars, two men who joined the greatest-ever conversations in their respective sports.

Michael Phelps, the Baltimore Bullet, won his eight gold medals in the pool and the *Star*'s assignment schedule ended up putting me at five of them. The only challenge was finding different ways to say essentially the same things about this amazing athlete.

The other superstar, probably even a bigger one given his charismatic performances, was Usain Bolt, who swept the three sprint golds (100 and 200 metres and 4 × 100-metre relay) in breathtaking style. The Jamaican women also flew all week and except for a dropped baton in the women's relay, Jamaica would have swept all six sprint golds. Meanwhile, the once-mighty Americans had been shut out, and that in itself was another story.

In that 100 final, as Bolt zipped past my seat, which was about 15 metres short of the finish line, he already was safely in front and cruising, spreading his arms and looking around. When his 9.69-second world-record time flashed, the only question was whether we had seen the greatest sprint in history. I surmised that basically the only greater run was yet to come, when he needed to bear down to the finish line and would go even faster. Donovan Bailey, who had been That Guy in 1996, was in the press section and suggesting Bolt had a 9.50 in him waiting to be released. Who could disagree?

(Aside here: people sometimes ask me to identify the greatest event I ever covered in my 40 years of witnessing top-level sport. Without being too specific, this event fits easily into my top five, for sure.)

One other story emerged from the Bird's Nest, the huge, new, 80,000-seat stadium that was the centrepiece of the extensive Olympic venue construction. It was deathly hot down in the bowels of the stadium, where the press rooms were, and one busy evening, I wandered upstairs for some fresh air. I was leaning on one of the walls, chatting with a colleague, and when it came time to leave, the back of my shirt was absolutely covered with concrete dust. I put my hand on the wall and started to flake off thumb-sized chunks of concrete. This did not promote much confidence in local construction practices. Ever since, I have expected to read a story about the Bird's Nest falling down, or being condemned.

The day after the Games ended, a half-dozen *Star* people went to tour the Great Wall and while it was touristy, simply walking it was a thrill, of course. But I couldn't understand how the same people who built this wonder of construction, for 4,000 miles over 1,000 years of basically hand labour, also built a stadium I could have started taking apart with my bare hands. It made no sense to me.

As far as Canadian results, the men's rowing eights happily rebounded from their disaster in Athens to win one of the country's three golds (in 302 events) and 18 total medals. This was up from the dozen won in Athens, which set off the usual round of back-patting by the Canadian Olympic Committee, but with the next Games scheduled for Vancouver, my suggestion was that the COC would do better to switch the focus from total medals won to gold medals won. Then again, as we were to reaffirm less than two years later, it was simply easier to move the goalposts after the fact.

VANCOUVER 2010

These turned out to be a different sort of Olympics for me and not only because Canadian athletes finally and emphatically shed the weight of previous home-game failures. After becoming the only country in history not to win a gold medal at home — in Montreal in 1976 — and then matching that dubious feat in Calgary in 1988, the home team rebounded with a sensational 14 gold medals, an Olympic Winter Games record. The capper was the men's hockey triumph, achieved on Sidney Crosby's overtime goal against the game U.S. side.

What was different for me was location. Given the pre-Games fears about travel up to the Alpine and sliding events in the mountains at Whistler, the *Star* decided to anchor two of us, myself and reporter Kevin McGran, in a condo at Whistler, leaving all other Olympic events to what we called the flatlanders.

This, as you can imagine, was not particularly heavy lifting and given that I had already accepted a buyout package from the newspaper and planned to depart full-time work at the end of the coming summer, this seemed an ideal way to work my 10th and final Olympics. After all, Whistler is a great little town, we were only minutes walk from a short bus ride to skiing or cross-country or a chairlift ride to the sliding centre. Plus, our condo had a hot tub and a propane grill. After years of covering Olympics in villages that featured beds resembling ironing boards, this was living large.

Alas, the incident that scarred these Vancouver Games, particularly in the world's view, happened the morning the opening ceremonies were to take place, down there in Vancouver. Along with several other journalists, I took in luge practice at the sliding centre, a new and ultra-fast track built for these Games. Canadian officials, proprietors of the Own the Podium program designed to heap Canadian medal totals as high as possible, had been openly boasting about restricting practice opportunities on Olympic facilities for non-Canadian athletes. These were certainly not the first Games where such restrictions were put in place; sportsmanship goes only so far.

One of those practising that morning was a young Georgian named Nodar Kumaritashvili. He had been mentioned, by name, by at least one Canadian coach as being among the sliders for whom practice restrictions could be a problem. There was a feeling that it might be too much track for him at this early stage of his young and promising career. Jeff Blair, then of the *Globe and Mail*, and I discussed this as we stood in one of the press viewing areas, up the track from the finish line, as Kumaritashvili set off. We watched his run on the large video screens, then looked on in horror as he lost control toward the finish line and was launched up and out of the track, slamming backward into a steel support pole, his head hitting first. The noise itself was awful, a dull thud followed by a lesser clatter as his sled bounced to a halt, then silence everywhere. Soon, screams and sobs filled the side of the hill.

It was clear almost immediately, at least to us, that he was dead. No one could survive that terrible impact, the way his head hit the pole. We moved down toward the victim and got close enough only to see that his helmet, split in the back, was full of blood. He was being given chest massage, but it was clear the poor kid didn't have a chance, even before the ambulance arrived.

I used my cell phone to call the paper and tell them I suspected we had a fatality and began dictating details for a quick website story. Once the press was tossed out of the area where the victim was, I collected quotes and more details from witnesses and kept filing to the paper's website.

Soon my BlackBerry began to whistle and pop with angry emails. Back at One Yonge, the *Star* website was using my early words along with a video showing the gruesome crash. I had no knowledge of what was on the website, being up on a mountain without internet capabilities. People were calling me every kind of name — blaming me personally for daring to show this video — although I had no idea what was being shown, or what video existed. (The *Star* soon stopped showing it, which only marginally cut down on the electronic hate mail.)

Official word of the young man's death was hours away. In the meantime, wildly inaccurate information was dispensed from official sources, including the fable that he was fine and had already left hospital. One colleague in Vancouver, whom I will not embarrass by naming, said she had good local sources that assured her Kumaritashvili was fine and only a little bit banged up. She naively began reporting that, despite my assurances that her information was not possibly correct, based solely on what I had seen.

There also became this matter of restricting the practice time of non-Canadian athletes and, as usual, the mandarins disappeared or backpedalled all they could. People who had been boasting about it the day before now were trying to deny they had done it. (In a related note, a Norwegian skier named Aksel Lund Svindal teed off on an anonymous Own the Podium zealot who had thrown Svindal off the Olympic hill months previously when he had been invited to join in training with Canadian Alpine skiers. Regardless, Svindal won silver in the downhill and gold in the Super-G while Canadians were completely shut out of Alpine medals in a terrible performance. Svindal didn't mention, but some of us did, that it had been a Norwegian coach, at a previous Olympics, who passed along a ski pole to Beckie Scott after she broke hers, thus helping her continue her run to a medal. Some people have vastly different definitions of sportsmanship.)

Back in Whistler, after the IOC and VANOC, the local organizing committee, confirmed the athlete's death, they then disgraced themselves by loudly maintaining that they were blameless, that the track was blameless, that it was strictly driver error. Surely there was some element of driver inexperience, but other tracks didn't kill young drivers who made mistakes. Within 24 hours, the Whistler track had been modified, with higher walls built toward the bottom and padding put on the steel poles. More significantly, the starting points for the coming races were lowered dramatically, so much so that many athletes griped. Alex Gough of Canada was extremely angry, given that she had practised on the track repeatedly from one starting point and now was forced to use one, as she said, "Where the 13-year-old girls start."

The effect of the accident, the first on-field death of an Olympic athlete in modern Games history, naturally left a heavy cloud over the Games, particularly in Whistler and especially at the sliding centre, where numerous wrecks in all events, most of them at the particularly difficult Turn 13 that the athletes quickly nicknamed 50-50 for their chances to get through it, resulted in everyone holding his or her breath until the flipped-over athlete got up and walked away. Some sliders simply couldn't perform to their capabilities, some lost sleep and many did what competitive athletes in speed sports almost never do: they spoke of their fears. Skeleton champion Melissa Hollingsworth, who had been as much of a pre-Games lock for a medal as any Canadian athlete, seemed particularly affected and missed the podium in her specialty. She handled her disappointment with grace, but we all felt her disappointment — and felt for her.

Four Canadians did eventually win sliding medals, a 1-2 finish in the women's bobsled the highlight, but Kumaritashvili never really left anyone's thoughts. In a wrap-up column, after a Canadian bronze medal in the four-man bobsled, mention was made of driver Lyndon Rush's habit of reciting scripture to calm himself in the starting blocks.

> *On this track, which carried with it a Games-long sense of further impending doom since the death of the young Georgian luger, whatever works is to be*

> *respected. It isn't often you hear high-performance athletes talk so openly and nakedly about fear, but plenty of them spilled it here the past two weeks. This was a scary place and there's a strong sense of relief, at least here, that it's over.*

It wasn't all doom and gloom, of course, even with the tragedy weighing everything down. Canada's Jon Montgomery won a skeleton gold medal and then went on a joyous, beer-fuelled and totally unscripted walk through town to the outdoor TSN studio. Hundreds of fans escorted and toasted him and it was wild and spontaneous fun; an entire town celebrating a gold medal and a gold medallist, and even the cops, watching all this booze flow in the streets, just smiled and made sure nobody got stupid.

One other moment came from the cross-country pit, where Norwegian Odd-Bjørn Hjelmeset furnished what might have been, pound for pound, the best quote ever received from any athlete in my four-plus decades of scribbling. Hjelmeset had a weak second leg, in the middle of Norway's silver-winning relay, and wasn't shy about explaining why.

"I skied the second lap and I fucked up today," he said. "I think I have seen too much porn in the last 14 days. I have the room next to [teammate Petter Northug] and every day there is noise in there. So I think that is the reason I fucked up today."

Then he added, unbidden and out of left field and referring to a bizarre public mea culpa made earlier that day several thousand miles away, "By the way, Tiger Woods is a good man."

Sometimes asking the simple question, "What happened out there?" will be a different kind of gold strike.

CHAPTER TWENTY-TWO

Mistakes? I've Made a Few

Anyone who stays in the newspaper business long enough will make mistakes, and I've certainly made my share. At various times I can blame lack of concentration, laziness, carelessness, pressure of deadlines, forgetfulness, poor note-taking, poor judgement, misremembering, confusion or garden variety stupidity. I can honestly say I never hit the "send" button knowing something was wrong, although many times I did hit that button when, it turns out, stories contained incorrect information.

I got scores wrong in games, although generally the copy desk, our last line of defence, would bail me out. This occurrence was more common than you might think, given the way we used to write stories on deadline, constructing them as the game went along and then going back in and filling in final details. Occasionally, a ninth-inning run or an empty-net goal might be neglected. Usually, this kind of error would snap my head off the pillow about 3 a.m. and make a night's sleep miserable while I worried whether the goof-up had been caught.

Most of my mistakes had to do with failure to adequately read fortunes and predict the future. So many times, things of which I was certain failed to come to pass. For instance, I thought Tiger Woods would come back from his run-in with that fire hydrant and the 2009 infidelity scandal that flatlined his major championship career, and he'd resume his lifelong hunt to surpass the 18 professional major titles won by Jack Nicklaus. After chronicling 13 of his 14 major championships, and seeing up close for a decade the way most of his competition seemed to absolutely melt when Woods was leading, I thought he would get at least some of his major-championship mojo back. Non-stop injuries interfered, certainly, and it didn't happen, at least for the first seven-plus years since that last win at the 2008 U.S. Open.

I badly underestimated the fallout from baseball's steroid scandals of the early 2000s. I always suspected Barry Bonds would be a lock for the Hall of Fame regardless of the overwhelming evidence of his juicing. Missed that one by a mile, apparently, and Bonds wasn't the only one I whiffed on. Try this paragraph on for size, in a 2003 column discussing Sammy Sosa's bust for using a corked bat:

> *Sosa isn't the first cheater and he won't be the last and he needn't worry about Cooperstown, either. Gaylord Perry thrived for 23 years with an illegal pitch and made the Hall of Fame, as Sammy surely will. He and baseball are embarrassed now, but long-term he won't be cork-screwed.*

Thirteen years later and still no induction. Nice call there, wasn't it?

One time at baseball's winter meetings, I pulled a dumb move and was embarrassed. The Blue Jays had agreed to terms with the agent for a middling relief pitcher, but the deal was on hold pending the pitcher's final approval. Except he was out in the bush somewhere on an off-season hunting trip, killing animals with soft brown eyes. Hmmmm. No way did I want to wait a day and let the competition sniff out that name first. So I parsed the list of free agents and came up with a couple of possibilities. One of them was a pitcher named Jay Howell, at the time a member of the Los Angeles Dodgers. I asked around and discovered that he had been on Toronto's radar. I worked a Dodger writer friend and came up with a home number and called it. Someone I presumed was Mrs. Howell said I couldn't talk to Jay. Sorry, he's not here. No, he's out on his annual hunting trip.

Well, that was enough for me. (Did I mention the part about me being lazy or careless or just stupid?) The next day's *Star* carried a couple of paragraphs from me about the newest Blue Jay, namely Jay Howell. Except, of course, it wasn't him. It was entirely somebody else. I ran a correction and felt like an idiot and once again vowed to myself to always, but always, get that second source to confirm. The other part of the story is that when it came to the vast majority of Americans playing big-league baseball in those days, huntin' and fishin' seemed to fill their off-seasons completely. At any given time, I'm guessing three-quarters of them are out doing one or the other. (Perhaps I exaggerate slightly.)

Part of the sportswriting dodge is setting up events and that naturally involves the occasional prediction. Occasionally, I guessed right about what would transpire. Just as often — meaning hundreds of times — I would misread all tea leaves and have no firm handle whatsoever (please see earlier mea culpas about Barry Bonds and Tiger Woods). For instance, after seeing

Oakland run all over Boston in the 1988 American League Championship Series, I slid down to Los Angeles to witness the Dodgers destroying the Mets to win the National League pennant, then declared the coming World Series to be no contest:

> *The Dodgers won the National League pennant last night and it's tempting to say Oakland Athletics won the World Series, too. Unless Orel Hershiser can pitch every day — and don't bet against him trying — Oakland might just kill these guys.*

Thanks to Kirk Gibson's miracle limp-off home run off Dennis Eckersley a couple of nights later, we all know who killed whom. Two years later, having seen Oakland once again stroll to the World Series (and win it in 1989, the intervening year), I boldly suggested the poor overmatched Cincinnati Reds might just as well stay home and read a book as show up in the World Series. Naturally, the Reds then swept the Athletics. As I got used to saying, "I get sick of being right."

Occasionally, a print proclamation made me correct, but only for a while. For instance, after a disappointing 1988 season, I suggested Pat Gillick had a small core of players, including Fred McGriff, whom he would not trade "for an extra year of life." That turned out to be true, except two years later he traded McGriff in the blockbuster for Roberto Alomar and Joe Carter. There being no internet around to record all the written foolishness, the readers seem to have forgotten that earlier declaration.

The arrival of the internet changed everything. Now, every single word that is published is fair game for comment or challenge, and two truisms seem to be firmly in place: when you are right, no one ever remembers and when you are wrong, no one ever forgets.

Typographical errors, which are simply an unfortunate part of doing business on a deadline, are never forgiven. Opinions are derided and ridiculed, facts are challenged and accused of masking an agenda. The level of anger, even hatred, is barely civil. We know all that.

A word about typos. Every now and then you get a good one that makes everyone laugh, at least until the online whackos get revved up. In my time, the best one I ever saw was in a football story, where the New York Jets somehow became the New York Jews. Some people went, as you can imagine, completely nuts.

The best typo I ever committed was in a cutline, when I was the overnight sports layout man and editor at the *Star* and the last man to touch the content for the (long since departed) afternoon edition. If there was a mistake, or a typo, it was on me. There was a good action shot from a hockey game, the goaltender doing the splits and the puck trickling off his toe and into the net. This I described in the cutline as, approximately, "Joe Blow's shot trickled down Fred Smith's leg and into the net." Except instead of typing "shot" I typed "shit" and there it was, in about 300,000 *Toronto Star*s, the shit running down the goalie's leg and into the net. The sports editor at the time, an ex-Marine named Paul Warnick, tried to give me hell later on, but he was laughing too hard.

Occasionally, well-meaning copy editors make a change that doubtless made sense to them at the time. For instance, Glen Abbey Golf Course outside Toronto contains a river named Sixteen Mile Creek. That is its name. At the *Hamilton Spectator* one day, that river came out as 23 Kilometre Creek, someone having helpfully converted to metric.

One time, writing about Phil Mickelson, who in this opinion is golf's $3 bill, I mentioned that his nickname among his fellow players is FIGJAM. That is an acronym for Fuck I'm

Good Just Ask Me. Because the *Star* is a family newspaper, I got around this (or so I thought) by explaining FIGJAM as Blank I'm Good Just Ask Me. I assumed readers could figure it out. Alas, our copy editor could not. He read what I wrote, decided it wasn't worth a phone call to clarify, and changed the acronym to BIGJAM. When I raised hell the next day, he accused me of somehow not knowing what letter the word Blank started with. I held my head, near tears.

One of my favourite nutty errors was a subject of discussion at the *Globe and Mail* when I was starting out. There was a legendary Toronto wrestler named Whipper Billy Watson who did tireless work for the Ontario Society for Crippled Children, as it was called then. One year, the society honoured Watson with a high-end gala dinner. The *Globe* had a snooty society columnist named Zena Cherry, who knew the forks, as we used to say about the swells with the high-society manners. Zena Cherry would know her way around charity dinners, for sure, but wrestlers? Might as well ask her to identify Martians.

The Whip attended with his wife. He was allowed to bring two guests, so he chose one of his great rivals at the time, who wrestled under the name of Lord Athol Layton. Now Athol Layton, who entered the ring wearing royal purple coronation robes and often delayed his matches while he enjoyed a spot of tea, was actually an Australian amateur boxer who had taken up wrestling. He was as far from Burke's Peerage as the rest of us. But that didn't stop the next day's *Globe* from printing, in Zena Cherry's column, that among the guests honouring Mr. Watson were the right honourable so-and-so and lieutenant-governor so-and-so and his honour such-and-such and "Lord and Lady Athol Layton." It had happened years before, but they were still chuckling about it at the *Globe* when I got there.

The greatest close-call error, one that would have launched

a gigantic lawsuit, happened at the *Globe and Mail* very early in my career. It was in the hot-type days, when newspaper pages were assembled individually within metal frames, using lines of type freshly made from molten lead. The type and headlines and pictures, in the form of engraved plates, were assembled by skilled compositors. The pictures, which came out of the engraving department, usually were the last addition to a page before it was sent to be made into the rollers that would fit on the printing press. One night, on the front page of the *Globe*, there was a story about the invasion of the Chinese cockroach, some new kind of marauding bug that had arrived on a ship in the harbour and was spreading across downtown. There was a one-column picture of said Chinese cockroach. In those days, one-column pictures were three inches deep and were called, for simplicity's sake, a "one by three." Elsewhere on the page was a story about a local city councillor, a respected individual named Ying Hope. It likewise was accompanied by a head shot of Mr. Hope, a "one by three." Under each picture was an indentifying cutline, sometimes called a caption. One said, naturally enough, "Ying Hope." The other said, equally understandably, "Chinese cockroach." They were on opposite sides of the page.

The compositor, a growly old cigar smoker, was pushing the otherwise-completed front page on its wheeled table toward a proof-making machine when he was handed the pair of one-by-three cuts, as the pictures were called. The top cut was the picture of Ying Hope. He said, out loud, "Who's the Chinaman?" The comp looked down, saw the word "Chinese" in the cutline and immediately assumed that's where Mr. Hope belonged. He put Ying Hope's picture above the words "Chinese cockroach" and the other cut, the cockroach, in the only other open space, the one reserved for Ying Hope. Didn't bother looking at either one closely. And away went the page to be made into printing plates, the two pictures located incorrectly.

A senior editor scurried upstairs with a page proof and the rest of the composing room departed for the dinner break, the front page always being the last page to leave the composing room floor. Moments later, from halfway down a hallway, came a blood-curdling scream and here came the editor, running like Usain Bolt. The mistake was caught and the plates were switched before they could do any damage.

Eventually the laughing stopped. But what an expensive and humiliating disaster it could have been.

Aside from typos and garbled stories and human error and carelessness and the rest, there's another kind of error that all media outlets made, which I would call the error of omission. That would be ignoring the items that don't fit an editor's desires. For instance, the *Toronto Sun*, whose founding sports editor was very close to Alan Eagleson, never printed even the charges filed against the former head of the hockey players' union. When Eagleson pleaded guilty, in a Boston court, to a number of charges, the *Sun* devoted only a handful of paragraphs to what was, in Canada, a huge story. That's a different kind of mistake. Other papers, the *Star* included, likewise would sometimes park stories that were inconvenient to its editorial position.

For instance, a couple of the higher-ups were very pro-Olympics for Toronto and backed the city's bid for the 2008 Summer Games in particular. I, on the other hand, was dead set opposed to it and opined regularly against them for various reasons that mostly had to do with the irresistible opportunity for corruption by the usual suspects. The only time, in my 33 full-time years at the *Star*, that I had a column killed was when the International Olympic Committee's evaluation panel was visiting Toronto to make its interim report on the city's suitability to play host to an Olympics. I wrote a please-not-us piece. It never saw the light of day, a call from the top that was not entirely unexpected. Sometimes publishers like to pretend they know better.

The only time I ever saw my newspaper publish something known to be flat-out wrong happened when I was sports editor, although it was on the letters page and not in the real newspaper. The letters page is one of those things that upper-level editors at a paper pretend to take seriously, but few working journalists pay much attention to on a regular basis. Most of the letters that get published in the *Star* have a trendy-lefty ring to them, at least in my opinion.

In April 1994, there was a women's world hockey championship played in Lake Placid, N.Y. The pinnacle of women's hockey was extremely limited, basically a Canada-U.S. showdown every time, but it was going to be included in the Olympics beginning in 1998. I thought we should cover it, so I dispatched Mary Ormsby to handle it. Guess what? Mary was the only journalist from a Canadian newspaper to attend. All the rest let the wire services handle it for them. Canada beat the U.S. to win the gold medal. Hooray and all that. The *Star* was there. Mary wrote good stuff. Good for us.

Now fast-forward several months. The NHL, having locked out its players in a salary dispute (and not the last one), was not operating. Television was looking for sports programming to fill the vast gaps and feed the hockey-starved masses. One evening TSN, the national sports channel, dragged out the tape of the gold-medal final from the previous April's world women's hockey championships and showed it on replay. Amazingly enough, just like all those months before, Canada beat the U.S. to win the gold medal.

Two days later, one of the compositors called me out to the back shop, as we called the composing room, and pointed to a letter already sitting in its place on the next day's letter page. This was a couple of hours to deadline. The letter was ripping the sports department and its Neanderthal and clearly misogynist sports editor. Why? For failing to run one word about Canada's tremendous win this week in the women's world championships. Imagine that, the letter said: Here are our brave Canadian women beating those nasty Americans and the sexist pigs at the *Star* ignore it. Oh, you damnable men! How dare you!

Well, I thought, this was idiotic. This stupid letter writer did not understand she was watching a replay from many months ago. Further, the *Star* had been the only paper in the country to cover the damned thing when it was happening, but now here I am getting called names for ignoring it.

Except our letters-page editor refused to pull it. She said no, that's this reader's opinion and it is going to run. She is entitled to her opinion and blah, blah. Naturally, I blew up and began using, shall we say, harsh language. But the letter ran. I followed it up the next day and, during the autopsy, which is held when a particularly insane error makes it into print, the managing editor zinged her for running such a stupid thing. Still, I was ashamed that the paper would knowingly run something it knew to be 100 percent incorrect. I still am. We made enough errors for all those other reasons, without making any on purpose.

CHAPTER TWENTY-THREE

The Most Honest Man

As much of a proud Canadian as I am, I would not profess to be much of a hockey fan. At least not as an adult.

As a kid, I knew every player in the six-team NHL, knew most of their numbers and could recite the makeup of the forward lines. Somewhere around the time I attained an age at which I discovered new essentials of life, like girls and alcohol, other items fell out of the rotation. Hockey was one of them. You could only take so much of a terrible Maple Leafs team and still want to pay attention.

Meanwhile, as the Leafs stayed lousy, team ownership — the dreary succession of Harold Ballard to Steve Stavro to Maple Leafs Sports and Entertainment — represented a deeply mired civic disgrace. They were not only awful on the ice, they were mostly awful to deal with, insatiable money-grabbers who would bilk, respectively, their own company, charities and taxpayers. No one could piss in your ear and tell you it was raining like a Maple Leaf owner.

A defenceman named Dmitri Yushkevich, a pretty decent defender, departed the Maple Leafs after a salary dispute and did us all in the typing pool a large favour. He identified Carlton Bear, the extremely unfunny and inconsequential mascot, as being the most honest man in the organization. Why? Because Carlton Bear cannot talk. "No one at Maple Leaf Sports and Entertainment denies the charges," I opined in the *Star*. "Nor does Carlton."

Once, the Leafs were in some kind of loose negotiations to acquire Eric Lindros. Not long before, while he was at his peak with the Philadelphia Flyers, I had referred to Lindros as Canada's "only man in the past, oh, 25 years to say no to Quebec." That was in reference to his draft-eligible avoidance of La Belle Province, and yes, there were a few outraged letters when I pointed out the reality. When the Leafs were trying to obtain him in late 2000, Lindros's concussion woes were in the process of completely derailing his once-promising career. He still had some value, although any deal eventually was snookered by Flyers' GM Bob Clarke, with whom Lindros was feuding. Here's how it came out in the run-up:

> *Yesterday, Lindros made clear his desire to join the Leafs. He actually suggested "it's a great organization" and right there you wonder if he has been wearing his helmet enough.*
>
> *This once was a great organization, sure. Then the owner went to jail, glorious history was ignored, the pedophilia scandal was exposed and, well, you know the stories. The only thing "great" about the organization is its loyal support from its long-starved customers.*

That pretty much summed everything up, and please note that was more than 15 years ago. Not much has changed in the interim, especially regarding starving fans.

There were, surely, some outstanding individuals to deal with over the years there. The players, mostly, were good-humoured and civil enough, even while being endlessly chewed on by the great media beast in Toronto. Bobby Hunter and Pat Park were always first-rate to deal with out of the front office. Coaches Mike Murphy, Pat Quinn and Paul Maurice understood that their responsibilities included dealing with the microphones and notepads and usually stayed on approachable simmer. Quinn, in particular, had a decent sense of humour and was always up for a little cigar talk in the (rare) offhand moments the job allowed him.

Late in 2001, a series of bobblehead dolls was being readied for souvenir sales for the 2002 Olympics. (Quinn was the coach of Team Canada.) My friend Michael Firestone had the contract to produce the bobbleheads, and each player, plus Quinn, had a prototype designed before mass manufacture began. Firestone gave me Quinn's prototype to show the coach one night. It would make an offbeat column, maybe. I got Quinn alone and showed him what he looked like in fibreglass. He looked at it for a long time, laughed and said, "I hope I look this good in the box one day."

One of Quinn's traits was an unwillingness to discuss specifics of injury, limiting disclosure to "upper body" or "lower body." This has become a plague across the league that is spreading to other leagues, as well. When the practice was in its infancy, I wrote: "Discerning the truth about injuries in Camp Quinn is only as difficult as, say, getting into Madonna's wedding."

I forget which wedding I was referring to.

When Quinn's heart issues slowed him down during one

playoff run, there was genuine concern among the press corps. We liked the big guy (most of us), and the issue was too close to home for some of us. After he had worked the bench in a crucial playoff loss to Carolina, then retreated to hospital for more treatment, I wrote:

> *Quinn's heart wasn't up to the stress of a post-game press conference. (Assistant coach) Rick Ley drew that straw. Why subject a guy freshly out of cardio care to Howard Berger, or any of us?*
>
> *Quinn's verticality is great to see. A guy who could lose a few pounds, smokes the odd cigar and likes a sip of single malt has a big fan here. Go Pat Go. Hope you're shot in bed at 99 by a jealous husband.*

(I should have paid more attention to what I was writing. Some 14 years later I was in the repair shop myself with basically the same kind of heart troubles as Quinn. Note that one of my first visitors was Howard Berger, then as now a pal from the press box. Shortly after I began my own rehab, sad news arrived that Quinn had passed. His time with the Maple Leafs included some success, a couple of decent playoff runs, and surely nobody has come close to equalling that since. Plus, Quinn was behind the bench for the team that won the gold medal at the Olympics for Team Canada and that's a legacy plenty of other coaches wish they had.)

Turning to the press box, there were some terrific plugged-in hockey journalists who understood the game, including Scotty Morrison, Bob McKenzie, Kenny Campbell, Damien Cox, John Shannon, Pierre LeBrun, David Shoalts, Elliotte Friedman and several others and that's merely part of the Toronto-based crowd. There also were guys who pulled punches, always protecting "the game" and loathe to criticize the way hockey was played. Far too many journalists defended, even promoted, fighting, including the mindless stuff staged by goons. Safety concerns, especially those centred on equipment, were underplayed, in this opinion. Likewise, the tenor of much hockey coverage was dictated by where a player was born. There was a built-in approval assigned to any "good Canadian boy." Meanwhile, European arrivals were mostly viewed with suspicion, as if they needed to demonstrate their bona fides to satisfy observers. It was automatically assumed non-Canadians "didn't care" about the Stanley Cup as much as someone born in Red Deer or Kingston. Meanwhile, if a Russian or a Czech, say, demonstrated the right stuff, he was said to "play like a Canadian."

It was all too much for me, although I suspect things weren't completely different in other sports, if you took a good look. Basketball writers would make open references to "soft" Europeans, after they began arriving in numbers, and baseball underwent its own transformation. The arrival of black and Latin players was long before my time, but it was during my stint writing baseball that Asian players began to show up in quantity. Like every new influx of faces, they seemed to arrive with a set of preconceived notions awaiting them and they needed to prove themselves in the games over here.

One item that proved significantly divisive among the hockey media was Alan Eagleson. There were old-timers who watched Eagleson consolidate his power atop the NHL Players Association years before and either couldn't or wouldn't believe he had stolen from the players he represented. There were many who vilified him for, as the *Globe*'s respected Roy McGregor termed it, "stealing from cripples." It is a shameful point for Canadian media that the investigation that finally sank Eagleson was led by a Boston-area newspaper and that when he finally was corralled, on a plea bargain, it was in a Boston courtroom. (A Toronto plea bargain on subsequent Canadian charges would follow the next day.) The day before the Boston court session, several of us flew to Boston to witness the official public humiliation of the former most powerful man in hockey. I ended up on the same plane as Eagleson, a row behind him in coach class, and got his little slice of what his life had become:

> *This is a guy who plans to stand up in court two days in a row and claim he's out of money and who really knows if he gots or not? No sense flying in first class if you plan to plead poverty.*
>
> *The CBC news came on the little TV sets and there . . . was the Eagleson story, in all its non-glory. He watched. Others watched him watching. Whatever footage they used, and some of it was old and some wasn't, he looked younger in it than he did last night. A lot.*

The next day, in a courtroom packed with retired NHL players, the story unfolded further:

> *Alan Eagleson stood, hands folded, in a courtroom so quiet you could almost hear the knitting needles clacking in the spectators' gallery.*
>
> *Some three dozen former NHL players, which officially now means three dozen Eagleson victims, crammed little courtroom No. 8 to see their former*

leader and in some cases (they thought) former friend say guilty three times to felony charges of stealing money, in some cases from them.

Nobody in the victims' grandstand had the pleasure of looking Eagleson in the eye, much less spitting into it.

And enough of all that. There was plenty to enjoy covering hockey, starting with the passion of both the players and fans, although without question I got more threats and invitations to do strange and painful things to myself from hockey fans than all other fan bases combined. It's an accepted truism among people who cover North American sports that hockey players, pound for pound, are the best to deal with, and I would agree with that. (Perhaps golfers are more genteel, but they seldom say anything worth hearing.) Now, access sometimes was restricted, but that had less to do with the players than with their official handlers in the media-relations department. For my money, players also had a pretty good idea of what was being written and said because they tended to read or hear it themselves, rather than rely on second-handed versions filtered through agents or acquaintances. For instance, one year the Leafs were looking to add a big name at the trade deadline, a Rob Blake or even a concussion-addled Lindros. They did not succeed, I noted:

The Leafs tried to pad the defence, but they can't even play anagrams right. They targeted Blake, as in Rob, and got Belak, as in Wade. Let's hope they don't trade for someone named Slindor.

A couple of days later, in the dressing room, I heard my name called and it was Belak. He looked at me and said. "Anagrams? Ha. Good one." That was the extent of it.

One other time the Leafs, in one of their incarnations when goal-scoring was at a premium, lost an overtime game, wasting a great goaltending effort with an acute inability to take advantage of their chances. "The way things are going," I wrote, "some of these guys couldn't score in a women's prison with a fistful of pardons."

The next day, at least a couple of them laughed, and a hand-lettered sign above an empty box said: prison pardons.

Tie Domi, a long-time fan favourite for his pugilistic ways, would jabber with reporters now and then and he provided one memorable exchange, after somebody somewhere had gotten into it with a mascot, of all things.

> *"When I was 15 I fought the mascot at Tillsonburg in Junior B. He was a big chicken [ed. note: literally, not figuratively]. Must have been about 6-foot-6. I beat the [feathers] out of him. Ripped his mask off. Broke his beak."*
>
> *What, inquiring minds wanted to know, was the ultimate insult? What was the final egg in that egg-on basket?*
>
> *"He called me pumpkinhead," Domi said, laughing at the memory.*

At the end of 1999 and early in 2000, a distressed Canadian dollar and the shameless owners of NHL franchises in Canada nearly convinced the federal government that Canadian NHL teams deserved government handouts — taxpayer cash — to survive. This idea, spearheaded by Ottawa Senators owner Rod Bryden, was totally preposterous and completely untrue, yet it was endlessly repeated by all concerned and transmitted as verifiable by a (mostly) compliant media. On the other hand, some of us felt the way I did:

> *How do all those taxpaying saps in Winnipeg and Quebec City feel now?*
>
> *Now that the Jets and Nordiques have gone, will it be easy for their fans to swallow seeing their hard-earned tax dollars going to subsidize already wealthy owners of other Canadian-based NHL teams?*
>
> *You people in Winnipeg, who poured millions and millions of municipal dollars down the rathole that eventually became the Phoenix Coyotes, how do you feel when you hear Rod Bryden tell everybody that this is about fairness?*
>
> *Ah, well. All you people know how our governments feel about the real issues these days. With people dying in hospital hallways, no doubt the solution soon will be to suggest we build more hallways.*

The government initially caved and announced it would fork over cash to these bums, but public outcry soon made them reverse course and pull the plug. Thankfully, this little corner of stupid was avoided.

But here's one corner that wasn't, a particularly dumb move by MLSE that involved Maple Leaf Gardens, the former home of the Leafs whose main floor had been converted into a grocery store. Ryerson University, which obtained use of portions of the building, got a terrific idea to rebuild some of it into a small arena for the school's hockey and basketball teams. (Architects and designers did a brilliant job, by the way. The conversion to what is now known as the Mattamy Athletic Centre is spectacular.)

MLSE went to court to order that the building not be referred to as Maple Leaf Gardens, even though it had a heritage designation that prevented the main marquee, containing that name, from being removed. Right. MLSE sued to prevent people from calling a historic landmark by its real name. Further, MLSE wanted the blue maple leaf on the roof painted over. Honest.

> *The profiteers at MLSE were concerned that having the name used would somehow damage the brand — as if their stewardship hadn't already turned a national institution into a laughingstock. (This had nothing to do with trying to excise memories of the pedophilia scandal that scarred the franchise and building in its later years; this was about protecting MLSE's right to make money.)*
>
> *MLSE didn't want Loblaws to build anything that would "compete" with the Air Canada Centre, insisting on non-competition clauses. When you look at MLSE teams, you understand the organization knows about non-competitiveness.*

That was almost 10 years ago. Some things never change.

CHAPTER TWENTY-FOUR

Laughter Is Allowed

David Cone was an outstanding pitcher whose addition to the 1992 Blue Jays was a critical component to the team's World Series victory. He also was a smart, funny guy with a fine appreciation for, and healthy attraction to, the glories of the female form. Late one spring training, when Cone was a higher-up in the players' association, a story moved on the wire about something to do with an impending strike or lockout. The desk called me and asked if I could get a comment from a player representative. This was before the days of cell phones. Where to find a major leaguer at 10 p.m. in spring training? Could it be done? In Cone's case, there was a good chance it could.

I jumped in the car at my Dunedin, Florida, hotel, drove most of the way across the causeway to Tampa and pulled in at an infamous strip bar called the Tanga Lounge. There, sitting at the bar behind a stack of dollar bills, was Cone, enjoying his evening. He explained the facts of the situation and provided a useful quote. Couldn't have been more helpful. As I left, he did feel obliged to make one request: "Uh, let's not say exactly where I was, okay?"

This was the same David Cone who, when playing for the Mets, was asked how he would prepare for the start against Los Angeles in the 1988 NLCS. Normally, somebody talks about charting pitches and viewing video and praying to the Good Lord and so on. Cone's response: "I'll get a good night's sleep — after I check out the mud wrestling at the Tropicana Hotel. I'll probably get to bed about 4 or 5. That'll be about right."

Imagine how Twitter would handle that joke these days.

This brings to mind Orlando Hernández, the Cuban defector who pitched for the Yankees in a couple of World Series. They used to bring the next game's pitchers into the press room before that night's game, to give people a chance to get a few parboiled quotes to write a set-up story. Someone asked El Duque how he would prepare for his start and he was too honest for his handlers: "I'll spend the day in bed with my woman."

Lou Piniella, long-time player and manager, always had a good sense of humour and liked a good line as much as the next guy. Once, when he managed a so-so Yankee team of the later 1980s, before or after one of Billy Martin's stints, he had a catcher named Don Slaught and an inconsistent reliever named Cecilio Guante. Guante had one of his wild nights and three or four pitches got through to the backstop during a Blue Jay victory. Someone asked Piniella later on about the catcher getting to know the fans in the front row and Piniella shook his head. "You can't write this," he told the assembled notepads, "but it looks like they bet the game."

Billy Martin, since somebody brought him up, was as edgy and unpredictable as you would think he was.

When the cocaine-in-baseball problem was at its peak in the 1980s and several players had been busted, I asked him to define the difference, to him, between booze and recreational drugs. Martin's eyes narrowed and he went off on a spree about booze being legal and drugs being a terrible scourge and so on. He rattled off a couple of his well-practised lines about drinking — "I never had a hangover; that's why I drank so much" — and mentioned that his mother, who just turned 86, had made her first visit to Yankee Stadium. "She made me vow a Catholic oath that I wouldn't drink until I was 21 — and I didn't," he said. "But I made up for it later."

On the opposite end of the spectrum was a one-time Blue Jay pitcher named Joe Johnson, a religious young man who always behaved himself. Like all players, he was constantly asked for autographs and Johnson obliged whenever possible. He liked to add a little biblical notation — his favourite passages, like John 3:3 — to his autographs.

"A couple of years ago, it was a verse in Romans," Johnson said. "I signed my name and added Rom 3:16. A couple of girls thought I was telling them my hotel room number."

The best line I remember getting from someone not in uniform came from Sandy Alderson, at that time the general manager of the Oakland Athletics. Baseball salaries were just starting to take off for the seven-figure stratosphere and Jose Canseco was among the players leading the upward charge. Except Canseco, who still was married, had just been photographed leaving Madonna's Manhattan apartment and the gossip pages were on fire. Someone asked Alderson about the development and he considered the question thoughtfully before suggesting, "Esther Canseco is about to become about the eighth-highest-paid player in baseball."

The great player and sportscaster Bob Uecker was widely

known for his great lines and he struck again one night in Milwaukee, when Tony Fernandez once again forgot to bat when it was his turn, which he did a few times as a Blue Jay. Kelly Gruber rushed up to hit when it should have been Fernandez and Gruber flied out. The Brewers chose to do nothing, which meant the game proceeded as scheduled, with Fernandez's spot simply left blank on the scoresheet.

"Is it really that easy?" wondered Uecker, whose shtick involved knocking his own abilities as a player. "If I'd known that, I'd never have come out of the dugout my whole career."

Spring training was never, ever taken seriously, except perhaps by a few kids trying to impress a manager, plus the statistics crowd, who think they see something in exhibition game numbers. One time against the Tigers, Al Leiter was pitching for the Jays. Detroit sent his brother, Mark, out to pinch run in the ninth inning and he worked his way around the bases to tie the game, which then went 13 innings, pissing off every veteran, to say nothing of a certain reporter who had a date with the dog track. After the game ended, the brothers united and Al lamented the wasted hour and a half. "If you'd just fallen down, we'd all be home by now."

David Wells, who was a loose horse as a rookie and as a veteran, was a fan of the great legends, particularly Babe Ruth and Joe DiMaggio. Once, on a day he was not scheduled to pitch for the Yankees, he heard DiMaggio was up in the owner's box with George Steinbrenner. Wells headed right up there, as he reported, "and there they were, having lunch. George, Joe, Phil Rizzuto and (Yankee partner) Barry Halper. I grabbed myself a sandwich and sat down. George's eyes bugged out. He thought I was crazy."

Wells was aware that DiMaggio often refused to sign autographs for players; he had arthritic hands and sometimes just did not feel up to signing. This time? As Wells told the story, "I told him to sign . . . or I'll head-butt him."

The supply of good lines, or stupid remarks that caused hilarity, are not limited to baseball. For instance, the first time I toured St. Andrews in Scotland, out walking the historic golf course

With son, Allan, on the Swilcan Bridge at St. Andrews, the day after the 2002 British Open at Muirfield. Allan was seven then.

that runs out to the sea and back, I was following two first-time visitors with, apparently, no sense of history's timeline. I will charitably say they were North American. One pointed out at the air force planes taking off and landing at Leuchers, across the estuary, and wondered why they had built this course so close to an air force base.

I mentioned this to Nick Faldo once and he said, "Yes, and I've heard people say they shouldn't have built Windsor Castle so close to Heathrow."

Augusta was a treasure trove of silliness at times, not surprising in a town that had a restaurant named the Wife Saver and at a golf club that for years featured a chairman named Hootie. One year, when Mike Weir and K.J. Choi, the popular Korean golfer, were near the top of a leader board, Cam Cole and I went out to see them finish at 18, then try to scrounge a few quotes. There was some question whether they would be brought into the interview room. After notable rounds, contenders were given the chance to accept or decline an invitation to the press centre. When it was 50-50 to be invited, as these two were this day, you had best get out there just in case. We checked with a press official outside the scoring tent and he reported that, yes, both would make stops at the press room. We turned to retreat the quarter mile to the press building. There were two green-jacketed members driving golf carts, tasked with whisking the golfers that quarter mile. With Cam and I standing there, one member said to the other, dividing the task at hand, "You take that po' little lefthanded Canadian boy and I'll take the Chinaman."

Naturally, we broke up. For the rest of my career, Weir was forever known, at least to Cam and me, as "that po' little lefthanded Canadian boy."

Bob Weeks, a terrific golf and curling reporter for TSN, always developed good stories and one early morning in Augusta, he turned into part of one with a line for the ages. It turns out that Joe Carter, the freshly retired former ball player who had always wanted to see a Masters, found his way to

Augusta early in Masters week. Lacking a reservation, it should be mentioned. Naturally, he couldn't find a hotel room and it was getting late. He put in a phone call to TSN's Rod Black, who was sharing a house with Weeks and a couple of other guys. Black offered Carter the house's couch and guided him to a late-night arrival. Carter stretched out on the couch and went to sleep.

Weeks, asleep during all this late-night drama, had no idea there was a rather large stranger sleeping on their couch the next morning as he descended the stairs. Cautiously, he peeked at the mystery man and thought, *You know, that looks a little like Joe Carter*. Upon closer inspection, he verified it was indeed Joe Carter, who seemed to be engaged in — shall we say? — a little creative scratching common to all men. Blurted out Weeksy, "Touch 'em all, Joe."

My other Augusta classic needs a name or two redacted, both to keep the lawyers' involvement to a minimum and also because the protagonist seems to have a different recollection. But it happened on the Sunday morning in 2000, with Mike Weir and Phil Mickelson tied on the edges of contention and playing together, and involves a first-year Masters reporter, a golfer and golf fan both, who woke up to a major birthday that morning. Now, our friend had a bad case of the birthday blues: here I am, my life half-over, in some stupid Georgia town. I should be home with my family, not working. Blah-blah-blah.

A little while later he got to the course and found out he had won the lottery for reporters and was entitled to play the golf course Monday morning. Perhaps 20 reporters win the lottery every year; he had beaten the odds in his first year, something others didn't do in 20 tries. Needless to say, his mood brightened. Life surely was not so bad all of a sudden. Happy birthday.

I went out to watch Weir and Mickelson. I like to locate myself down the fairway, record where the players' tee shots land, then head up to the green to await their approaches. The fans were lined up four or five deep at the ropes, as is usual at Augusta. I was behind them, watching the tee shots land. One hit. The other hit. I scribbled my notes and turned to go. Approaching from the press room was our friend. I said, referencing the recently announced lottery postings, something like, "Congratulations. Playing tomorrow, eh? Good for you."

He responded, "Yeah, it's my birthday and I woke up feeling lousy. My life is half-over and I'm stuck here and all that. But now? The sun is shining. A Canadian is in contention. I win the lottery and I'm playing the big course tomorrow. The only way this day could be better is if (a famous golfer's famously beautiful wife) gave me a blow job."

I froze. I knew this famous golfer's famously beautiful wife happened to be about eight feet behind me. I never turned around. I took a step to my left, at which point he could now see past where I had been standing. A look of jellied horror crossed his face. Clearly, he just saw her for the first time. Instead of turning and heading toward the green, I walked toward the tee box as fast as I could, then back to the press room. TV would be just fine today, thanks. I didn't wish to get involved in this one. I have no idea if she heard or didn't hear or pretended not to hear or what. Being blameless in all this, I was not going to stick around and find out. Later on, he asked me if I knew she was within earshot. My answer then was the same as now: I never want to know. And don't get me involved. I didn't say it.

Mind you, there were many times I wish I had said what others did. Two f'rinstances: Mark Whicker, a long-distance friend from the *Orange County Register*, came up with a line worthy of bronzing. It concerned former U.S. president Bill Clinton spending the night at Greg Norman's house in Florida. Something happened and Clinton took a tumble and damaged a knee and departed on crutches. Might have undergone surgery, too. We were debating what might have happened and Whicker arrived at one certainty: "Well, we know he didn't trip over any green jackets."

The other came from Steve Milton of the *Hamilton Spectator*, who had a scything sense of humour at times. He also was a CFL devotee. During a period in the mid-'90s the Canadian league was dipping its toe into expansion to the United States as a means of revenue generation necessary for survival. About the same time, Alan Eagleson, disgraced former head of the NHL Players Association, was unable to enter the United States because of outstanding warrants for his arrest on several charges stemming from his looting operations. Milton put the two together and suggested the CFL name Eagleson as commissioner in order to put a stop to all talk of U.S. expansion. Very smooth.

Occasionally, situations brought the laughs. For instance, during the Blue Jays 1993 season, a trip to Minnesota was about to commence. Someone had screwed up, though, and forgot to load the beer on the plane. This is only a middling-sized deprivation, but it was widely noticed by the travellers. No problem, the pilot suggested to Cito Gaston, the manager, as they waited for the plane to be loaded for takeoff. We have time for someone to run over to the nearest 7-Eleven and buy a few six-packs before we take off.

This obviously was a U.S.-based pilot. Gaston explained that convenience stores in Ontario did not sell beer and, this being Sunday evening, the local beer stores were closed. No problem, the pilot retorted, we'll just fly over to Buffalo in 15 minutes and stop and load up at the 7-Eleven there. I'll adjust the flight plan right now. Gaston considered the offer and suggested they were fine without suds for two hours to Minnesota and let's get going. Thanks very much.

One of the situations that broke me up was watching Kenny Williams run the bases during his brief time with Toronto in 1990 and 1991. Now, this was a man who went to Stanford University, where he caught passes for John Elway. He later became a successful general manager with the White Sox and won a World Series with them. Plus, he fleeced his former team badly by trading a damaged-goods pitcher named Mike Sirotka, who never did pitch for the Jays, then winning the grievance filed by the Jays over the deal. So he had to be somewhat sharp, although when he got on the base paths he was anything but.

Once, while killing time watching another game on TV in the Jays clubhouse, a hitter was called out on a bang-bang play at first base after sliding into the bag. I expressed thoughts on such a dumb move. Kenny disagreed.

"It's the fastest way to get to the bag, to slide," he insisted. Now I disagreed.

"Kenny, do you ever see Ben Johnson and Carl Lewis slide into the tape at the end of the 100-metre dash? It's deceleration. Batters are better off accelerating down the line, not decelerating."

That argument was not well received by Kenny, who pondered it and then said, "If that's the case, why do we slide into second?"

"Because you'll be out in left field and tagged!" I said, possibly too loudly, while mentally scratching Stanford off the list of potential universities for any children I would have in the future.

One day in 1991, Kenny went in to pinch run for somebody. This was not long after he had gotten confused and went back and forth on the bases and finally steamed around third base and, while looking elsewhere, ran smack into third base coach John McLaren and knocked him cold. On this occasion, at least, no one lost consciousness:

> *Williams, who can do some amazing things out there (and just ask John McLaren) got himself into a rundown, trapped off second base on a routine ground ball to short. It didn't turn out to be too damaging, but who knew that at the time?*
>
> *In Williams's previous pinch-running assignment, he was picked off first by Dennis Eckersley as the potential tying run in the ninth inning. This is tougher than it sounds, in that Eckersley had two and only two pickoffs in his Oakland career. One was Williams last week. The other was a Chicago outfielder back in 1987. Yes, it was Ken Williams that time, too.*

Back in those days, the Jays dabbled in the rule V draft and would carry kids who seldom played. One was Willie Canate, an occasional outfielder, who in 1993 was stashed on the disabled list when required. The Jays called the reason "a persistent intestinal disorder," which is a pretty difficult malady to argue with from a distance. One day Willie missed the memo; the Jays put him on the DL for that stomach trouble while Willie, as I noted:

> *. . . was strolling around the clubhouse grazing from a bag of Frito-Lay's finest. Good old potato chips.*

Sounds like the right kind of medicine for a problem down in the engine room. What is next? Cake and ice cream? Will Willie go on the birthday party diet, or what?

When John Gibbons was in his first stint as manager of the Blue Jays, he didn't get along with a lefthanded pitcher named Ted Lilly. This is strange since the affable Gibbons, who has a tremendous sense of humour, seems to get along with just about everybody. This day, though, the two actually came to blows after Lilly was pulled from the third inning of an 8-0 drubbing and said something that caused Gibbons to chase after him. As I explained it:

It's possible that Ted Lilly did indeed punch John Gibbons in the schnozz the other night. Of course, Gibbons would have had to put his nose belt-high down the middle for Ted to hit it squarely.

Yes, every now and then, something would happen that would cause me to write a snarky line. Snarky, but funny, at least to my possibly twisted sense of humour. For instance, in the 1996 American League playoffs against the Yankees, the Texas Rangers kicked the ball around to the point that my column led off thusly:

If the original Texans had defended like this, the battle of the Alamo would have lasted 10 minutes and the world would have been spared 160 years of obnoxious Texas BS.

Five days later the Yankees knocked out Texas and one of the reasons was a 12-year-old fan named Jeffrey Maier who reached over the outfield wall and interfered with a catchable fly ball that was incorrectly ruled a home run for the Yankees. It looked familiar to me:

> *Seeing young Jeffrey Maier almost catch that fly ball the other day in Yankee Stadium brought back memories . . . of the 1996 Blue Jays outfield.*
>
> *Listen the 12-year-old did not mean to do one thing wrong. He saw a baseball coming at him and he tried to catch it. Just like Shawn Green would.*

The year before, while the baseball labour dispute droned on, the one that already had caused the 1994 postseason to be cancelled, U.S. President Bill Clinton attempted to conciliate the dispute. He was not successful, but it was worth a column to a grateful scribbler:

> *Bill Clinton pulled out his Solomonic sword and threatened to cut the baseball baby in half. What happened instead is that both sets of mothers — I use the word in its abbreviated form — acted rather unbiblically and turned their backs on the baby (and) now we have, slowly twisting in the wind, one President of the U.S.*
>
> *Granted, the quality of occupant of the White House perhaps isn't what it used to be. They used to get Washington and Jefferson and Abe Lincoln and the Roosevelt twins and Marilyn Monroe's boyfriend in the Oval Office. Now it's a guy who practically had to become president before he'd stop dating.*

There was another notable labour dispute, this one in 2012, that concerned National Football League referees. It played out very publicly in a league already absorbing all kinds of PR dents over such matters at the time as Bountygate, the rise of concussion science and the attendant lawsuits from damaged former players. As a bettor, I was always suspicious of football referees and their evil cousins, namely racing judges, baseball umpires and hockey and basketball officials. When the "regular" NFL referees, their strike freshly settled, were welcomed back with long, loud and loving receptions from fans, that was all too much for me, especially coming in a country, I suggested, "that couldn't properly officiate its own presidential election 12 years ago."

> *It was touching to see the returning referees greeted with hugs by players and standing ovations from customers Thursday evening in Baltimore. By Monday evening, it will be acceptable to once again question the eyesight and intent, if not parentage and scruples, of these same officials.*
>
> *What follows comes from someone with decades of scars inflicted by Red Cashion, Tommy Bell, Phil Luckett, Gerry Austin, Armen Terzian and other personal financial assassins wearing zebra shirts. When I die, I expect Jerry Markbreit to do the right thing and send flowers. These guys seldom threw a flag without hitting me in the wallet.*
>
> *So seeing "real" referees back doesn't exactly generate tears of warmth here. It's kind of like that old analogy about having enough monkeys and enough typewriters and time and one of them eventually writing Hamlet. I say give those replacement guys*

enough games and they too will come up with a Tuck Rule, a Jerome Bettis Coin Toss, a Holy Roller, the Seattle-Pittsburgh Super Bowl or the Ed Hochuli/ Jay Cutler Dead Ball Call. Among many other felonies.

Not that I held a grudge, or anything.

CHAPTER TWENTY-FIVE

Luckiest Man

What else to call myself except maybe the luckiest man in town after 40 years of witnessing outstanding sporting events, up close, in two dozen countries and on every continent — except Antarctica, and they don't play many games there.

I went around the world a few times on someone else's dime. Other than travel that went from tolerable to mostly gruesome thanks to the way the world changed after 9/11, a sentiment that everyone who travels for a living will understand, I pretty much enjoyed the whole thing.

Lucky, though. Not only in the larger sense, but sometimes in the specific, are-you-serious sense. Like the time I took a day flight to London for the British Open. Usually I took the overnight flight, which departs Toronto in the early evening and lands about breakfast time. This day, because I was driving to Sandwich, down in Kent, I decided to try the day flight, which left Toronto about 10 in the morning and got to London about 10 at night. Then it would be an easy two-hour jaunt down to Royal St. George's. I got off the plane and went to the rental car desk and showed the clerk my reservation. He hummed and hawed and said sorry, but they didn't have any cars left.

"Well," I said to him. "This won't fly. I have a reservation. I need a car. What are you driving?"

The guy diddled around on the computer and grumbled and said, "I shouldn't do this, but I do have one car available. I have to let you have it for the price we quoted you for your reservation."

It was a brand new Jaguar, a $90,000 item, still smelling of *eau de new car*, which is man's favourite perfume. Geez, what a score. A beautiful Jag for the price of some Euro pisspot. I flipped the guy my American Express gold card, the one I always used when I rented cars because it pays for the insurance. I thought to myself, *How good is this?*

So away I went. This thing was purring on the motorways, cruising around 90 miles an hour. I spent the next 10 days having a great time, tooling around the countryside, giving writer pals rides around the south of England, trailing large clouds of cigar smoke, all the time thinking, *I'm the goddamn governor's son.*

When the trip was over, I returned the car to the lot at Heathrow Airport. At that point, someone comes out and does a walk-around, to make sure there are no chunks out of the vehicle. The man looked at the car, looked at my rental contract, looked at the price quoted and whistled. "How did you get this car for that price?" I gave him the explanation, he muttered his congratulations and I flew home.

Fast-forward about two months and here came a letter from American Express. "Dear Mr. Perkins. As a valued customer of

American Express for more than 30 years . . ." it began. It went on to "remind" me that as the fine print in my American Express literature clearly states, insurance is available on rental cars, but only on rental cars with a retail value of less than $60,000 (or some similar number.) As such, it continued, please note that the car rented on July the whatever — my Jag! — has a value that far exceeds our limits and therefore was not covered by us during the rental period. Please make note of this situation in the future. Yours very truly, etc.

Yowsah. I was wheeling around England like a maniac for 10 days in an expensive car with, it turns out, ZERO insurance. And got away with it. That's what I mean by lucky.

Here's one more example, from a splendid night in Paris after the 2006 Turin Olympics. I took the high-speed train up to Paris the day after the closing ceremonies for a couple of days of R&R before flying home. Exactly 24 years before, I had spent a glorious evening in Paris with colleague Jim Proudfoot, after we had covered the Albertville Winter Games. We had a magnificent dinner at Jim's favourite Paris restaurant, a seafood place on Rue George V, then took in the revue at the Crazy Horse before strolling home behind fine cigars. One of my best nights ever on the road and there were plenty of great ones.

Jim had died five years before, in 2001, but in his honour I decided to at least eat at the same place. I found the same restaurant, had a magnificent meal and told the proprietor, who had certainly been around long enough to preside over both my visits, about that first night nearly a quarter century before. He brought out a bottle of brandy and we toasted Jim's memory. Eventually, he presented me with the cheque, I tossed him my *Toronto Star*–issued credit card, added an extravagant tip to the bill, which was something like 115 euros, and bade my host a warm farewell. I fired up a honking grand cigar and ambled up

George V toward the Champs Élysées, once again suggesting to myself that I was, indeed, the governor's son.

I had gone a few blocks, contemplating the greatness of things like Paris and crisped baby octopus and Romeo Y Julieta and so on, when I heard my name. "Monsieur Perkins. Monsieur Perkins. Arrêt."

Here, puffing up the street, came my new restaurant friend. Waving something and calling to me.

"Problem," he said. "Problem with your credit card. Please return immediately."

What the hell. Had the *Star* given me a dud card? Why would 115 euros, plus tip, set bells ringing?

I went back, where the problem was outlined: I had signed not for 115 euros (plus tip). They had steered the decimal point to the wrong place and I had signed for 11,500 euros, or about $20,000 in Canadian money. It was a hell of a meal, but not that good.

We went through the process of cancelling the first transaction, which I had blindly approved while apparently lost in my own little cloud of brandy mixed with contentment. Thankfully, we got it all sorted out, but I thought of some poor *Star* bean-counter somewhere, checking the numbers in a couple of days and risking a stroke when this one arrived. Imagine the fun if they hadn't found me and I had tried to sort this out days later in a trans-Atlantic phone call. How easy would that have been?

Like I said and always will — lucky guy.

ACKNOWLEDGEMENTS

Blame my cardiologist. If he'd let me play golf last summer, I'd have been out enjoying myself instead of sitting around idly, going nuts. But this tome was not entirely written in self-defence. The smooth urgings of agent Brian Wood, who arrived bearing a timely offer from the alphabet jockeys at ECW, persuaded me to type up the stories from a newspaper working life of 40 years, an existence all but unavailable to journalists now given the industry's terminal afflictions. Appreciation goes to Jack David, editor Laura Pastore and the crew at ECW who steered a rookie author around a strange new world. Further kudos are due to researcher extraordinaire Astrid Lange, who waded through an ocean of words to help me find a few of the good ones.

I also need to thank the *Globe and Mail* for starting me off on my newspaper cruise and the *Toronto Star* for the rest of the journey, one that took me in a working capacity to every continent at least once, as long as we don't count Antarctica and who really does? I was fortunate enough to work at the *Star* when it was, in the old phrase, a great metropolitan daily, one that spared no expense to cover important events and knew what a good story was without benefit of focus groups. Gerry Hall was the first *Star* sports editor who thought I could help out from this side of the keyboard and, subsequently, Phil Bingley, Steve Tustin and Graham Parley apparently agreed with him. All deserve my gratitude. So, too, do my hundreds of co-workers over the years and the outstanding journalists who were companions on the road. They, more so than the athletes we covered, were my heroes. For many years, my travel averaged 90 nights a year, with gusts to 120 in Olympic years. That means my wife Debra deserves limitless thanks for holding down the home fort almost single-handedly, particularly after our son Allan arrived. None of it could have happened the way it did without her support. Allan, always a source of pride, helped out by reading and correcting a few of the chapters here. Those two know how much love is directed their way.